PRAISE FOR
TWILIGHT *of the* ELITES

A *FOREIGN POLICY* FAVORITE READ OF 2012
A *MOTHER JONES* STAFF PICK FOR BEST NONFICTION OF 2012
AN INC.COM TOP FIVE BUSINESS BOOK OF 2012
A *KIRKUS REVIEWS* BEST NONFICTION BOOK OF 2012

"A perceptive and searching analysis of the problems of meritocracy."
—*Foreign Affairs*

"An elegant, original argument that will make both cynics and idealists reconsider their views of how, and whether, our society works. If Americans believe in anything, it's our meritocracy. Hayes is brave to question it so forcefully."
—*Commonweal*

"[A] stunning polemic.... Hayes's book is the rare tome that originates from a political home (the left) and yet actually challenges assumptions that undergird the dominant logic in both political parties. This is not mealy-mouthed centrism. It is a substantive critique of the underlying logic of both Barack Obama and Mitt Romney—the logic of meritocracy."
—TA-NEHISI COATES, *Baltimore Sun*

"A great read.... *Twilight* uses a wide variety of academic and journalistic work, balancing a deep, systemic critique of society with detailed and empathetic reporting about those most affected by elite failure."
—MIKE KONCZAL, *Dissent* magazine

"Engrossing…thoughtful critiques of what's gone wrong with America's ruling class."
—TheAtlantic.com

"Compellingly readable, impossibly erudite, and—most stunningly of all—correct."

—AARON SWARTZ, CrookedTimber.org

"I was myself very impressed by the level of execution in this book."

—TYLER COWEN, Marginalrevolution.com

"An extended meditation on why the great hope and change revolution of 2008 has so far left the inequitable status quo a little bit too intact."

—Salon.com

"*Twilight of the Elites* is an engaging, insightful book. I finished it in less than twenty-four hours, and I encourage you to pick up a copy."

—Forbes.com

"An engaging read that addresses the question of whether a meritocratic elite can really stay meritocratic over extended periods of time."

—DANIEL W. DREZNER, ForeignPolicy.com

"A potent articulation of a society's free-floating angst, *Twilight of the Elites* stakes its claim as the jeremiad by which these days will be remembered."

—WashingtonMonthly.com

"You should really get yourself a copy of *Twilight of the Elites*."

—*Daily Kos*

"Raises demanding questions about a nation that is both enamored with and troubled by its elites."

—Reason.com

"Chris Hayes is a gift to this republic. The brilliance he shows us each week on MSNBC has now been complemented by this extraordinary book. Beautifully written and powerfully argued, it will force you to rethink everything you take for granted about 'merit.' And it will show us a way to a more perfect nation."

—LAWRENCE LESSIG, Roy L. Furman Professor of Law and Leadership, Harvard Law School and author of *Republic, Lost*

"In *Twilight of the Elites*, Hayes shows us what links the bailout of investment bankers but not mortgage holders, the useless public conversation in the run-up to the Iraq war, and the Catholic Church's harboring of child rapists: our core institutions are no longer self-correcting and have become committed to protection of insiders at all costs. Read this and prepare to be enraged."

—CLAY SHIRKY, author of *Here Comes Everybody* and *Cognitive Surplus*

"A provocation; a challenge; and a major contribution to the great debate over how the American dream can be restored."

—DAVID FRUM, contributing editor, *DailyBeast/Newsweek*

TWILIGHT *of the* ELITES

America After Meritocracy

CHRISTOPHER HAYES

BROADWAY PAPERBACKS
NEW YORK

Copyright © 2012 by Christopher L. Hayes

All rights reserved.
Published in the United States by Broadway Paperbacks, an imprint of the
Crown Publishing Group, a division of Random House, Inc., New York.
www.crownpublishing.com

BROADWAY PAPERBACKS and its logo, a letter B bisected
on the diagonal, are trademarks of Random House, Inc.

Originally published in hardcover in the United States by Crown Publishers,
an imprint of the Crown Publishing Group,
a Division of Random House, Inc., New York, in 2012.

Library of Congress Cataloging-in-Publication Data
Hayes, Christopher, 1979–
Twilight of the elites : America after meritocracy / Christopher Hayes.
— 1st ed.
p. cm.
1. Elite (Social sciences)—United States. 2. Business and politics—United
States. 3. Corporate power—United States. 4. Power (Social sciences)
5. United States—Politics and government—21st century. 6. United States—
Economic conditions—21st century. 7. United States—Social conditions—
21st century. I. Title.
HN90.E4H39 2012
305.5′20973—dc23   2012002435

ISBN 978-0-307-72046-7
eISBN 978-0-307-72047-4

Printed in the United States of America

Book design by Lauren Dong
Cover design by Ben Wiseman
Cover photography © Ryan McVay/Getty Images

7 9 10 8

First Paperback Edition

To my mom and dad,
who taught me how to see the world.

Contents

Chapter 1

THE NAKED EMPERORS

Now see the sad fruits your faults produced,
Feel the blows you have yourselves induced.

— RACINE

AMERICA FEELS BROKEN.

Over the last decade, a nation accustomed to greatness and progress has had to reconcile itself to an economy
that seems to be lurching backward. From 1999 to 2010, median
household income in real dollars *fell* by 7 percent. More Americans
are downwardly mobile than at any time in recent memory. In poll
after poll, overwhelming majorities of Americans say the country
is "on the wrong track." And optimism that today's young people
will have a better life than their parents is at the lowest level since
pollsters started asking that question in the early 1980s.

It is possible that by the time this book is in your hands, these
trends will have reversed themselves. But given the arc of the past
decade and the institutional dysfunction that underlies our current extended crisis, even a welcome bout of economic growth
won't undo the deep unease that now grips the nation.

The effects of our great disillusionment are typically measured
within the cramped confines of the news cycle: how they impact
the President's approval rating, which political party they benefit
and which they hurt. Most of us come to see the nation's problems
either as the result of the policies favored by those who occupy the

opposite end of the ideological spectrum, or as an outgrowth of political dysfunction: of gridlock, "bickering," and the increasing polarization among both the electorate and the representatives it elects.

But the core experience of the last decade isn't just political dysfunction. It's something much deeper and more existentially disruptive: the near total failure of each pillar institution of our society. The financial crisis and the grinding, prolonged economic immiseration it has precipitated are just the most recent instances of elite failure, the latest in an uninterrupted cascade of corruption and incompetence.

If that sounds excessively bleak, take a moment to consider America's trajectory over the first decade of the twenty-first century.

The Supreme Court—an institution that embodies an ideal of pure, dispassionate, elite cogitation—handed the presidency to the favored choice of a slim, five-person majority in a ruling whose legal logic was so tortured the court itself announced it could not be used as precedent. Then the American security apparatus, the largest in the world, failed to prevent nineteen men with knives and box cutters from pulling off the greatest mass murder in U.S. history. That single act inaugurated the longest period of war we have ever known.

Just a few months later Enron and Arthur Andersen imploded, done in by a termitic infestation of deceit that gnawed through their very foundations. At the time, Enron was the largest corporate bankruptcy in the history of the nation, since eclipsed, of course, by the carnage of the financial crisis. What was once the hottest company in America was revealed to be an elaborate fraud, aided and abetted by one of the most trusted accounting firms in the entire world.

And just as Enron was beginning to be sold off for scraps in bankruptcy court, and President Bush's close personal connection to the company's CEO, Ken Lay, was making headlines, the Iraq disaster began.

Iraq would cost the lives of almost 4,500 Americans and 100,000-plus Iraqis, and $800 billion, burned like oil fires in the desert. The steady stream of grisly images out of the Middle East was only interrupted, in 2005, by the shocking spectacle of a major American city drowning while the nation watched, helpless.

As the decade of war dragged on, the housing bubble began to pop, ultimately bringing about the worst financial panic in eighty years. In the wake of the bankruptcy of Lehman Brothers in September 2008, it seemed possible that the U.S. financial system as a whole would cease to operate: a financial blackout that would render paychecks, credit cards, and ATMs useless.

In those frenzied days, I watched Federal Reserve chairman Ben Bernanke and Treasury secretary Hank Paulson defend their three-page proposal for a Troubled Asset Relief Program (TARP) in front of a packed and rowdy Senate hearing room. When pressed on the details by members of the Senate Banking Committee, Bernanke and Paulson were squirrelly. They couldn't seem to explain how and why they'd arrived at the number they had (one Treasury staffer would tell a reporter it was plucked more or less at random because they needed "a really big number").

Watching them, I couldn't shake a feeling in the pit of my stomach that either these men had no idea what they were talking about or they were intentionally obfuscating because they did not want their true purpose known. These were the guys in charge, the ones tasked with rescuing the entire global financial system, and nothing about their vague and contradictory answers to simple questions projected competence or good faith.

Washington managed to pass the bailout for the financial sector, and while Wall Street would soon return to glory, wealth, and profitability, the rest of us would come to learn in gruesome detail all the ways in which the source of its prosperity had, in fact, been the largest Ponzi scheme in the history of human civilization.

The cumulative effect of these scandals and failures is an inescapable national mood of exhaustion, frustration, and betrayal. At the polls, we see it in the restless, serial discontent that defines the current political moment. The last three elections, beginning in 2006, have operated as sequential backlashes. In 2006 and 2008, Democrats were able to point to the horrifyingly inept response to Katrina, the bloody, costly quagmire in Iraq, and, finally, the teetering and collapsing economy. In 2010, Republicans could point to the worst unemployment rate in nearly thirty years—and long-term unemployment rates that rivaled those of the Great Depression—and present themselves as the solution.

Surveying the results of the 2010 midterms on election night, Tom Brokaw alluded to the collapse of trust in institutions in the wake of a war based on lies and a financial bubble that went bust. "Almost nothing is going the way that most people have been told that it will. And every time they're told in Washington that they have it figured out, it turns out not to be true."

At a press conference the day after Democrats faced a "shellacking" in the 2010 midterm elections, Barack Obama recounted the story of meeting a voter who asked him if there was hope of returning to a "healthy legislative process, so as I strap on the boots again tomorrow, I know that you guys got it under control? It's hard to have faith in that right now."

And who could blame him? From the American intelligence apparatus to financial regulators, government failures make up one of the most dispiriting throughlines of the crisis decade.

As citizens of the world's richest country, we expend little energy worrying about the millions of vital yet mundane functions our government undertakes. Roads are built, sewer systems maintained, mail delivered. We aren't preoccupied by the thought that skyscrapers will come crashing down because of unenforced building codes; we don't fret that our nuclear arsenal will fall into the wrong hands, or dread that the tax collector will hit us up for a bribe.

It is precisely because of our expectation of routine competence that government failure is so destabilizing.

"We've created this situation where we've created so much mistrust in government," Ivor van Heerden told me one night in a seafood restaurant in the coastal town of Houma, Louisiana. For years van Heerden was deputy director of the LSU Hurricane Center, which issued a series of dire warnings about the insufficiencies of the levee system in the run-up to Katrina. After the storm, van Heerden was fired by LSU, because, he suspects, he was so outspoken in his criticism of the Army Corps of Engineers.

"You have these politicians that are selling this mistrust," he said in reference to the ceaseless rhetoric from conservatives about government's inevitable incompetence. "And the federal government sure as hell hasn't helped."

And yet the private sector has fared no better: from the popping of the tech bubble, to Enron, WorldCom, and Global Crossing, to the Big Three automakers, to Lehman Brothers, subprime, credit default swaps, and Bernie Madoff, the overwhelming story of the private sector in the last decade has been perverse incentives, blinkered groupthink, deception, fraud, opacity, and disaster. So comprehensive and destructive are these failures that even those ideologically disposed to view big business in the best light have had to confront them. "I've always defended corporations," a Utah Tea Party organizer named Susan Southwick told me. "'Of course they wouldn't do anything they knew was harming people; you guys are crazy.' But maybe I'm the crazy one who didn't see it."

The dysfunction revealed by the crisis decade extends even past the government and the Fortune 500. The Catholic Church was exposed for its systematic policy of protecting serial child rapists and enabling them to victimize children. Penn State University was forced to fire its beloved football coach—and the university president—after it was revealed that much of the school's sports and administrative hierarchy had looked the other way while former assistant football coach Jerry Sandusky allegedly raped and abused young boys on its own property. Even baseball, the national pastime, came to be viewed as little more than a corrupt racket, as each week brought a new revelation of a star who was taking performance-enhancing drugs while owners, players, and union leadership colluded in a cover-up. "I'm 31, an Iraq war veteran, a Penn State graduate, a Catholic, a native of State College, acquaintance of Sandusky's, and a product of his Second Mile foundation," wrote Thomas Day, days after the Penn State scandal broke. "And I have fully lost faith in the leadership of my parents' generation."

The foundation of our shared life as Americans—where we worship, where we deposit our paychecks, the teams we root for, the people who do our business in Washington—seems to be cracking before our very eyes. In our idle panicked moments, we count down the seconds until it gives out.

In the course of writing this book, I spoke to hundreds of Americans from all over the country, from Detroit to New Orleans, Washington to Wall Street. I traveled to those places where institutional failure was most acute, and spoke with those lonely prophets who'd seen the failures coming, those affected most directly by their fallout, and those with their hands on the wheel when things went disastrously off course. No one I talked to has escaped the fail decade with their previous faith intact. Sandy Rosenthal, a New Orleans housewife radicalized by the failure of the levees during Katrina, founded Levees.org in order to hold the

Army Corps of Engineers to account, and she described her own disillusionment in a way that's stuck with me: "We saw how quickly the whole thing can fall apart. We saw how quickly the whole thing can literally crumble."

The sense of living on a razor's edge is, not surprisingly, most palpable in those areas of the country where economic loss is most acute. On a freezing cold January night in 2008, I accompanied the John Edwards campaign bus on a manic, thirty-six-hour tour of New Hampshire, and in the wee hours of the morning on primary day we stopped in the small former mill town of Berlin, New Hampshire. Murray Rogers, the president of the local steelworkers union and himself a laid-off millworker, was one of those who came out to greet the campaign bus as it rolled into the Berlin fire station at 2 A.M. When I asked him why he was there, he told me it was because he felt like no one in government cared about the fate of the millworkers of New Hampshire . . . with the exception of Edwards. When his mill had closed, he'd written to all the Democratic primary candidates. Edwards, he said, "offered to come and help us; he wrote a letter to the CEO because of the poor severance package they gave us. None of the others even offered to come." When news of Edwards's appalling personal behavior hit the papers, I immediately thought of Murray Rogers. Who would be Rogers's champion now?

In Detroit, the national capital of institutional collapse, the feeling of betrayal and alienation suffuses public life. "Just drive around," a local activist named Abayomi Azikiwe told me in 2010. "It's just block after block after block of abandoned homes, abandoned commercial structures." Officially unemployment was about 28 percent, he said, but the real figure was closer to 50 percent. "This is ground zero in terms of the economic crisis in this country. They say the stimulus package saved or created about two million jobs. We really don't see it." As hard hit as Detroit is, it's also probably the region of the country (with the exception of the tip of Lower Manhattan) that has most directly benefited from federal government intervention in the wake of the crash. In many ways the bailout of the automakers was a stunning success, but like so many of the Obama administration's successes, it is one only understood counterfactually: things could be much worse. But if this is what success looks like, what hope do the rest of us have?

"I can't remember when I last heard someone genuinely optimistic about the future of this country," former poet laureate Charles Simic wrote in the spring of 2011. "I know that when I get together with friends, we make a conscious effort to change the subject" from the state of the country "and talk about grandchildren, reminisce about the past and the movies we've seen, though we can't manage it for very long. We end up disheartening and demoralizing each other and saying goodnight, embarrassed and annoyed with ourselves, as if being upset about what is being done to us is not a subject fit for polite society."

That emotional disquiet plays in different registers on the right and the left, but across the ideological divide you find a deep sense of alienation, anger, and betrayal directed at the elites who run the country. "I'm an agent for angst," one Tea Party organizer told me, "and the whole Tea Party movement is an agent for angst." The progressive blogger Heather Parton, who goes by the screen name Digby, has dubbed the denizens of the Beltway who arrogate to themselves the role of telling Americans what to think the "Village," and it was Village mentality, a toxic combination of petty obsessions with status and access to power, that in her view produced the disaster in Iraq and the financial crisis that followed. In Parton's telling, the Village is "a permanent D.C. ruling class who has managed to convince themselves that they are simple, puritanical, bourgeois burghers and farmers, even though they are actually celebrity millionaires influencing the most powerful government on earth."

It's not just the activist base of the left and the right who have recognized the widespread elite failure; more and more individual elites have broken ranks to acknowledge their own responsibility. Rob Johnson is a good example of this new kind of class traitor. With a résumé that boasts a Ph.D. in economics from Princeton and years at the infamous Soros Quantum fund, Johnson has a uniquely intimate perspective on American elite failure: "For years, the right has worshipped markets and now they have reason to be skeptical," he told me. "Meanwhile, the left has romanticized government and now they have reason to be skeptical. So what you've got now is a society that is demoralized because they have nothing to believe in."

"Go all the way back to Sumerian civilization," Bill Clinton instructed a crowd of global jet-setters at the 2011 World Economic Forum in Davos, "and you'll see that every successful civilization builds institutions that work, that lift people up and reward people for their greatness. Then, if you look at every one of those civilizations, all those institutions that benefited people get long in the tooth. They get creaky. The people ruling them become more interested in holding on to power than the purpose they were designed for. That's where we are now in the public and private sector."

The Davos crowd seemed unmoved by this rare dose of honesty. But then, the mood of Davos that year was a strange mix of cluelessness, self-importance, and repressed shame. Hours after Clinton gave that speech, a European economist who had spent the last three decades consulting with a major American investment bank admitted to me that he, too, had lost faith in his own profession, and in the competence of the global ruling elite gulping down cocktails at the bar on all sides of us. "In retrospect we were all illiterate! I include myself in that. Larry Summers and Bob Rubin thought they were intellectual masters of the universe. Alan Greenspan, too. But the emperor had no clothes!"

In the early 1970s, Vietnam and Watergate provoked such national paroxysms of self-doubt and distrust that both Gallup and the General Social Survey began asking Americans how much trust they had in their major institutions—big business, public schools, the Supreme Court, and about a dozen others.

Writing in the *New York Times* on April 8, 1970, James Reston observed: "Behind all the questions of politics, ideologies and personalities . . . lies the larger issue of public confidence and trust in the institutions of the nation. . . . That trust does not exist now. The authority of the Government, of the church, of the university, and even of the family is under challenge all over the Republic, and men of all ages, stations and persuasions agree that this crisis of confidence is one of the most important and dangerous problems of the age."

But what was viewed at the time as a nadir of public trust turns out to have been its high-water mark. By 2007—even before the financial crash—both Gallup and the General Social Survey showed public trust in nearly every single major institution at or near an all-time low. Twelve of sixteen institutions measured by Gallup recorded their all-time low in public confidence in the aughts, while seven were at their all-time high in the seventies. Those institutions that have lost the most trust are also the most central to the nation's functioning: banks, major companies, the press, and, perhaps most troublingly, Congress.

According to Gallup, Congress is the least trusted institution in the country: just 12 percent of respondents expressed a "great deal" of trust in it. Harvard law professor Lawrence Lessig, who studies campaign finance and congressional corruption, notes that the British Crown was almost certainly more widely trusted in the colonies at the time of the revolution. Approval ratings of Congress lag behind Paris Hilton and the United States going communist.

A 2010 Pew survey revealed that trust in government in general was at the lowest level since Pew started measuring it in 1978. But "while anti-government sentiment has its own ideological and partisan basis," Pew noted, "the public also expresses discontent with many of the country's other major institutions." The ratings for Congress were just as low as they were for "large corporations (25% positive) and banks and other financial institutions (22%)." And the marks were "only slightly more positive for the national news media (31%), labor unions (32%), and the entertainment industry (33%)."

The least trusting are those who came of age in the aughts. A 2010 study conducted by the Harvard Institute of Politics asked more than three thousand millennials whether they thought various institutions did the right thing all the time, most of the time, some of the time, or never. Of the military, the Supreme Court, the President, the United Nations, the federal government, Congress, traditional media, cable news, and Wall Street executives, only one—the U.S. military—was believed to do the right thing all or most of the time by a majority of respondents.

You can construct a whole host of theories to explain this evaporation of trust. One of the most common, particularly popular with those who find themselves the target of distrust and anger, is that the twenty-four-hour news cycle and the frenetic intensity of the Internet eat away at people's faith by sensationalizing mistakes and insinuating nefarious motives.

Former Republican senator Bob Bennett, who was ousted by the Tea Party over his support of TARP, made precisely this case to me in explaining his own plight: "The moral for that story is: if people will read responsible publications and commentators . . .

and they have a sense of respect for institutions and those of us who labor in those institutions, then we're OK. But if you get all of your information from the blogs, then you're just angry because we're lying to you."

There is no question that we have access to more information than ever before. The deluge of twenty-four-hour cable news and the Internet can obscure as much as it clarifies, and the explosion of prying electronic eyes in camera phones and Internet gossip sites means that every failing, every misstep, no matter how small or human or pathetic, can be and often is reported and obsessed over. In another era, we probably would never have seen Anthony Weiner's crotch shot, and—let's be honest—the republic isn't any better off for us having had that privilege.

A natural consequence of the proliferation of news sources is a more balkanized political landscape. CBS's Walter Cronkite would speak to nearly 20 million people every night during his heyday, an audience larger than all three network evening newscasts combined in 2010. As the audience has dispersed, distrust in the media has skyrocketed. In 1979, newspapers were one of the most trusted institutions in America, with ratings over 50 percent; today they're one of the least. The same goes for TV news.

Declining trust in the mainstream media isn't helped by the simple fact that it hasn't performed particularly well during the past ten years. By and large the media managed to miss the two most consequential stories of the decade—the manipulation of intelligence that led to the Iraq War, and the growth of the housing bubble and associated financial chicanery that would ultimately cause the crash.

But after surveying the wreckage of the fail decade, it takes some willful delusion to blame the media or an ungrateful public for our predicament. We do not trust our institutions because they have shown themselves to be untrustworthy. The drumbeat of institutional failure echoes among the populace as skepticism. And given both the scope and the depth of this distrust, it's clear that we're in the midst of something far grander and more perilous than just a crisis of government or a crisis of capitalism. We are in the midst of a broad and devastating crisis of authority.

WHEN YOU bring your car to your mechanic because it's making a worrisome noise, you trust that he's knowledgeable enough to figure out what's wrong and scrupulous enough not to rip you off. On all things auto-related, your mechanic is an authority. In public life, our pillar institutions and the elites who run them play the mechanic's role. They are charged with the task of diagnosing and fixing problems in governance, the market, and society. And what we want from authorities, whether they are mechanics, money managers, or senators, is that they be competent—smart, informed, able—and that they not use their authority to pursue a hidden agenda or personal gain.

We now operate in a world in which we can assume neither competence nor good faith from the authorities, and the consequences of this simple, devastating realization is the defining feature of American life at the end of this low, dishonest decade. Elite failure and the distrust it has spawned is the most powerful and least understood aspect of current politics and society. It structures and constrains the very process by which we gather facts, form opinions, and execute self-governance. It connects the Iraq War and the financial crisis, the Tea Party and MoveOn, the despair of laid-off autoworkers in Detroit to the foreclosed homeowners in Las Vegas and the residents of the Lower Ninth Ward in New Orleans: nothing seems to work. All the smart people fucked up, and no one seems willing to take responsibility.

The key both to Barack Obama's political success and to his

political setbacks lies in his ability to connect to our core sense of betrayal and his inability to deliver us from it. Obama's 2008 campaign promised that he would take the voter's hand and lead her out of the bewildering forest of confusion and darkness into the light of a new, hopeful era. And he was uniquely positioned to make this case, both because of his biography—a testament to American institutions at their meritocratic best—and because of his record.

Obama only had a fighting chance at the nomination because of the credibility bestowed by his appearance at a 2002 rally opposing the invasion of Iraq, where he referred to the impending invasion as a "dumb war." When all the smart people got it wrong, including his many rivals for the nomination, he got it right. He, alone among the leading contenders, was able to see that the emperor had no clothes. Hillary Clinton and her husband came to symbolize the Establishment, and Barack Obama was there to dislodge it. He invoked, time and time again, the great social movements in American history that attacked the authority of the unjust institutions that preserved the status quo. And he advanced a critique of American politics at the end of the Bush years that homed in on the fundamental dysfunctions, improper dependencies, and imbalances of power that had led to the mess we were in.

On Iraq he said that he didn't "want to just end the war," but rather to "end the mind-set that got us into war in the first place." He spoke of the way lobbyists and campaign contributors had been allowed to "rig the system," and said the very reason he was running for president was to challenge it. He vowed to "fundamentally change the way Washington works," and his campaign seemed to make good on that promise. It revolutionized the way campaigns were run by pushing power downward, allowing volunteers an unprecedented amount of authority and, in so doing, channeling people's exhaustion with failed institutions and their hopes for someone in power they could finally genuinely trust.

But as much as Obama spoke to the desire of Americans for reconstruction, and reform, he also cultivated the support of those members of the elite who had grown disgusted with and weary of the Bush administration, and who longed for restoration of authority rather than a revolution from below. Barack Obama may have constantly invoked his years as a community organizer, but he spent just as much time at Harvard Law. The latter formed him as much, if not more, than the former.

In his very first speech as president, Obama avoided castigating the establishment and instead urged Americans to trust in it once again. He acknowledged that there was a "sapping of confidence across our land; a nagging fear that America's decline is inevitable, that the next generation must lower its sights." But rather than use the speech to explain just how and why our confidence was sapped, he instead announced that sheer will and determination would be the key to repairing our broken trust. "[O]ur time of standing pat, of protecting narrow interests and putting off unpleasant decisions—that time has surely passed," he said. "Starting today, we must pick ourselves up, dust ourselves off, and begin again the work of remaking America."

Obama then quoted the ultimate authority, Scripture, to pronounce that "the time has come to set aside childish things" and genuflected to tradition: "Our challenges may be new. The instruments with which we meet them may be new. But those values upon which our success depends—honesty and hard work, courage and fair play, tolerance and curiosity, loyalty and patriotism—these things are old. These things are true."

Obama's preoccupation with authority and its reconstitution has continued through his presidency. In his 2010 State of the

Union, he addressed the crisis of authority head-on. "Unfortunately," he said, "too many of our citizens have lost faith [in] our biggest institutions—our corporations, our media and, yes, our government. . . . No wonder there's so much cynicism out there, no wonder there's so much disappointment." That same year Obama pollster Joel Benenson noted to a *New York Times Magazine* reporter that though confidence in the President was below 50 percent, it was still much better than a lot of the other traditional sources of social authority. "We are in a time when the American public is highly suspect of any institution," he said, "and President Obama still stands above that."

In 2008, trust in a number of institutions, most notably the presidency, shot up, born on a wave of optimism ushered in by the beginning of the Obama era. For a year, trust in the President as an institution was above 50 percent. But by 2010 it had plummeted back down toward Bush levels in the immediate aftermath of Hurricane Katrina.

Part of the reason for that decline was that despite his campaign promises to take on the "system," the President has operated safely within it. His approach to our broken institutions has been an attempt to will them back into functioning through sheer determination, hoping to initiate a virtuous circle in which improved institutional performance leads to increased trust and involvement, which would in turn improve institutional performance. Such an outcome has not yet materialized, though Lord knows it's not for lack of effort.

The reason is that three decades of accelerating inequality have produced a deformed social order and a set of elites who cannot help but be dysfunctional and corrupt. Most of us don't see it that way, because we get elites wrong. We don't acknowledge that our most fundamental, shared beliefs about how society should operate are deeply elitist. We have accepted that there will be some class of people that will make the decisions for us, and if we just manage to find the right ones, then all will go smoothly.

To recover from the damage inflicted by the Crisis of Authority, we will be forced to reconstruct and reinvent our politics, a process that has, in a sense, already begun. Andrew Smith, an organizer with Occupy Wall Street, told me one fall evening in 2011 that the movement is not "Left or right, but up or down." Amid drums and whoops and chants of "We! Are! The 99 percent!" he leaned in and said, "I realize that's scary for some people."

Beyond left and right isn't just a motto. Those most devoted to the deepest kinds of structural reform of the system are insistent that they do not fall along the traditional left-right axis. Just as elite failure claims a seemingly unrelated number of victims—the Palm Beach retiree bankrupted by Bernie Madoff and the child left homeless after his mother's home was foreclosed—so, too, will you find that among those clued in to elite failure, left/right distinctions are less salient than those between what I call insurrectionists and institutionalists.

Paul Krugman is one prominent example of an insurrectionist. A man who was once a defender of elite consensus and persuasive technocracy against the popular foes, he has come to believe there is something very wrong with the very people who compose the elite. At the beginning of the new millennium, it seemed to him the the beginning of the *The Great Unraveling,* it seemed with mature, skillful economists who do what had to be done, the policies; they would us who considered we thought that b but that it would the fail decade ha opinion and what

tories of au
time. *The New*
alism's most acces
multitudes) and in 200
scientist Hugh Heclo, who
Brooks writes that "the insti
those who came before and built

approvingly cites such insurrectionist heroes as the radical author Naomi Klein, something that would have been unthinkable a decade before.

The insurrectionists not only think there is something fundamentally broken about our current institutions and the social order they hold up, but they believe the only way to hold our present elites accountable is to force them to forfeit their authority. Insurrectionists see the plummeting of trust in public institutions as a good thing if it can act as a spur for needed upheaval and change. The insurrectionists want a rethinking of some of our major institutions—our government, our corporations, our civil society.

On the other side are the institutionalists, who see the erosion of authority and declining public trust as a terrifying trend. Like Edmund Burke, the institutionalists look on aghast as pillar institutions are attacked as decadent and dissolute by the uninformed rabble. Part of what horrified Burke about the French Revolution, as he told the British parliament in 1790, was that the revolution had laid waste to the entire institutional landscape of the ancien régime. The revolutionaries, Burke explained, had "pulled down to the ground their monarchy; their church; their nobility; their law; their revenue; their army; their navy; their commerce; their arts; and their manufactures" leaving the door open to "an irratio-nal, unprincipled, proscribing, confiscating, plundering, ferocious, ly and tyrannical democracy."

itutionalists live in fear of a society without central reposi-thority, one that could collapse into mob rule at any *York Times* columnist David Brooks is institution-ible advocate (the *Times* op-ed page contains 9 he laid out its vision. Citing the political wrote the book *On Thinking Institutionally*, utionalist has a deep reverence for up the rules that he has temporarily taken delivery of . . . Lack of institutional awareness has bred cynicism and undermined habits of behavior."

Most people who, like Brooks, occupy coveted positions at the heart of our pillar institutions—from university presidents to CEOs—are institutionalists by disposition. Nearly every member of the United States Senate from both parties is an institutionalist (there's no institution quite so dysfunctional and quite so loved by its members as the United States Senate). In his farewell speech to that body, retiring senator Chris Dodd (D-CT) decried the fact that "Americans' distrust of politicians provides compelling incentives for Senators to distrust each other, to disparage this very institution, and disengage from the policy making process." He hoped, he said, that they would resist that temptation and rather embrace their institution's unique features, the same ones that critics contended were making self-governance near impossible.

A big part of the institutionalist catechism, discernible in Dodd's defensiveness about his own institution, is that the people at the center of power are doing a better job than they're given credit for. At Davos in 2011, while Clinton alluded to elite failure, JPMorgan Chase chief executive Jamie Dimon defended bankers from the mob mentality of a resentful public. "I just think this constant refrain 'bankers, bankers, bankers'—it's just a really unproductive and unfair way of treating people," he said during one session. "And I just think people should just stop doing that."

What divides the institutionalist from the insurrectionist is a disagreement over whether the greatest threat we face is distrust—a dark and nihilistic tendency that will produce a society bankrupted of norms and order—or whether the greater threat is the actual malfeasance and corruption of the pillar institutions themselves.

But even the most ardent institutionalists have to admit that things aren't working. "My own trust in our political leaders is at a personal low," David Brooks wrote on the *Times'* website in 2010. "And I actually know and like these people. I just think they are trapped in a system that buries their good qualities and brings out the bad."

Ultimately, whether you align yourself with the institutionalist or the insurrectionist side of the debate comes down to just how rotten you think our current pillar institutions and ruling class are. Can they be gently reformed at the margins or must they be radically overhauled, perhaps even destroyed and rebuilt?

Barack Obama seemed to suggest he was on the side of those who favored radical overhaul, but he has governed as a man who believes in reform at the margins. This is the heart of why his presidency has been so frustrating for so many: He campaigned as an insurrectionist and has governed as an institutionalist. And how could he do anything but? He is, after all, a product of the very institutions that are now in such manifest crisis. The central tragic irony of the presidency of Barack Obama is that his election marked the crowning achievement of the post-1960s meritocracy, just at the moment that the system was imploding on itself.

Like all ruling orders, the meritocracy tends to cultivate within its most privileged members an abiding devotion. Many of the figures who feature most prominently in this era's chronicle of woe, are, like Obama himself, products of the process of elite formation we call the meritocracy, the interlocking institutions that purport to select the brightest, most industrious, and most ambitious members of the society and cultivate them into leaders: Ben Bernanke, son of a pharmacist and substitute teacher in South Carolina; Ken Lay, raised by a preacher and a farmer in Missouri; Angelo Mozilo, CEO of Countrywide and son of a Bronx-born butcher, first in his immediate family with a college degree; Major League Baseball commissioner Bud Selig, son of a first-generation Romanian immigrant who owned a Milwaukee car-leasing business; Goldman

Sachs CEO Lloyd Blankfein, raised in a Brooklyn housing project; Condoleezza Rice, daughter of a Birmingham minister.

Recruitment into the top ranks of the meritocracy also cultivates a disposition to trust one's fellow meritocrats and to listen closely to those who occupy the inner circle of winners. This faith in the expertise and judgment of the elites has been the Achilles' heel of the Obama administration. "Obama's faith lay in cream rising to the top," writes Jonathan Alter in his chronicle of Obama's first year, *The Promise.* "Because he himself was a product of the great American postwar meritocracy, he could never fully escape seeing the world from the status ladder he had ascended."

Twilight of the Elites is the story of how the same order that produced that magical election night, when the American dream seemed most impossibly alive, also produced the crisis we now face. It's a story that begins during the last Crisis of Authority, the iconic, long period of social upheaval we refer to as "the sixties." That period represented what would be the high point for economic equality in the country. Labor unions were strong, wages steadily rising, and basic components of middle-class life—health care, housing, and higher education—accessible to more households than ever in the nation's history.

But the country was also grossly unequal along lines of race, gender, and sexual orientation, and controlled by a relatively small, self-contained set of white Anglo-Saxon men. By waging a sustained assault on the establishment responsible for perpetuating the Vietnam War, patriarchy, and racial discrimination, the social movements of that era permanently transformed American society for the better.

In place of the old WASP Establishment, America embraced meritocracy, an ideal with roots that reach back to the early years of the republic. To the old catechism of self-determination and hard work, the meritocracy added some new chapters. By opening the doors to women and racial minorities, while also valuing youth over seniority and individual talent over the quiet virtues of the Organization Man, it incorporated the demands of the social movements of the 1960s. But whatever the egalitarian commitments of the social movements that brought about the upheaval of the time, what emerged when the dust had settled was a model of the social order that was more open but still deeply unequal.

The meritocracy offered liberation from the unjust hierarchies of race, gender, and sexual orientation, but swapped in their place a new hierarchy based on the notion that people are deeply unequal in ability and drive. It offers a model of society that confers vastly unequal compensation and resources on the bright and the slow, the industrious and the slothful. At its most extreme, this ethos celebrates an "aristocracy of talent," a vision of who should rule that is in deep tension with our democratic commitments. "Meritocracy," as Christopher Lasch once observed, "is a parody of democracy."

Over the last thirty years our commitment to this parody of democracy has facilitated accelerating and extreme economic inequality of a scope and scale unseen since the last Gilded Age. There are numerous reasons for the explosion of inequality—from globalization, to technology, to the corruption of the campaign finance system, to the successful war on organized labor—but the philosophical underpinning for all of this, the fertile soil in which it is rooted, is our shared meritocratic commitment. Fundamentally we still think that a select few should rule; we've just changed our criteria for what makes someone qualified to be a member in good standing of that select few.

It is precisely our collective embrace of inequality that has produced a cohort of socially distant, blinkered, and self-dealing elites. It is those same elites who have been responsible for the cascade of institutional failure that has produced the crisis of authority through which we are now living. While each specific institutional failure—Major League Baseball, Enron, Iraq—was the product of a complex set of specific, sometimes contingent causes, the consistent theme that unites them all is elite malfeasance and elite corruption.

WHATEVER MY own insurrectionist sympathies—and they are considerable—I am also stalked by the fear that the status quo, in which discredited elites and institutions retain their power, can just as easily produce destructive and antisocial impulses as it can spur transformation and reform. Call it my inner David Brooks. When people come to view all formal authority as fraudulent, good governance becomes impossible, and a vicious cycle of official misconduct and low expectations kicks in. In neighborhoods where institutions routinely fail, where the quality of life is low and prospects for improvement dim, distrust is the norm. When I visited Genaro Rendon, an organizer with the Southwest Workers Union, in his East San Antonio offices in the spring of 2010, his organization was mobilizing to make sure the undocumented residents of the neighborhood were all being counted in that year's census. Distrust makes it a hard sell. "Who's going to feel confident about the government coming to your home to do door knocking around the census? People don't know what it means or why they should fill it out. Or that it will bring better representation." Distrust in the government leads to undercounting; undercounting leads to underrepresentation; underrepresentation produces a government whose policies adversely impact the people Rendon is trying to organize, thereby confirming their initial distrust. In cities around the country, the unsolved murder rate in poor, minority neighborhoods is much higher than the average, at least in part because residents are justifiably skeptical of any cooperation with the police and their investigations. The result of the mutual distrust between cops and citizens is impunity for murderers and a cycle of violence and vengeance.

Mary Johns, the editor in chief of *Residents' Journal*, the community newspaper written by and for residents of Chicago's notorious public housing projects, told me she'd learned from experience that institutions were not to be trusted. Johns spent most of her adolescence on the streets, before eventually ending up in public housing at the age of twenty-nine with five kids. She was relieved to have housing, but the conditions were shocking: "We and our children walking around in ankle-deep water, because of pipes that busted," she told me. "In the winter." She said she'd make a call for repairs and leave the apartment, only to come back and find the water still there.

Faced with such obvious incompetence, it's natural to be suspicious of the institution's motives: surely the Chicago Housing Authority would be capable of stopping flooding if they wanted to. Since they haven't, it must mean they don't want to. They must be trying to flood their own residents. Conspiratorial thinking feeds on distrust of institutions and draws sustenance from elite malfeasance. And for this reason it takes on an extra potency among those accustomed to poor institutional performance.

In the same way the Great Recession has introduced much of middle America to the grinding despair that was for decades the norm among the poor and marginalized, so, too, has the Crisis of Authority projected onto the national scrim images of elite corruption and incompetence that have made up the scenery of life in poor neighborhoods for ages. The broken pipes are no longer confined to public housing residents; we are all ankle-deep in the water.

Such betrayals produce a cumulative effect. They prompt citizens to adopt a corrosive skepticism about the very legitimacy of the project of self-government. Outside the United States, a robust development literature shows that poor institutional performance, distrust of those institutions, corner-cutting, and petty corruption like tax evasion, all feed one another in a vicious circle. Under these conditions often people turn toward authoritarian solutions, hoping to trade a dysfunctional system with democratic input for a functional one without it. In Pakistan, a nation beset by corruption, crony government, and poor provisioning of basic public goods, the army is by far the most trusted institution. In the past, military coups have been welcomed by much of the populace as deliverance.

And sure enough, the military is now the most trusted institution in all of American life, according to every poll on the topic, having managed to gain confidence from the public over the course of the decade. In the 2009 General Social Survey, the majority of Americans reported "a great deal" of trust in the armed forces. The only other institution that has seen its reputation improve and also commands "a great deal" of confidence from most Americans is the police. So while our legislative branch, the foundational pillar of our republic, is the least trusted institution in the country, our standing army and police forces are the most. Increasingly, we trust the men with the guns, not the men in suits.

The sound you hear is the founders rolling over in their graves.

In addition to the authoritarian threat, there is another insidious possibility: that endemic elite failure will prompt the populace to retreat into denialism. As distrust spreads from institution to institution like a contagion, it can render the entire social structure of publicly accessible knowledge unusable. If the experts as a whole are discredited, we are faced with an inexhaustible supply of quackery.

To take one small but acute example of how this plays out, look at the dramatic decline in childhood vaccinations in the United States, due to fears that—contrary to the scientific consensus—they cause autism. In California the number of kindergartners whose parents requested vaccination exemptions doubled between 1997 and 2008. From 1970 to 2000, thanks to vaccinations, the number of annual reported whooping cough cases in the United States hovered around 5,000 a year. In 2010, it spiked up to 27,500 cases. A 2010 outbreak of the illness killed ten infants in California.

A similar dynamic is at play in our terrifyingly apathetic response to global warming. Certain political issues do not require elite mediation: you can tell unemployment is a problem without reading the latest figures from the Labor Department, because it's quite likely someone you know is out of work. But that doesn't hold for global warming, which I would argue is the single most pressing challenge our civilization faces. No one is equipped to perceive the steady increase of average global temperature over several decades. Here, we need elites and experts to tell us it's happening and that we have to take steps to prevent it. Implementing corrective policy on the scale necessary requires, as a precondition, a robust and widely shared level of public trust that climate scientists and the political leaders who favor a carbon policy are telling us the truth.

But the crisis of authority makes that impossible. By the end of the fail decade, belief among Americans in the basic, scientific consensus on climate change was plummeting. A comprehensive Pew poll on the issue released in October 2009 found that only 57 percent of people thought there was evidence of warming, down from 71 percent the previous year. The number of people who thought climate change was a serious problem was down to just 35 percent.

In order to doubt the science of climate change you must be-

lieve in a vast conspiracy to deceive, one that involves thousands
of scientists, bureaucrats, and journalists. And implausible as this
may be, it is precisely the theory that prominent media figures are
selling to their audiences. In 2010, Rush Limbaugh told his 15 million listeners that the list of untrustworthy institutions extended
way past Al Gore. He described "government, academia, science,
and media" as making up what he called the four corners of deceit.
"Those institutions," he told his listeners, "are now corrupt and
exist by virtue of deceit. That's how they promulgate themselves; it
is how they prosper."

Think about what it would mean to dispatch the duties of citizenship while discounting every single piece of information that
emanated from government, academia, science, or the media.

The nation has experienced crises of authority before, in the
wake of the great crash of 1929 and during Vietnam, and they have
created the conditions for periods of reformation. Social change is
a two-step process. In the first stage, those seeking change must
convince the public that the current system, with its hierarchies
and concentrated power, should not be trusted. In the 1960s,
antiwar student protesters convinced the public not to trust the
pronouncements of the commander in chief on the war's progress;
Civil Rights protesters convinced the public that the Southern
segregationist order was morally bankrupt; and feminists convinced women they didn't have to submit to the commandments
of the patriarchy.

In the second stage, once those who oppose the status quo succeed in weakening the authority of the existing order, they are able
to bring about new social and legal structures that actually reduce
its power. That is, more or less, what's happened during each period of social reform in the country's history. The decline in authority of the national security state was followed by the end of the

Vietnam War, the elimination of the draft, and the new oversight of intelligence and covert operations precipitated by the Church Committee. The decline of the patriarchy was followed by women entering the work force en masse, and the bridge in Selma led to the Voting Rights Act.

At the moment we are caught in a strange limbo between stage one and two. While the pillar institutions of American life are now, almost without exception, viewed with deep skepticism by the American public, these institutions remain largely unreformed, helmed by the same elites who screwed them up in the first place. The men who oversaw baseball's scandal-ridden steroid era still run the sport. The same bishops who lied about and covered up serial sexual abuse of minors are still running dioceses around the country. In Washington, the very architects of disaster—the pundits who sold the Iraq War, the prophets of deregulation, the corrupt and discredited lobbyists and merchants of influence—return time and again, Terminator-like, to the seats of power. We've swapped out the party in charge in three successive elections, and yet the country's key unelected power brokers remain unchanged.

In the case of Wall Street, the situation is even worse. Thanks to unprecedented government assistance, Wall Street has managed to increase its economic and political power. Bonuses and profits are near record levels, as is the money the financial services industry is spending on lobbying and donating to campaigns. Just a year after they induced the worst financial crisis in eighty years, Illinois senator Dick Durbin was moved to tell an interviewer that banks' influence on Capitol Hill was so great that "they frankly own the place."

The American body politic is sick. We are stalked, as a patient with a fever might be, by the maddening sensation that things aren't right. Because the country manages to function—the ATMs work, the planes get people where they need to go, crime is the lowest it's been in decades—it's tempting to simply hope that national convalescence is right around the corner. But the longer this Crisis of Authority persists, the more it runs the risk of metastasizing into something that could threaten what we most cherish about American life: our ability to self-correct, to somehow, even seemingly against all odds, make the future better than the past.

Chapter 2

MERITOCRACY AND ITS
DISCONTENTS

*The existence of an upper class is not injurious, as long as it is
dependent on merit.*

— RALPH WALDO EMERSON

WHETHER WE THINK ABOUT IT MUCH OR NOT, WE
all believe in meritocracy. It is embedded in our very
language: to call an organization, a business, or an institution "meritocratic" is to pay it a high compliment; to call it
bureaucratic is to insult it. On the portion of its website devoted
to recruiting talent, Goldman Sachs tells potential recruits that
"Goldman Sachs is a meritocracy." It's the first sentence.

While faith in America's meritocratic promise is shared up
and down the social hierarchy and across the political spectrum,
it is particularly strong among those who have scaled its highest
heights. Naturally the winners are tempted to conclude that the
system that conferred outsize benefits on them knew what it was
doing. So even as the meritocracy produces failing, distrusted institutions, massive inequality, and an increasingly detached elite,
it also produces a set of very powerful and influential leaders who
hold it in high regard.

It's for this reason that I find the story of Justin Hudson so remarkable. In 2010, the eighteen-year-old Hudson delivered a commencement address to his fellow graduating seniors at Hunter College High School in Manhattan. The school embodies the meritocratic ideal as much as any institution in the country. It is public and open to students from all five boroughs of New York City, but highly selective. Each year, between 3,000 and 4,000 students citywide score high enough on their fifth-grade standardized tests to even qualify to take Hunter's entrance exam in the sixth grade; only 185 are offered admission. (About forty-five students, all from Manhattan, test into Hunter Elementary School in kindergarten and automatically gain entrance to the high school.)

Hunter is routinely ranked one of the best high schools in the nation. In 2003, *Worth* named it the highest-ranking public feeder school, and *Newsweek,* in a 2008 evaluation of high schools, named it one of eighteen "public elites." In 2007, the *Wall Street Journal* identified Hunter as sending a higher percentage of its graduates to the nation's top colleges than all but one of its public peers. That year, nearly 15 percent of the graduating class received admission to one of eight elite universities that the *Journal* used for its analysis. The school boasts an illustrious group of alumni, from famed Civil Rights activist and actress Ruby Dee, to writers Cynthia Ozick and Audre Lorde, to Tony Award winners Robert Lopez (composer and lyricist, *The Book of Mormon* and *Avenue Q*) and Lin-Manuel Miranda (composer and lyricist, *In the Heights*), to *West Wing* writer and producer Eli Attie, to Supreme Court justice Elena Kagan.

Because its students certainly don't need an extra incentive to be maniacally obsessive about achievement, Hunter does not rank them. There is no valedictorian. Instead, a faculty committee selects a commencement speaker based on drafts submitted by aspirants. In 2010, the faculty chose Hudson, a black student from

Brooklyn headed to Columbia University in the fall, to give the address. He started out with standard expressions of gratitude and nostalgia. And then he pivoted.

"More than happiness, relief, fear, or sadness," he told the crowd, "I feel guilty."

He continued:

> I feel guilty because I don't deserve any of this. And neither do any of you. We received an outstanding education at no charge based solely on our performance on a test we took when we were eleven-year-olds, or four-year-olds. We received superior teachers and additional resources based on our status as "gifted," while kids who naturally needed those resources much more than us wallowed in the mire of a broken system. And now, we stand on the precipice of our lives, in control of our lives, based purely and simply on luck and circumstance. If you truly believe that the demographics of Hunter represent the distribution of intelligence in this city, then you must believe that the Upper West Side, Bayside, and Flushing are intrinsically more intelligent than the South Bronx, Bedford-Stuyvesant, and Washington Heights, and I refuse to accept that.
>
> ... We are talking about eleven-year-olds. ... We are deciding children's fates before they even had a chance. We are playing God, and we are losing. Kids are losing the opportunity to go to college or obtain a career, because no one taught them long division or colors. Hunter is perpetuating a system in which children, who contain unbridled and untapped intellect and creativity, are discarded like refuse. And we have the audacity to say they deserved it, because we're smarter than them.

The parents in the crowd were, not surprisingly, a bit taken aback. The teachers offered a standing ovation. Jennifer J. Raab, the president of Hunter College and herself a graduate of Hunter High School, stayed seated.

The critique Hudson offered was not a glancing attack at a deficiency of Hunter, but rather an assault on its very core. What animates the school is a collective delight in the talent and energy of its students and a general feeling of earned superiority. In 1982, a Hunter alumnus profiled the school in a *New York* magazine article called "The Joyful Elite" and identified its "most singular trait" as the "exuberantly smug loyalty of its students."

That loyalty emanates from the deeply held conviction that Hunter is one of the most genuinely meritocratic institutions in existence. Unlike elite colleges, which use all kinds of subjective measures—recommendations, résumés, writing samples, parental legacies, and interviews—in deciding who gains admittance, entrance to Hunter rests on a single "objective" measure: one three-hour test. If you clear the bar, you're in; if not, you're out. There are no legacy admissions, and there are no strings to pull for the well connected. If Michael Bloomberg's daughter took the test and didn't pass, she wouldn't get in. There are only a handful of institutions left in the country about which this can be said.

Because it is public and free, the school pulls kids from all over the city, many of whom are first-generation Americans, the children of immigrant strivers from Korea and Russia and Pakistan. Half the students have at least one parent born outside the United States. For all these reasons Hunter is, in its own imagination, a place where anyone with drive and brains can be catapulted from the anonymity of working-class outer-borough neighborhoods to the inner sanctum of the American elite. "I came from a family where nobody went to college. We lived up in Washington Heights. We had no money," says Raab. "It was incredibly empowering." When she surveys the current student body, she says, "It gets me very sappy about the American dream. It really can come true. These kids are getting an education that is unparalleled, and it's not about where they come from or who they are."

In 1990, at the age of eleven, I, like Justin Hudson, stood on a line of sixth graders outside an imposing, converted armory on Manhattan's Upper East Side nervously anticipating a test that would change my life. When I got to Hunter, I discovered a place completely different from all the pop-cultural representations of high school life I'd come across. There was no football team and there were no cheerleaders. There were cliques, of course, and social hierarchies, but nerdiness wasn't a distinguishing feature, or a liability: good grades conferred status. It was something of a bohemian redoubt, where angst and rebellion were expected, tolerated, and even tacitly endorsed. The school culture had little patience for seniority or "wait your turnism." At Hunter what mattered most was that you were bright, talented, and self-confident; order, rules, and everything else were secondary.

It was at Hunter that I absorbed the open-minded, self-assured cosmopolitanism that is the guiding ethos of the current American ruling class. I learned that the world is yours for the taking, that you can go anywhere and, with the right amount of cultural capital, do anything. On the first half day in September during seventh grade, my new friends (drawn from the ranks of Manhattan's professional classes and today still some of the people in the world I'm closest to) shepherded us into cabs in order to make a matinee screening of Steven Spielberg's film *Hook* playing at a theater a mere ten blocks away. I don't think I'd ever been in a cab before, and I anticipated that the fare would be a hundred dollars. We might as well have been hopping into a private jet to spend the weekend in Bermuda.

Hunter's approach to education rests on two fundamental

premises. First, kids are not created equal: Some are much smarter than others. And second, the hierarchy of brains is entirely distinct from the social hierarchies of race, wealth, and privilege. That was the idea, anyway. But over the last decade, as inequality in New York has skyrocketed and competition for elite education has reached a fever pitch, Hunter's single entrance exam has proven to be a flimsy barrier to protect the school's meritocratic garden from the incursions of the world outside its walls.

Thanks to the socioeconomic makeup of New York City's children, and the vastly unequal quality of the schools across lines of neighborhood, class, and race, Hunter has never had a student body that matched the demographic composition of the city in which it resides. White and Asian students have always been over-represented, and they certainly were when I entered the school in 1991. But the phenomenon has intensified in recent years, leaving teachers and admissions officials worried that on its current path, the school could, before long, have its first entering class without a single black or Latino student.

According to the *New York Times*, the entering seventh-grade class was 12 percent black and 6 percent Hispanic in 1995, but just 3 percent black and 1 percent Hispanic by 2009. The rest of the students were split about evenly between Asian and white. Many teachers and even administrators at the school have grown increasingly worried about the lack of black and Latino students, particularly in a city that is 25 percent black and 27.5 percent Latino, so much so that in 2010 the debate landed on the front page of the *New York Times* with the headline DIVERSITY DEBATE CONVULSES ELITE HIGH SCHOOL. "The teachers are disconcerted," says social studies teacher Irving Kagan (who also happens to be Elena's brother). But both the administration and (perhaps not surprisingly) the current student body are wary of reform as well. "When you look at what happens in the classrooms," Raab tells me, rattling off examples of remarkable Hunter student achievements, "I do think you have to say the test is effective in selecting for a certain kind of intelligence." "Honestly, [admissions] is based, and should be based, entirely on merit," one junior told the school newspaper, *What's What,* in a 2010 article titled "Graduation Speech Ignites Heated Debate." "People work their butts off to get in."

Kyla Kupferstein Torres also graduated from Hunter, but she sees the question of merit as a bit more complicated. Before being hired by her former school and becoming director of admissions, Kupferstein Torres worked for a variety of New York City private schools and prep programs that sought out and nurtured high-achieving black and Latino students from underserved areas of the city. She dismisses the idea that Hunter's entrance exam provides for a "perfect meritocracy." "What does meritocracy mean?" she asks. "There is no such thing as a level playing field. . . . There's always going to be some kind of advantage."

Kupferstein Torres then runs through the origins of standardized testing and its original promise. Her account closely tracks that laid out in Nicholas Lemann's *The Big Test,* the definitive history of the Educational Testing Service (ETS) and its signature Scholastic Aptitude Test. Before the SAT, America's elite colleges were closed off to immigrants, Catholics, and Jews. Rather than evaluate candidates "on the merits," admissions boards at Harvard, Yale, Princeton, and the rest used an amorphous set of subjective judgments about "character" and other intangibles to tell if someone really was a "Harvard man." The result was that WASP boys with C averages from prominent families were admitted to Harvard while overachieving Jewish boys from Brooklyn were kept out. Enter the SAT: with an objective measure of the "merit" of the applicant in hand, the nebulous subjectivity of the admissions procedure would be eliminated in favor of an equal, accessible, and objective metric.

Testing, then, in its early incarnation, struck a democratic blow against the barricaded and entrenched elite. But only up to a point. "The rhetoric that accompanied the birth of the ETS was one of mass opportunity and classlessness," Lemann writes, "yet the main purpose of the organization was to select the few not to improve the lives of the many." It worked. At first Jews, then other non-WASPS began to flow into the Ivy League, and the newcomers permanently transformed the makeup of the American elite.

Hunter, which admits students solely based on their performance on a single test, preserves in amber the aspirations of the earliest SAT proponents. "We're still using this method of identifying children of so-called merit," says Kupferstein Torres. And it has yielded predictable results. "The overwhelming majority of students offered admission through our test process are Asian and white," she says.

I asked Kupferstein Torres to explain why Hunter was admitting fewer and fewer black and Latino students. "There are certain things that emerge immediately," she says, pointing to the dismantling of affirmative action at Hunter (about which more in a moment) and the persistent and growing inequality of opportunity in New York City. On top of that, she notes, "There was no test prep culture thirty years ago. Stanley Kaplan—the founder of Kaplan Test Prep—was probably tutoring one person."

The test prep industry for national standardized tests like the SAT is now a booming, multimillion-dollar business, and it is at least part of the reason (along with wide variety in school quality and parental educational attainment) that one of the best ways to predict a student's SAT score is to look at his parents' income: the more money they make, the higher the score is likely to be.

When I was eleven there was no test prep industry for the Hunter entrance exam, but that's no longer the case. Elite Academy is just one of several so-called cram schools in Queens, where sixth graders go after school, on weekends, and during winter break to memorize vocabulary words and learn advanced math in preparation for the Hunter admissions test. According to the *New York Times,* Elite and others like it have "imported the year-round enrichment programs of the Far East, giving students the chance to forfeit evenings, weekends, summer break and winter vacation for test preparation." Parents pay $2,550 for the fourteen-weekend Hunter test prep package, and $540 for a special five-day crash course. The school's motto is "Where the smart get smarter," and in 2010 its website boasted that all eight students who'd been enrolled in the Hunter test prep courses had gained admission to the school. (Keep in mind only about 6.5 percent of students who take the test gain admission.) Meanwhile, the wealthier precincts of Manhattan are home to a flourishing tutoring industry, where parents who can afford the $90-an-hour price hire private tutors for one-on-one sessions with their children.

According to numerous people I spoke with at Hunter, the majority of students who make it into the school these days are the product of some kind of test prep regimen. Kupferstein Torres doesn't blame them. "They're doing the right thing to get the prize that we promised at the end of the process," she says. "That's what we told them to do: do well on tests."

Justin Hudson's condemnation of the Hunter model helped push out into the open a conflict among the school's teachers, administrators, and alumni. For some, The Test is what makes Hunter, and any alternative will corrupt and sully this very special place. For others (and I place myself in this latter group) it is simply unacceptable, in New York City of all places, to be running an elite, public educational institution that admits hardly any black or Latino students.

Ironically, it's those who favor altering the admissions procedures that have tradition and history on their side. In 1965, the school's administrators at the City University of New York directed it to "identify and develop gifted students who come from economically and socially disadvantaged groups in our society." While there is essentially no written record of the school's admissions procedures over the years, a 1982 *New York* magazine feature describes an admissions procedure in which a certain number of slots were set aside for students of color who'd scored near, but below, the threshold for entrance. They, along with the elementary school students who had failed to score above the threshold, were then enrolled in a special intensive summer training course to get them up to speed.

Such procedures no longer exist. Hunter, like both the educational system at large and society more broadly, has moved backward, away from a concern with diversity and more equitable outcomes and toward a pristine and simple model of equal opportunity: everyone takes the same test. No "preferences."

This seems, at first, a strange contradiction. In the 1980s, when there was less inequality, more was done to mitigate it, and yet now, at a time when the playing field is as uneven as it's ever been, Hunter clings to a far more austere vision of meritocracy than it did in the past. In this way, Hunter is a near perfect parable for how meritocracies tend to devolve. While it rejects, with a kind of bracing austerity, any subjective aspects of admission, its hard-line dependence on a single test is not strong enough to defend against the larger social mechanisms of inequality that churn outside its walls. The result is that just 10 percent of Hunter High School's students are poor enough to qualify for free or reduced-price lunch in a city where more than 75 percent of all public school students do. The playing field may be level, but certain kids get to spend nights and weekends practicing on it in advance of the competition.

THE CONCEPT of meritocracy is so essential to our ideas about American exceptionalism that it's surprising to learn the word itself is an import. It was coined by Michael Young, Labour member of parliament and social critic, in his 1958 book, *The Rise of the Meritocracy.*

Written as a history of British political, social, and economic development from the perspective of an academic writing in 2034, the book details the development of a new social system in Britain that upended the old British caste system. In its place, the British Labour government creates the meritocracy, which swaps out the aristocratic elite for a ruling class composed of bright and industrious members of all classes. "Today," the author of the monograph from the future tells us, "we frankly recognize that democracy can be no more than aspiration, and have rule not so much by the people as by the cleverest people; not an aristocracy of birth, not a plutocracy of wealth, but a true meritocracy of talent."

The education system begins testing all children, and the score becomes their defining identity, faithfully reproduced on their national identity card. So as to make sure that smart kids having an off day aren't overlooked, the government eventually allows for people to petition for retesting. The bright children are segregated early on and put in special schools that are lavished with resources. Meanwhile, in order to mirror the meritocracy constructed by the government around public education, businesses adopt a similar ethos internally, doing away with seniority as a criterion of evaluation and replacing it solely with merit.

As Young imagined it, these twin trends are powered by increasingly "scientific" measures of merit, whether in intelligence testing for children or productivity measurements for employees.

The new order takes a while to consolidate, but once it does it confers huge advantages to the society. It no longer wastes the talent of exceptional members of the working class who were formerly left to languish in menial factory jobs that did not adequately utilize their abilities, and it does not squander precious educational dollars and teacher resources on the dull or lazy members of the aristocracy.

While the term he invented is now the name of our shared social ideal, the grand irony is that Young intended to conjure a grim dystopia. In 2001, he wrote that he was "sadly disappointed" with how *The Rise of the Meritocracy* had been received. "The book," he noted, "was a satire meant to be a warning (which needless to say has not been heeded) against what might happen" if "those who are judged to have merit of a particular kind harden into a new social class without room in it for others."

Here in the United States, "meritocracy" was adopted as the perfect name for the American system of testing, schooling, and social differentiation that, in the wake of the social upheaval of the 1960s, would produce a new, more diverse elite to replace the inbred Eastern WASP establishment.

But of course, long before Young coined the phrase and Americans adopted it, something like "meritocracy" had always been near the core of the American ideal. Alexis de Tocqueville painted a picture of a place in which the old barriers to entry of birth, land, and title had been washed away, a society where each man could achieve as much as his talent and determination would yield him: "The Americans never use the word peasant," he noted, "because they have no idea of the peculiar class which that term denotes."

But while our founders were skeptical of the British Crown they overthrew, they were not particularly egalitarian. Many longed to simply replace one hierarchy with another. In 1813, Thomas Jefferson wrote the following in a letter to his friend John Adams:

I agree with you that there is a natural aristocracy among men. The grounds of this are virtue and talents. . . . May we not even say that that form of government is best which provides most effectually for a pure selection of these natural aristoi into the offices of government?

This letter would, a century later, serve as inspiration for Harvard president James Bryant Conant as he set up the system of modern-day college admissions that is the mechanism by which today's "natural aristocracy" is identified and nurtured.

This desire for rule by the "natural aristocracy" is the other half of our peculiar ideological inheritance as Americans. For all we associate the revolution with a battle for democracy, of the four governing institutions the founders created—the Supreme Court, the Presidency, the Senate, and the House of Representatives— only one, the House, was directly elected. Senators were chosen by state legislatures, the President by the electoral college, and justices of the Supreme Court by the President (with the consent of the Senate). In *Federalist* 10, James Madison famously drew a distinction between a democracy and a republic, placing the entity created by the new constitution squarely in the latter camp.

But Tocqueville presciently noted that once America began extending the franchise it would be impossible to stop short of universal suffrage—"The gradual development of the principle of equality is, therefore, a providential fact"— and indeed the arc of American history has bent toward broader democracy: the electoral college never became the independent deliberative body the framers envisioned, senators came to be directly elected, and suffrage was eventually extended to every nonconvicted citizen eighteen years of age and older.

At different crucial points, in the midst of unrest often brought about by social movements, the terms of the social contract that binds elites to ordinary citizens have been renegotiated. Andrew Jackson's insurgent campaign and founding of the Democratic Party was the first conquest of the rabble over the elites, but it would be a recurring theme: Reconstruction, the progressive/populist revolts at the turn of the twentieth century, the labor battles of the New Deal, and the upheavals of the 1960s are but a few examples.

But there is a countervailing trend to this process of democratization. As American history has moved toward wider and wider circles of legal enfranchisement, it has also moved (unavoidably) in the direction of bigness and complexity. Thomas Jefferson conceived of the nation as rooted in relative administrative simplicity, pastoral landscapes, and a threadbare state. If the cornerstone of the republic was to be the yeoman farmer, independent and self-sufficient, there would be little need for bureaucracy and layers of administration. But growth, technology, or, in short, progress, has massively expanded the complexity of the state, society, and institutions. The more complex a society, the more specialization develops: doctors, lawyers, auto mechanics, portfolio managers, water quality experts, and on and on.

In this context, elites emerge as a set of specialized experts to whom key decisions are outsourced.

As the administrative reach of the federal government exploded in the post–New Deal era, sociologist C. Wright Mills identified what he called the "Power Elite" as the overlords of the Cold War industrial order. "As the circle of those who decide is narrowed," he wrote, in reference to the increasingly interlocked worlds of politics, business, and defense that emerged out of World War II, "as the means of decision are centralized and the consequences of decision become enormous, then the course of great events often rests upon the decisions of determinable circles."

So while the history of enfranchisement moves steadily—if

slowly—in the direction of inclusion, the social contract must also accommodate the fact that management of affairs of state and market grow evermore complex and specialized. The result is a cycle of populism, anti-elite revolt, and oligarchic retrenchment, with each new ruling elite displacing its predecessor. "History," as the Italian political economist Vilfredo Pareto once said, "is the graveyard of aristocracies." And so it was for the Eastern Establishment that Mills chronicled. Its hold on power was thoroughly (and forever) disrupted by a number of social upheavals that culminated in the 1960s. As famously chronicled in David Halberstam's *The Best and the Brightest,* Vietnam permanently destroyed the credibility of the "Wise Men" who straddled the upper echelons of both private business and public service. It was these most visible members of the American Establishment who had staffed both Kennedy's and Johnson's administrations, who had overseen the disastrous course of events in Southeast Asia, and who continued to defend their actions and their own rightful place at the decision-making table as the country increasingly rebelled.

That rebellion was driven by the demographics of the baby boom and the unprecedented mass prosperity of the postwar era that flooded America's institutions of higher education with the largest cohort in history. It wasn't so much that the old institutions of elite formation were discarded—Harvard is still Harvard—but that they were increasingly populated by young, bright overachievers who came from outside the narrow Northeastern Protestant aristocracy that had been the core of the former Establishment.

The meritocratic elite is more diverse than its predecessor, as racial minorities and women have been allowed into its institutions. And it places a greater value on high levels of educational attainment, advanced degrees, and professional schools. Where the Establishment emphasized humility, prudence, and lineage, the meritocracy celebrates ambition, achievement, brains, and self-betterment. Barack Obama, a multiracial child of a single mother, graduate of an elite prep school, Columbia University, and Harvard Law, is the ultimate product and symbol of this system. He is its crowning glory.

Meritocracy represents a rare point of consensus in our increasingly polarized politics. It undergirds our debates, but it is never itself the subject of them, because belief in it is so widely shared. In a February 2007 speech, Federal Reserve chairman Ben Bernanke sketched it out this way: "A bedrock American principle," he said, "is the idea that all individuals should have the opportunity to succeed on the basis of their own effort, skill, and ingenuity.... Although we Americans strive to provide equality of economic opportunity, we do not guarantee equality of economic outcomes, nor should we."

The more succinct articulation of this vision is the mythical "level playing field" metaphor, which has become a staple of the political rhetoric of both parties. When an Indian tycoon casually suggested to Thomas Friedman that the explosion of the Internet, cheap computing, and fiber-optic cables meant that "the playing field is being flattened," Friedman had happened upon the uniting conceit for his bestseller *The World Is Flat.* What Friedman is actually describing and effusively praising is a kind of neoliberal globalized version of meritocracy where Indian and Chinese software engineers play the role that hard-studying Jews from Brooklyn once did when they crashed the gates of Harvard.

Michael Young paints the meritocracy as an idea that originated on the left but came to devour it. In *The Rise of the Meritocracy* he wryly notes in a footnote that the origin of the "unpleasant term, like that of 'equality of opportunity' is still obscure. It seems to have been first generally used in the sixties of the last century in small circulation journals attached to the Labour Party." In his 2001 *Guardian* op-ed, Young noted that the mechanisms of meritocracy robbed the working class of potential leaders. The working classes, he wrote "have been deprived by educational selection of many of those who would have been their natural leaders, the able spokesmen and spokeswomen from the working class who continued to identify with the class from which they came."

Traditional left politics, the kind that powered the Labour Party in Britain and the labor movement in the United States, depend on class-consciousness, a kind of solidarity that the meritocracy subverts. The select group of young bright stars of the working class and the poor is taught an allegiance to their fellow meritocrats. They come to see their natural resting place as atop a vastly unequal hierarchy. Those on the bottom who make it to the top rise from their class rather than with it. It is a fundamentally individualistic model of achievement.

Crucially, however, the appeal of such a system extends far beyond the relatively small number of the poor and the working class who are able to actually capture the brass ring at the top. Like the lottery, the meritocracy allows everyone to imagine the possibility of deliverance, to readily conjure the image of a lavish and wildly successful future. So that even if the number of kids from the South Bronx who end up at Goldman Sachs is trivial, even if the number of college grads from rural America who get into Harvard Law School is vanishingly small, the dream of accomplishment for our children is the one thing we all share.

Ultimately the meritocratic creed finds purchase on both the left and right because it draws from each. From the right it draws its embrace of inequality—Edmund Burke once noted acidly that "the levelers . . . only change and pervert the natural order of things"—and from the left it draws its cosmopolitan ethos, a disregard for inheritance and old established order, a commitment to diversity and openness and hostility to the faith, flag, family credo of traditional conservatism. It is "liberal" in the classical sense.

The areas in which the left has made the most significant progress—gay rights, inclusion of women in higher education, the end of de jure racial discrimination—are the battles it has fought or is fighting in favor of making the meritocracy more meritocratic. The areas in which it has suffered its worst defeats—collective action to provide universal public goods, mitigating rising income inequality—are those that fall outside the meritocracy's purview. The same goes for conservatives. Those who rail against unions and for reduced taxes on hedge fund bonuses have the logic of meritocracy on their side, yet those who want to keep gay men and women from serving openly in the military do not.

Within the framework of a system that seeks equal opportunity rather than any semblance of equality in outcomes, it is inevitable that the education system will be asked to do the heavy lifting. Young predicted as much in his book. And as inequality steadily increases, we ask more and more of the educational system, looking for it to expiate the society's other sins.

This is why, if there is a single consensus in our contentious politics, it is about the importance of education: "Think about every problem, every challenge, we face," George H. W. Bush said in a 1991 speech. "The solution to each starts with education." Bill Clinton explicitly argued that education was the solution to stagnating wages and flat-lining incomes: "We are living in a world where what we earn is a function of what we learn." And Barack Obama has made this particular theme something of an obsession: "In a global economy where the most valuable skill you can sell is your knowledge, a good education is no longer just a pathway to opportunity—it is a prerequisite."

Even George W. Bush, arguably the most conservative president since the Great Depression, centered his 2000 campaign on his brand as someone who could deliver to America the fulfillment of its meritocratic promise. Remember that the central plank of the supposedly new compassionate conservatism was his education record in Texas and his plans to implement something similar at the national level. Upon taking office, Bush worked with Massachusetts senator Ted Kennedy on crafting and passing No Child Left Behind, which increased federal funding of education in exchange for a set of national standards. It was the legislative embodiment of the grand left/right consensus on education and merit. "There's no greater challenge," the President said at the bill signing event in a middle school in Hamilton, Ohio, "than to make sure that every child . . . every single child, regardless of where they live, how they're raised, the income level of their family, every child receive a first-class education in America." Like the two presidents who preceded him, and the one who followed, Bush paid into the myth that education will level the playing field.

Because education is so central to the meritocracy in both theory and practice, we tend to associate it most closely with those highly selective institutions of higher learning—Harvard, Yale, Princeton—that most reliably produce our presidents, senators, and cabinet members. But there are two distinct but related pathways of meritocratic achievement in American society. The other ladder into the upper echelons, the one that allows certain people to bypass the credentialing of elite institutions, is the world of business. If you make enough money, people care a lot less where you went to school.

There has always been something of a populist streak in those who achieved their elite status through entrepreneurial moxie rather than through establishment channels. In an address to college students in 1885, Andrew Carnegie, a Scottish immigrant who worked his way up from the factory floor, lamented the fact that businesses now hired janitors, because it meant that entry-level businessmen would unfortunately miss "that salutary branch of a business education" that involved sweeping the floors as part of one's initial duties.

The original idea behind the meritocracy (before it even had the name), as crafted by its Harvard proponents in the earliest days, was to select a fit, bright *governing* elite. But it also now plays a large role in selecting the titans of industry. Today, the big financial firms are staffed almost exclusively by graduates of elite universities. In *Liquidated,* her exquisite ethnography of Wall Street, Karen Ho documents the degree to which elite educational institutions and Wall Street have fused into a sort of educational industrial complex: "I found not only that most bankers came from a few elite institutions, but also that most undergraduates ... assumed that the only 'suitable' destination for life after Princeton ... was first investment banking and second management consulting." Between 2000 and 2005 about 40 percent of Princeton students who chose full-time employment upon graduation went to Wall Street. Harvard featured similar numbers.

And it's not just Wall Street. The most notably successful tycoons of our own era, Microsoft's Bill Gates, Google founders Sergey Brin and Larry Page, and Facebook's Mark Zuckerberg, are all products of the most elite educational institutions in existence. Gates and Zuckerberg both ditched Harvard to pursue their business dreams, but their pre-Harvard educations took place at some of the most elite, expensive prep schools in the nation.

Thanks in large part to the private equity revolution of the 1980s and 1990s, American business around the country has been remade in Wall Street's image. Writing in *New York* magazine, Benjamin Wallace-Wells noted that by 1999 "American CEOs looked very different from [their] predecessors ... genial paternalists, spending their careers at a single company." More and more, the new breed of CEOs "were pure meritocrats—well-educated, well-compensated, moving frequently between jobs and industries, trained to look ruthlessly for efficiency everywhere."

BECAUSE OUR meritocratic ideal is so foundational, public figures rarely expend much rhetorical energy making affirmative arguments in its favor. We simply assume it in the same way we assume that global dominance should be an American prerogative. But if one is pushed to actively defend the meritocracy, there are two different ways to justify it—the moral case and the practical case—each compelling in its own way.

The moral justification for meritocracy is straightforward: the meritocracy gives everyone what he or she deserves. Effort and talent are rewarded, ignorance and sloth punished. People are not discriminated against due to contingent, inessential features like skin color, religious affiliation, or gender, but rather due to their essential features: their cognitive abilities and self-discipline. In a meritocracy, people are judged not on the color of their skin, but on the content of their character.

This crucial distinction between the contingent and essential features—between skin color and intelligence—appeals to some of our most profound moral intuitions about justice and desert. If confronted with the story of a boss who refused to promote a black employee because of her skin color, we would be outraged. If the same boss refused to promote an employee because she took longer to complete projects or performed her functions poorly, we would see this as entirely unremarkable, even commendable.

But if we're focused exclusively on the moral question of desert, of those traits that are within our control and those that are not, the line between the two grows blurry under closer inspection. What we call intelligence, along with work habits, diligence, social abilities, and a whole host of other attributes we associate with success, seem to emanate from some alchemical mix of genetics, parental modeling, class status, cultural legacies, socioeconomic peers, and early educational opportunities. As one Hunter student told one of the school papers about the Hunter test: "It's the easiest way to see who was lucky enough to get a good elementary school education and who wasn't."

So just what is the precise relationship between merit and just apportionment of rewards and resources? How do we separate the contingent from the essential? It's not so easy. Distinguishing between the two rests on all kinds of normative assumptions and highly inconclusive empirical work about nature and nurture. "The idea of meritocracy may have many virtues," philosopher Amartya Sen writes, "but clarity is not one of them."

At their most extreme, defenders of the status quo invoke a kind of neo-Calvinist logic by saying that those at the top, by virtue of their placement there, must be the most deserving. Karen Ho describes this "meritocratic feedback loop" as common on Wall Street, where the finance industry's "growing influence itself becomes further evidence that they are, in fact, 'the smartest.'"

Likewise, those who most strenuously defend our uniquely non-redistributive form of American capitalism attack redistribution as representing, fundamentally, a moral transgression. In the eyes of conservatives: The government does not deserve the money it takes through taxes, the person who "earned it" does. Speaking on National Public Radio's show *Fresh Air* with Terry Gross, conservative anti-tax activist Grover Norquist likened progressive taxation, in which the rich pay a higher percentage of their income than others, to Hitler's treatment of the Jews. In both cases, he said, you had a society singling out a group of people.

The second argument in favor of meritocracy, and to my mind the more compelling, is not that it is necessarily fair, but rather that it is efficient. By identifying the best and brightest and putting them through resource-intensive schooling and training, we produce a set of elites well equipped to dispatch their duties with aplomb. By conferring the most power on those best equipped to wield it, the meritocracy produces a better society for us all. In rewarding effort and smarts, we incentivize both.

At the level of theory, this is a fairly noncontroversial proposition. People should get jobs and positions based on their ability to do the jobs. The ranks of airline pilots should be staffed with those who are best at flying, the ranks of surgeons with those best at performing surgery. And so on. Such a social order obviously benefits us all by keeping us clear of plane crashes and mangled operations. The broader social theory of meritocracy simply extends this logic: We have lots of complicated and difficult tasks in our society—managing the Federal Reserve, designing financial derivatives, overseeing corporate mergers and acquisitions—and those functions should be done by those best able to do them well.

But if that's the most compelling theoretical argument for meritocracy, it is also just that—an argument in theory. The reality is that meritocracy in practice is something different. The most fundamental problem with meritocracy is how difficult it is to maintain in its pure and noble form. In this, Michael Young's prophecy got it wrong. The meritocracy of his imagination fails because it works too well: It is able to measure merit with such precision and hews to the rules so well that the dullard scions of the wealthy find themselves thrown down into the drone class along with the others who test poorly. Ultimately, they are able to foment an uprising, based partly on the umbrage they feel from their unjust dispossession.

In reality our meritocracy has failed not because it's too meritocratic, but because in practice, it isn't very meritocratic at all.

THE IRON LAW OF MERITOCRACY

Let's return to Hunter as a case study. The problem with my alma mater is that over time the mechanisms of meritocracy have broken down. With the rise of a sophisticated and expensive test preparation industry, the means of selecting entrants to Hunter has grown less independent of the social and economic hierarchies in New York at large. The pyramid of merit has come to mirror the pyramid of wealth and cultural capital.

How and why does this happen? I think the best answer comes from the work of a social theorist named Robert Michels, who was occupied with a somewhat parallel problem in the early years of the last century. Born to a wealthy German family, fluent in French and Italian, Michels studied under Max Weber and achieved academic renown as the master's star pupil. During his time in the academy he came to adopt the radical socialist politics then sweeping through much of Europe.

At first, he joined the Social Democratic Party of Germany, but he ultimately came to view it as too bureaucratic to achieve its stated aims. "Our workers' organization has become an end in itself," Michels declared, "a machine which is perfected for its own sake and not for the tasks which it could have performed." Michels then drifted toward the syndicalists, who eschewed parliamentary elections in favor of mass labor solidarity, general strikes, and resistance to the dictatorship of the Kaiser. But even among the more militant factions of the German left, Michels encountered the same bureaucratic pathologies that had soured him on the SDP, and he came to believe the problem was deeper than the nature of one individual party. Despite their democratic principles and their commitment to egalitarianism, the parties of the left were never able to embody those principles in the actual practice of party governance. For parties of the right, which were committed to inequality, concentrated power, and rule by few, it was not surprising to find hierarchical party structures dominated from on high. But why, Michels wondered in his classic book *Political Parties,* were parties of the left, those most ideologically committed to democracy and participation, as oligarchic in their actual functioning as the self-consciously elitist and aristocratic parties of the right?

Michels's grim conclusion was that it was impossible for any party, no matter its belief system, to actually bring about democracy in practice. Oligarchy was inevitable. "The most formidable argument against the sovereignty of the masses," Michels came to believe, "is . . . derived from the mechanical and technical impossibility of its realization." For any kind of political party, or, indeed, for any institution with a democratic base, to consolidate the legitimacy it needs to exist, it must have an organization that delegates tasks. The rank and file will not have the time, energy, wherewithal, or inclination to participate in the many, often minute, decisions necessary to keep the institution functioning. In fact, effectiveness, Michels argues convincingly, requires these tasks be delegated to some kind of permanent, full-time cadre of leadership: "In the great industrial centers, where the labor party sometimes numbers its adherents by tens of thousands, it is impossible to carry on the affairs of this gigantic body without a system of representation."

As this system of representation develops its bureaucratic structure, it imbues a small group of people with enough power to delegate tasks and make decisions of consequence for the entire membership. "Without wishing it," Michels says, there grows up a great "gulf which divides the leaders from the masses." The leaders now control the tools with which to manipulate the opinion of the masses and subvert the organization's democratic process. "Thus the leaders, who were at first no more than the executive organs of the collective, will soon emancipate themselves from the mass and become independent of its control."

All this flows inexorably from the nature of organization itself, Michels concludes, and he calls it "The Iron Law of Oligarchy": "It is organization which gives birth to the dominion of the elected over the electors, of the mandataries over the mandators, of the delegates over the delegators. Who says organization says oligarchy."

For those committed to democracy, trade unionism, and all other sundry forms of left/progressive organizations, Michels's account is dispiriting to say the least. But it is also prescient and profound. Though Michels would later turn to the right, becoming a devoted supporter of Benito Mussolini, whom he saw as a vessel for a genuine working-class sensibility, the Michels who wrote *Political Parties* was still proudly a man of the left. He recognized the challenge his work presented to his comrades and viewed the task of democratic socialists as a kind of noble, Sisyphean endeavor, which he described by invoking a fable. In it, a dying peasant tells his sons that he has buried a treasure in their fields. "After the old man's death the sons dig everywhere in order to discover the treasure. They do not find it. But their indefatigable labor improves the soil and secures for them a comparative well-being."

"The treasure in the fable may well symbolize democracy," Michels wrote. "Democracy is a treasure which no one will ever discover by deliberate search. But in continuing our search, in laboring indefatigably to discover the undiscoverable, we shall perform a work which will have fertile results in the democratic sense."

In order for it to live up to its ideals, a meritocracy must comply with two principles. The first is the Principle of Difference, which holds that there is vast differentiation among people in their ability, and that we should embrace this natural hierarchy and set ourselves the task of matching the hardest working and most talented to the most difficult, important, and remunerative tasks.

The second is the Principle of Mobility. Over time, there must be some continuous competitive selection process that ensures that performance is rewarded and failure punished. That is, the delegation of duties cannot be simply made once and then fixed in place over a career or between generations. People must be able to rise and fall along with their accomplishments and failures.

This has different meanings in different contexts. In the context of an organization, like, say, Enron or Major League Baseball, the principle means that there is no such thing as tenure or seniority, that performance ultimately determines one's status and placement in the hierarchy. When a slugger loses his swing, he should be benched; when a trader loses money, his bonus should be cut.

At the broader social level it means we expect a high degree of social mobility. We hope that the talented children of the poor will ascend to positions of power and prestige while the mediocre sons of the wealthy will not be charged with life-and-death decisions. Over time, in other words, society will have mechanisms that act as a sort of pump, constantly ensuring that the talented and hardworking are propelled upward, while the mediocre trickle downward.

But this ideal, appealing as it may be, runs up against the reality of what I'll call The Iron Law of Meritocracy. The Iron Law of Meritocracy states that eventually the inequality produced by a meritocratic system will grow large enough to subvert the mechanisms of mobility. Unequal outcomes make equal opportunity impossible. The Principle of Difference will come to overwhelm the Principle of Mobility. Those who are able to climb up the ladder will find ways to pull it up after them, or to selectively lower it down to allow their friends, allies, and kin to scramble up. In other words: "Whoever says meritocracy says oligarchy."

Hunter is a good example. Its foundational premise—one shared by several other New York high schools designed for the intellectually gifted—is an acceptance, even a glorification, of inequality. As an institution, it has been set aside to nurture and educate the brightest minds in the city. Hunter also takes great institutional pride in pulling in these bright minds from all five boroughs and not simply cultivating the children of Manhattan's ruling class as its private-school rivals do. The problem is that, over time, the inequality in the city at large has produced mechanisms—most significantly the growing test prep industry—that largely subvert the single method whereby mobility is achieved.

We've seen the same thing happen in elite colleges, though there it takes a very different shape. American universities are the central institution of the modern meritocracy, and yet, as Daniel Golden documents in his devastating and meticulous book *The Price of Admission,* atop the ostensibly meritocratic architecture of SATs and high school grades is built an entire tower of preference and subsidy for the privileged:

> At least one third of the students at elite universities, and at least half at liberal arts colleges, are flagged for preferential treatment in the admissions process. While minorities make up 10 to 15 percent of a typical student body, affluent whites dominate other preferred groups: recruited athletes (10 to 25 percent of students); alumni children, also known as legacies (10 to 25 percent); development cases (2 to 5 percent); children of celebrities and politicians (1 to 2 percent); and children of faculty members (1 to 3 percent).

This doesn't even count the advantages that wealthy children have in terms of private tutors, test prep, and access to expensive private high schools and college counselors adept at navigating the politics of admissions. All together this layered system of preferences for the children of the privileged amounts to, in Golden's words, "affirmative action for rich white people." It is not so much the meritocracy as idealized and celebrated but rather the ancient practice of "elites mastering the art of perpetuating themselves."

A pure functioning meritocracy, like that conjured by Michael Young, would produce a society with growing inequality, but that inequality would come along with a correlated increase in social mobility. As the educational system and business world got better and better at finding inherent merit wherever it lay, you would see the bright kids of the poor boosted to the upper echelons of society, with the untalented progeny of the best and brightest relegated to the bottom of the social pyramid where they belong.

But the Iron Law of Meritocracy makes a different prediction, that societies ordered around the meritocratic ideal will produce inequality without the attendant mobility. Indeed, over time, a society will grow both more unequal and less mobile as those who ascend its heights create means of preserving and defending their privilege and find ways to pass it on across generations. And this, as it turns out, is a pretty spot-on description of the trajectory of the American economy since the mid-1970s.

The sharp, continuous rise in inequality is one of the most studied and acknowledged features of the American political economy in the post-Carter age. Paul Krugman calls it "The Great Divergence," and the economist Emmanuel Saez, who has done the most pioneering work on measuring the phenomenon and recently received the prestigious John Bates Clark Medal, has written, "The top 1% income share has increased dramatically in recent decades and reached levels which had not been seen . . . since before the Great Depression."

In 1928, the top 10 percent of earners captured 46 percent of national income. That was the highest share that the top tenth captured for nearly eighty years, until 2007, when we returned to the wealth distribution of the country on the eve of the Great Depression. The top 1 percent did even better. Between 1979 and 2007, nearly 88 percent of the entire economy's income gains went to the top 1 percent.

One of the most distinctive aspects of the rise in American inequality over the past three decades is just how concentrated the gains are at the very top. The farther up the income scale you go, the better people are doing: the top 10 percent have done well, but have been outpaced by the top 1 percent, who in turn have seen slower gains than the top 0.1 percent, all of whom have been beaten by the top 0.01 percent. As Jacob Hacker and Paul Pierson put it in their book *Winner-Take-All Politics*, even the top 1 percent, "while seemingly an exclusive group, is much too broad a category to pinpoint the most fortunate beneficiaries of the post 1970s income explosion at the top." Adjusted for inflation, the top 0.1 percent saw their average annual income rise from just over $1 million in 1974 to $7.1 million in 2007. And things were even better for the top 0.01 percent, who saw their average annual income explode from less than $4 million to $35 million, nearly a *ninefold* increase.

It is not simply that the rich are getting richer, though that's certainly true. It is that a smaller and smaller group of über-rich are able to capture a larger and larger share of the fruits of the American economy. America now features more inequality than any other industrialized democracy. In its peer group are countries like Argentina and other Latin American nations that once stood as iconic examples of the ways in which the absence of a large middle class presented a roadblock to development and good governance.

So: income inequality has been growing. What about mobility? While it's much harder to measure than inequality, there's a growing body of evidence that at the same time inequality has been growing at an unprecedented rate, social mobility has been declining. In a 2012 speech, Alan Krueger, the chairman of President Obama's Council of Economic Advisers, coined the term "The Gatsby Curve" to refer to a chart showing that, over the past three decades, "as inequality has increased . . . year-to-year or generation-to-generation economic mobility has decreased."

The most comprehensive attempt at divining the long-term trends of social mobility over several generations is "Intergenerational Economic Mobility in the U.S., 1940 to 2000," a complex paper by economists Daniel Aaronson and Bhashkar Mazumder of the Federal Reserve Bank of Chicago. After a series of maneuvers that qualify as statistical pyrotechnics, they conclude that "mobility increased from 1950 to 1980 but has declined sharply since 1980. The recent decline in mobility is only partially explained by education."

Another pair of economists, from the Boston Federal Reserve, analyzed household income data to measure mobility over three decades, rather than intergenerational mobility. They found that in the 1970s, 36 percent of families stayed in the same income decile. In the 1980s, that figure was 37 percent, and in the 1990s it was 40 percent. In other words, over time, a larger share of the families were staying within their class through the duration of their lives.

A study carried out by economist Tom Hertz of more than six thousand American families over two generations found that of those born into the bottom income quintile, 42 percent remained in it, while only 6 percent made it to the top bracket. Someone born into the top bracket of American society is seven times as likely to end up there as someone born into the bottom. Hertz notes that race is a crucial factor in mobility, particularly for those in the lowest income bracket. "The gap between median black family income and median white family income hasn't changed in twenty years," he told me. "That is not a society moving toward equality. It's a society that's reproducing inequality by race."

Part of this is likely due to the rise of the war on drugs and mass incarceration, which disproportionately impacts African Americans. A report based on the research of Bruce Western and Becky Pettit, published by Pew, looked at the effect that our criminal justice policies have on social mobility. It found that incarceration dramatically reduces earnings after release, as well as the prospects for children of those incarcerated. The report notes that "1 in every 28 children in the United States—more than 3.6 percent—now has a parent in jail or prison. Just 25 years ago, the figure was only 1 in 125. For black children, incarceration is an especially common family circumstance. More than 1 in 9 black children have a parent in prison or jail, a rate that has more than quadrupled in the past 25 years."

Not only is America less mobile than it used to be, it is less mobile than nearly every other industrialized democracy in the world. "Compared to the same peer group," Pew's Economic Mobility Project reports, "Germany is 1.5 times more mobile than the United States, Canada nearly 2.5 times more mobile, and Denmark 3 times more mobile." They find that the only other country with similarly low levels of mobility is our sibling in meritocracy, the birthplace of the word itself, the United Kingdom.

And yet, in one of the grand ironies of American public opinion, the United States is still the place where the meritocratic faith burns brightest. "In Europe," the *Economist* noted, "majorities of people in every country except Britain, the Czech Republic, and Slovakia believe that forces beyond their personal control determine their success. In America only 32% take such a fatalistic view." Since 1983 an occasional CBS News/New York Times poll has asked people: "Do you think it is still possible to start out poor in this country, work hard, and become rich?" In 1983, 57 percent answered yes, and by 2007 the number had risen to 81 percent. Even in 2009, after the worst financial crisis in recent memory, and epidemic levels of unemployment, the overwhelming majority of those surveyed (72 percent) still held on to this singular faith.

It is remarkable that as faith in so much about the American project disintegrates, this one belief endures, even as the facts do more and more to undermine it. But I think this is more than mere coincidence. A deep recognition of the slow death of the meritocratic dream underlies the decline of trust in public institutions and the crisis of authority in which we are now mired. Since people cannot bring themselves to disbelieve in the central premise of the American dream, they focus their ire and skepticism instead on the broken institutions it has formed.

MUCH OF the enduring value of Michels's analysis of political parties comes from his prophetic understanding of the end point toward which certain socialist parties were heading. His theory predicted that a true dictatorship of the proletariat would keep the dictatorship and lose the proletariat, as happened in Russia just a few years after his book was published. "The socialists might conquer," he prophesied, "but not socialism, which would perish in the moment of its adherents' triumph."

In our own case, the end point is nowhere near as violent or dire. But if The Iron Law of Meritocracy has corrupted a society founded upon the twin principles of difference and mobility, we might ask what kind of social order would result.

It would be a society with extremely high and rising inequality yet little circulation of elites. A society in which the pillar institutions were populated by and presided over by a group of hypereducated, ambitious overachievers who enjoyed tremendous monetary rewards as well as unparalleled political power and prestige and yet who managed to insulate themselves from sanction, competition, and accountability, a group of people who could more or less rest assured that now that they have achieved their status, now that they have scaled to the top of the pyramid, they, their peers, and their progeny will stay there.

Such a ruling class would have all the competitive ferocity inculcated by the ceaseless jockeying within the institutions that produce meritocratic elites, but face no actual sanctions for failing at their duties or succumbing to the temptations of corruption. It would reflexively protect its worst members, it would operate with a wide gulf between performance and reward, and would be shot through with corruption, rule-breaking, and self-dealing as those on top pursued the outsize rewards promised for superstars. In the way the bailouts combined the worst aspects of capitalism and socialism, such a social order would fuse the worst aspects of meritocracy and bureaucracy.

It would, in other words, look a lot like the American elite circa 2012.

Chapter 3

MORAL HAZARDS

*The bargain has been breached. . . . The American people do not
think the system is fair, or on the level.*

—JOE BIDEN

O N THE MORNING OF FEBRUARY 18, 2010, ANDREW
Joseph Stack woke in his home in the quiet, leafy neighborhood of North Austin, Texas. A self-employed software consultant and a part-time bassist in a local band, Joe, as his friends called him, started the day by setting fire to his house. He then drove to the local plane hangar where he kept his single-engine Piper Dakota. He loaded in an extra fuel tank, taxied to the runway, and, when cleared for takeoff, uttered his last words to the control tower: "Thanks for your help. Have a great day."

Just a few minutes later he aimed his plane at an office building where 190 local Internal Revenue Service officers worked, and crashed into it, killing himself, injuring fourteen, and murdering IRS manager Vernon Hunter.

Before he killed himself, Stack posted a three-thousand-word suicide note on his personal website. His paranoid yet oddly articulate prose touched off a round of finger-pointing about just which "side" of the political spectrum Stack belonged to. No sooner did local television station KVUE-TV arrive at the scene than the national media began hustling to assign their own caption to his suicide/murder. *Daily Kos* referred to him as an "anti-tax terror-ist," and the *Washington Post*'s Jonathan Capehart noted that "his alienation is similar to what we're hearing from the extreme ele-ments of the Tea Party movement." The director of the Southern Poverty Law Center's Intelligence Project connected the attack to "an explosive growth of anti-government militias and so-called Pa-triot groups over the past year," whose central idea is that "taxes are completely illegitimate." The right wing responded in kind. A car-toonist on *RedState* pointed out that Stack approvingly paraphrased Marx and criticized capitalism. Conservative writer John Lott la-beled Stack a "leftwing nut," and Rush Limbaugh remarked that Stack's note sounded "just like any liberal Democrat." (It did not.)

In truth, Stack's note oscillates wildly between both extreme ends of the political spectrum. He was quite clearly disturbed, and possibly in the grip of genuine mental illness. But his rage took a shape we can immediately recognize. The suicide note is an expres-sion of a raw nihilistic insurrectionism. Stack came to the conclu-sion that each and every pillar institution in American society had rendered itself irredeemable. He railed against the "vulgar, cor-rupt Catholic Church," and politicians, whom he called "thieves, liars, and self-serving scumbags." He launched invective at bureau-crats, "big business," unions, Enron, and health insurance and drug companies alike. The entire society, he had concluded, was rigged against people like him: "Starting at early ages we in this country have been brainwashed to believe that, in return for our dedication and service, our government stands for justice for all."

But it was all a poisonous lie.

Why is it that a handful of thugs and plunderers can commit unthinkable atrocities (and in the case of the GM executives, for scores of years) and when it's time for their gravy train to crash under the weight of their gluttony and overwhelming stupidity, the force of the full federal government has no difficulty coming to their aid within days if not hours?

The note is also shot through with self-pity. Everyone seems to be conspiring against him. "The cruel joke," he concludes, "is that the really big chunks of shit at the top have known this all along and have been laughing at and using this awareness against fools like me all along."

Joe Stack was a lone, bitter solipsist. His hopes to begin a full-scale violent insurrection were always preposterous, and his death registered little more than profound heartache for the family and loved ones of the man he murdered.

But it turns out that he also had a pretty legitimate grievance.

What appears to have prompted Stack's descent into violence was a drawn-out battle with the IRS over the taxes on his own computer consulting small business, and proper reporting thereof. The government was insisting he owed taxes and Stack was insisting he didn't.

At the heart of the dispute was an obscure section of the tax code—Section 1706 of the 1986 Tax Reform Act, which Stack cited in his note. The law, according to the *New York Times,* "made it extremely difficult for information technology professionals to work as self-employed individuals, forcing most to become company employees." Because Stack was a self-employed computer programmer, he'd run smack-dab into this provision and failed to adequately comply with the requirements it imposed. The provision was originally pushed through by Daniel Patrick Moynihan, who wanted to deliver a $60 million tax break to New York–based IBM. In order to deliver the tax cut, he had to find somewhere else in the code to raise $60 million. So he proposed a rule requiring software engineers to be employed as payroll employees rather than contractors.

The new requirement raised little revenue and created a lot of hassles. A year later Moynihan proposed its repeal, and was subsequently joined by seventy other senators. Somehow, though, the law remained in place. Its effect, according to a Washington lawyer who follows the issue, has been disastrous. "This law has ruined many people's lives, hurt the technology industry, and discouraged the creation of small, independent businesses critical to a thriving domestic economy," the lawyer Harvey J. Shulman told the *Times* in 2010, after Stack's death. "That the law still exists—even after its original sponsors called for its repeal and unbiased studies proved it unfairly targeted a tax-compliant industry—shows just how dysfunctional and unresponsive Democratic and Republican Congresses and our political system have been, even on relatively simple issues."

IBM, of course, got to keep its tax break.

As manifestly disturbed as Stack was, legions of Americans went through their own process of disenchantmant followed by radicalization over the course of the decade. Susan Southwick, a fifty-year-old Utah Tea Party organizer, grew up in a family so loyally Republican that her grandmother had a collection of stuffed elephants. But in the latter days of the Bush administration she says she "started getting disillusioned and feeling not so good about my government." For her, this was a first. "I've always been accepting and trusting," she told me. "And back when Bush was taking a lot of flack, I thought well, he knows more than me and he's got his reason. You know: you kind of trust authority."

Then came the financial crisis, and the bailouts.

"It threw me over the ledge. Are you kidding me? I just couldn't believe they were going to bail out these banks. I thought people are out of control; people are crazy. This is stupid. People need to succeed or fail on their own without help of our government." At that moment, something about Southwick's worldview began to

TWILIGHT *of the* ELITES

fundamentally change; some innocence she'd carried with her all her adult life died.

Southwick says she had always been a trusting person, always been inclined to think the best about people, particularly those working in government and other positions of authority. But the bailout vote made her question all of that. Maybe she'd been a sucker all along, or maybe the most cynical interpretation was the correct one. "You start to see some injustices, and things that make you go 'what?' and you start to realize maybe you kind of had the blinders on. I don't want to believe anyone's doing anything wrong deliberately, but with what's happened over the last several years, it's hard to maintain that position when you see the government and the corporate world acting the way they are."

Southwick became an activist and organizer. She joined the Tea Party, built an influential e-mail list, trained volunteers, and got herself elected as a delegate to the state's party convention. In a move that shocked the political world, she and her comrades ousted Utah's three-term Republican senator Bob Bennett, a man who had voted for and continued to defend the bank bailout. It was, to her mind, a rare case of just deserts.

THE LEGITIMACY of a hypercompetitive social order such as our own derives from a shared sense that everyone is playing by the same rules, that there is an inherent fairness to the terms of the social contract, and that the system basically manages to confer the most benefits on the most deserving. Under the guidelines of the American meritocratic ethos, vastly unequal outcomes are fine, so long as the process that produces them is fair—as long as the rules of the game create a "level playing field" such that everyone is subject to the same rewards and sanctions, regardless of station.

Most Americans have internalized the general sense that

there's a more or less proportional relationship between what you put into life and what you get out of it.

This is a very old American idea. In 1867, the founding editor of *The Nation* magazine, Irish-born Edwin Lawrence Godkin, compared the militancy of European striking workers to their more muted American counterparts and concluded that the ferocity of class sentiment in Europe was unknown in the United States because American laborers all felt as if they were part of the same basic order as the bosses. "The social line between the laborer and the capitalist here is very faintly drawn," he noted. "Most successful employers of labor have begun by being laborers themselves; most laborers hope . . . to become employers."

The conviction that in America those at the top and those at the bottom are equal under the eyes of the law is one of our most fundamental and cherished national creeds. But nearly everywhere you look, this basic principle of fairness is ignored or violated. To take just a few basic examples: We live in a country in which the vast majority of Americans are subject to what's called "at will" employment, which means they can be fired at any time for almost anything—wearing the wrong tie, calling the boss "dude," or sneaking a free Slurpee while closing up the gas station. And yet while U.S. employment declined by 8.8 million during this recent recession, just a handful of bank CEOs have lost their jobs for the roles they played in creating the crisis. Many who did, most notably Ken Lewis of Bank of America, were shown the door with multi-million-dollar pension plans or golden parachutes. Even Dick Fuld, the disgraced former CEO of the now defunct Lehman Brothers, left his job having exercised nearly half a billion in options before his company sailed over the subprime precipice.

This imbalance is more than simply economic: it is embedded in the current machinery of American justice. America incarcerates a larger percentage of its citizens than any other nation on earth (including China). With less than 5 percent of the world's population, we account for nearly 25 percent of the world's prison population. Yet the same mighty prosecutorial apparatus that churns through so many Americans has almost entirely spared the ranks of bank managers who oversaw the very institutions that nearly brought the whole system down.

Joe Stack saw his plight in this context. The IRS accused him of being a tax cheat and brought the full force of the state down on him for subverting the rules. And yet: the rules themselves were rigged; they had been twisted into a rope by powerful interests and slung around his neck. Stack came to believe this to be true not just in tax law, but in every single part of American life: the rich and powerful blatantly flouted the law without sanction, bending the law to their own benefit or simply writing the law themselves, while guys like him couldn't catch a break.

A society in which cheaters, shirkers, and incompetents face no sanction, where bad behavior meets reward, is a morally hazardous one. In economics, the term "moral hazard" refers to the perverse incentives that can arise when agents are insulated from the cost of their actions: A hypochondriac with a health insurance plan that covers the full cost of doctor's visits will make more appointments than one who has a sizable co-pay; a banker who knows at some level that the cost of catastrophically bad bets will ultimately be picked up by the government has far less incentive to avoid blowing everything up while in the zealous pursuit of the highest yield possible.

One way to understand the financial crisis is as the natural result of moral hazard: major financial institutions only took the risks they did because at some institutional level they assumed that if things went terribly wrong the government wouldn't let them fail. Whether or not that was the case before the crisis, it's undeniable that the unprecedented actions undertaken by the federal government after the crisis demonstrated definitively that the government will step in to prevent the failure of institutions big and powerful enough to bring down the entire system.

If no one on Wall Street is held accountable for the crash, then what incentive is there not to grab another stack of chips and sit back down at the poker table? The same principle extends beyond Wall Street: an institution that rewards the reckless will act as a spawning ground for recklessness.

CHEATERS NEVER WIN

Before the subprime crisis and the widespread mortgage fraud made Wall Street the symbol of corporate perfidy, there was Enron. It's funny now to think of Enron as the largest corporate bankruptcy of all time, because it's been supplanted by several victims of the financial crisis. But at the time Enron was the biggest corporate scandal (and biggest threat to the Bush presidency) the country had ever seen. Fifty-six hundred people lost their jobs. Sixty billion dollars in stock market value evaporated, and $2.1 billion in pension plans disappeared. And for good measure the scandal managed to take down Arthur Andersen, one of the five largest and oldest accounting firms in the nation.

But before Enron was Enron, the symbol of corporate deception, hubris, and elite failure, it was a fast-growing energy concern, pioneering new business models. And a story from the firm's early days provides a grim bit of foreshadowing of what was to come.

In 1987, the firm's vice president of internal auditing, David Woytek, and his colleague discovered a pattern of suspicious financial transactions emanating from Enron's oil trading desk. When confronted, the two men who ran the trading division—Louis Borget and Thomas Mastroeni—gave a suspicious story about funneling money into their personal accounts in order to move profits from 1986, which was a banner year, to 1987, thereby smoothing out earnings over time. The explanation seemed to Woytek implausible and absurd, but the kicker was this: in support of their contention, the two traders had provided the auditors, and, ultimately, Enron CEO Ken Lay, with bank records that had clearly been doctored to remove the suspect transactions.

When, at a climactic meeting with Lay, Woytek presented the evidence of forged documents, he was shocked by Lay's response: Lay didn't punish the traders or fire them. Instead, he told them he didn't want to see them doing something like this again and ordered Woytek up to the oil trading offices for a few weeks to monitor its practices and conduct an audit.

Eventually, though, the very profitable trading desk complained so vociferously about the auditors hanging over their shoulder that Woytek and company were sent packing. The end result of the whole affair was, in the short term, nothing. Lay didn't fire the traders for their forged bank records, or the unaccounted-for $250,000 transfer to personal accounts (or the company car that one of them sold, pocketing the proceeds). Later that year, the Enron Oil unit would blow up, taking on enormous losses, thanks in part to Borget and Mastroeni, who ultimately pled guilty to fraud and tax crimes.

But the message of the entire story was clear: if you're profitable, you can break the rules. Signals like that ripple out through an organization: corners are cut, rules broken, and everyone can see the benefits that redound to those who do the cutting and breaking.

In his encyclopedic chronicle of the Enron debacle, Kurt Eichenwald describes the organizational vision of Enron's Jeff Skilling, who rose from chairman of Enron's finance division to be chief operating officer of the entire company, this way:

> Skilling thought he was on his way to building a perfect meritocracy, where smart, gifted—and richly compensated—people would be pitted against one another in an endless battle for dominance, creating a free flow of ideas that could push the business past its competitors.

And whatever you did in pursuit of "dominance" was fine so long as you won. Skilling used to brag about an Enron vice president named Louise Kitchen who had explicitly ignored multiple orders from Skilling not to start an Internet trading business. She went ahead and did it anyway. The business unit would prove to be wildly profitable, and its success insulated Kitchen from any reprimand from above. Skilling would often tell this story to subordinates, with the lesson being clear: you can break the rules as long as it makes money.

Enron prized performance and rewarded stars with outsize bonuses; it ruthlessly purged those it felt did not perform. One executive described the hypercompetitive, talent-obsessed approach of Enron this way: "We hire very smart people and we pay them more than they think they are worth." With big rewards at the top for performance, there was also brutal punishment at the bottom for those perceived to be slacking. As a matter of policy, Enron would routinely fire people in the bottom 10 percent of its workforce after biannual reviews, a practice known as "rank and yank." (Goldman Sachs, among other companies, employs a similar policy.) This *Survivor*-like human resources policy emanated from Skilling's former employer McKinsey, and (unsurprisingly perhaps) *McKinsey Quarterly* singled out the policy in 1997 for playing a large role in Enron's success.

At its best Enron marshaled the energizing force of meritocratic competition, reducing the importance of seniority, connections, and office politics. Former employees who managed to thrive
in this setting still, to this day, speak highly of it. Pravin Jain, who
ran Enron's telecom operation in Brazil and spent four years as an
executive of the company, says he'd never seen a business run like
Enron: "I thought Enron was a fabulous experiment in applying
some of the basic tenets of capitalism to how you put together an
organization. . . . The energy they generated in the company, I had
never seen anything like it before."

"It was an exhilarating atmosphere," recalls former Enron VP
Sherron Watkins. "There was a sense that if you came up with a good
idea, you could get a budget and do it." The brutal logic of "rank and
yank" actually worked, according to Watkins: "It really kept dead
wood from hanging around. Someone who was just a favored child
of some manager, they couldn't keep those types around."

If the name Sherron Watkins rings a bell, it should. She was
one of the few senior Enron employees, if not the only one, to
emerge from the entire drama with her reputation intact. In August 2001, disturbed by the company's books, she sent Ken Lay a
memo containing what would become a famous prediction: "I'm
incredibly nervous that we will implode in a wave of accounting
scandals."

Watkins's lawyer Phil Hilder recalled that when she first
walked into his office, shortly after Enron had started to capsize,
and told him her story, he was incredulous. "Here you have an
individual telling a story about the best and brightest, a company
that had hired the top law firm in the state, top accounting company in the world and all these Ivy League MBAs, all being involved in one capacity or another or turning a blind eye to cooking
the books. I knew either this woman was a lunatic or I was sitting
on a corporate nuclear bomb that was going to explode."

When I met Sherron Watkins at Hilder's office in Houston in spring 2010, it was Saint Patrick's Day and she was suited up in green, a cross dangling from her neck, arranging plans on her cell phone for celebrating the holiday later that day. There's a very short list of recipients of *Time* magazine's Person of the Year who struggle to find work, but Watkins is on it. "Whistle-blower," she says, "might as well be synonymous with troublemaker."

The whistle-blowing (a term she and her lawyer are both hesitant to use since her memo was entirely internal) made her a star witness at the congressional hearings into Enron that later landed her on the cover of *Time*. It also created a new career for her as a professional business ethicist. Since Watkins can no longer make a living as a CPA, she now draws her income from traveling the country and talking to business groups about how to avoid becoming the next Enron. It's something of a growth industry. On the day we met in the spring of 2010, the report from the Lehman Brothers' bankruptcy investigator was released, describing a set of off-balance-sheet transactions at the firm eerily similar to Enron's off-balance-sheet shenanigans.

Watkins's theory of the malfeasance at Enron, and the epidemic of corporate fraud that's followed in its wake, is bracingly straightforward: "It's all one thing: it's compensation." The amount of money at stake for executives, she argues, is so large it induces misconduct: "Money makes a lot of people rationalize behavior that they normally would not participate in."

Competition and outsize monetary reward are just one-half of the fraud equation. The other is lack of regulatory oversight and an internal culture of corruption. On that front, Watkins is pessimistic about the ability of outside entities, whether they be the financial press or regulators, to crack open the kind of systemic fraud that was going on at Enron. Ultimately, she says, it's a matter of the institution itself setting boundaries. "The controls, the better practices have to come from within. There has to be a tone at the top."

Enron promised large rewards for performance and harsh penalties for failure. And it prided itself on the fact that its employees would rise or fall based solely on their performance, not on connections, seniority, office politics, or anything else. But the absence of a culture of accountability meant that it produced cheating along with performance.

This wasn't unique to Enron. In fact, one of the lessons of the decade is that intensely competitive, high-reward meritocratic environments are prone to produce all kinds of fraud, deception, conniving, and game rigging. And there's no single more symbolically potent example of this phenomenon than our disgraced national pastime.

The story of steroids in baseball is more often than not told as a morality tale with a rogues' gallery of villains—Roger Clemens, Alex Rodriguez, Barry Bonds—who are called out by a swarming press to be berated and humiliated, and to tearfully apologize for their sins and seek redemption. It's an emotionally satisfying drama, but not particularly edifying. Because the story of Major League Baseball isn't about any one person's misconduct, but the story of a systemic breakdown that created institution-wide incentives for fraud and a total failure of accountability. It is, in other words, the story of Enron, the story of the housing bubble and the crash, the story of much of the decade as a whole.

To understand the steroids era, you first need to understand Marvin Miller, the man who turned the Major League Baseball Players Association into one of the country's most effective unions. For the majority of baseball's history, the players union was a toothless beast. Owners more or less owned players outright; they were able to trade, hire, and fire at will. There was no free agency, and though the league was quite profitable (the only legal monopoly in the country), most players merely scraped by, working odd jobs in the off-season to make ends meet. It was a classic system of exploitation, one the owners were single-mindedly committed to maintaining.

Enter Miller. "The beginning was absolutely the worst because to the hard-line owners of that day unionism was treason, there's no other way to describe it," Miller, now in his nineties and combative as ever, recounts. "For very wealthy people who owned franchises, baseball was a respite of the tensions and problems elsewhere; here you could control everything: no unions, a reserve clause that made the players prisoners, no grievance procedure, no salary arbitration, no nothing."

Then a respected labor representative for the United Steelworkers, Miller was chosen by a player search committee that was casting around for an effective leader with experience in contracts and pension plans. He immediately went to work impressing upon his players the rudiments of union consciousness—solidarity—and putting it into practice with a series of strikes. By 1968, Miller had negotiated baseball's first collective bargaining agreement, raising baseball's minimum salary for the first time in twenty years. Four years later the players struck for the first time. It would be the first of many. In each strike the union held, the owners conceded, and the players walked away with concrete and valuable contract improvements. If the median American wage earner had been able to join a Marvin Miller union, that wage earner would have seen his or her inflation-adjusted wages increase from $4,938 to $62,717 over the same period of time (1966 to 1982). Not surprisingly, the union became highly trusted by its members.

Then in 1985, in response to the union's victories, the owners engineered a conspiracy to steal back millions from the players.

Meeting secretly, they struck a deal not to competitively bid for the services of free agents, artificially suppressing the salaries on the market. The union got wind of the arrangement, sued, and the owners ultimately ended up paying hundreds of millions of dollars to players in settlements.

The collusion episode confirmed for Miller's successor, Donald Fehr, that the owners were implacably intent on suppressing their members' salaries by any means necessary. "It poisoned the well of what was already a fairly toxic relationship," recalls former commissioner Fay Vincent. Vincent entered baseball from the movie business as the second in command to commissioner and former Yale president Bart Giamatti. When Giamatti died unexpectedly in 1989, Vincent took the reins. "The union-management problem dominated everything when I came to baseball."

By the mid-1990s, having been bested and bested again, the owners resolved to precipitate a confrontation with the players they would finally win. In preparing for this fight, they came to see Vincent as an obstacle. In 1990, during a period of intense labor-management tension, Vincent had stepped in as a neutral third party, facilitating negotiations that ultimately avoided a work stoppage. This time, though, the owners didn't want negotiation. "They thought if they got into a major confrontation with the union, I might get involved and order them to make a deal or go back to work or permit the union to play," he told me.

If there was going to be a no-holds-barred brawl with the union, it was important that there not be an independent referee: The league's commissioner was empowered by the league's by-laws to act "in the best interest of the sport" even if that meant penalizing owners for misconduct, as Vincent did the Yankees' George Steinbrenner. (Steinbrenner had paid a small-time gambler $40,000 to dig up dirt on former Yankees outfielder Dave Winfield in response to Winfield suing Steinbrenner for breach of contract.) In other words, in an institutional landscape defined by a ceaseless war between labor and management, the commissioner stood as the only quasi-independent representative of the sport's long-term interests. He was the closest thing baseball had to a regulator. So in 1992, when Milwaukee Brewers owner Bud Selig led a group of owners in a putsch against Vincent, what they were doing was deregulating—putting one of their own foxes in charge of the proverbial henhouse.

Vincent, who now lives in Vero Beach, has watched the steroid scandal unfold with no small amount of horror. "I think I would have figured out earlier than Selig did that steroids were a problem," he told me. "In 1991, I put out a memo banning steroids. I was onto the fact it was an emerging issue." Vincent also had some real experience as an actual regulator. "I came from the SEC. I was a lawyer. I was basically a trouble expert. I knew more about trouble than most people."

Once the owners ditched Vincent, they went right after the union. In the summer of 1994, they demanded a number of preposterous concessions from the players, and after a series of acrimonious back-and-forths, the union struck. Four weeks into the strike, new commissioner Selig declared that the rest of the season, including the World Series, would be canceled for the first time in the game's 113-year history. Though the owners got the showdown they wanted, the outcome they'd hoped for eluded them. In the end, the union and management agreed to a contract and the union marched on, unbroken.

Neither side emerged from the strike with its reputation intact. Through two world wars and the Great Depression, the World Series had never been canceled. The strike demoralized the league, decimated the fan base, and imperiled the league financially. Both management and the players emerged from the fracas sullied, each side viewed as spoiled rich brats. That is, until 1998, when the greatest home run race in the history of the sport between Mark McGwire and Sammy Sosa revived baseball's fortunes.

DRUGS HAVE always been a part of baseball. It's no small thing to play 162 games in 180 days as major leaguers are expected to, and a little chemically created energy was viewed as a necessary boost. For decades, "greenies," or amphetamines, were ubiquitous in major-league locker rooms. In the 1980s, the league wrestled with something of a cocaine epidemic among its players. (There's also the amazing and surreal tale of Dock Ellis pitching a no-hitter in 1970 for the Pittsburgh Pirates while tripping on LSD.) But while steroids have been part of other athletic endeavors for years—the biochemically engineered East German Olympic team, modern track and field, and cycling, just to name a few—before 1989, they remained largely absent from baseball.

Then things changed. During the World Series–less October 1994, President Clinton signed into law the Dietary Supplement Health and Education Act of 1994 (DSHEA), which created an unregulated carve-out of the FDA's jurisdiction for the nutritional supplement industry. One of the areas that experienced the most explosive growth was weight-lifting supplements sold in stores like General Nutrition Centers.

With legal weight-lifting supplements now available, the line between banned and legitimate substances became somewhat blurred, and supplements made their way into locker rooms. Players union president Donald Fehr points to supplement deregulation as the root of baseball's problems with banned substances. "As long as we have this enormously unregulated [supplement] industry in which there is little or no federal inspection," he said in 2009, "you'll have these kinds of problems."

But DSHEA was just one component. Even before its passage,

a few steroids pioneers had entered baseball and, like successful entrepreneurs who'd soon find their product aped by the competition, changed the league forever. The most famous of these is José Canseco. In his controversial (though in retrospect largely vindicated) memoir *Juiced,* Canseco describes his own personal steroids learning curve. As an undersized minor leaguer, Canseco had good speed and a graceful swing but little else. In his hometown Miami, while still in the minors, he hooked up with a weight-lifting buddy who got him access to a variety of anabolic drugs.

By his own telling, Canseco threw himself into learning about combinations of drugs and used himself as a guinea pig. The results were obvious to everyone who played with him. In his memoir, former Yankee pitcher David Wells recalls facing Canseco in the minors, before he'd begun chemical enhancement and thinking "This guy could Hula Hoop inside a Cheerio." A year later, when Wells next faced Canseco things had changed: "I was stunned to find that 'the Idaho skinny guy' had somehow grown up to become a freaking Macy's balloon. Brand new biceps ripped out from under his uniform sleeves. Thick slabs of beef padded his formerly bony frame. . . . Seven innings and two 450-foot moon shots later, I still had no idea what to make of this new improved mutant. Was this kind of supersize growth spurt even possible? What the hell was this monster eating?"

An environment as intensely competitive as baseball produces a very rapid and intense form of evolution: those who do not perform quickly find themselves back in the minors, while those who succeed are imitated. Under these conditions, adaptations spread quickly: when players notice a technique, strategy, or piece of equipment that gives a fellow player a competitive advantage they appropriate it for themselves. This happens with everything from elbow pads, which sluggers now use to protect their exposed arm as they crowd the plate, to the kinds of gloves they wear and bats they swing.

This sort of adaptive drive is at its strongest when there are massive piles of money at stake, and in the world of poststrike major-league baseball, few achievements brought in more money than hitting home runs. All players had to do was look at Canseco. As a rookie in 1986 he earned $75,000. But his slugging prowess earned him fame, fawning press attention, and a contract of $1.6 million (three times the league average) just three years later.

Canseco accelerated the spread of chemical enhancement by converting himself into a chemical evangelist. He would give fellow players tips on what to use when and even taught them how to inject themselves. (The motivation for this is a touch obscure, but in his memoir, Canseco comes across as needy and desperate for recognition and acclaim.)

When Canseco moved from Oakland to the Texas Rangers in 1992, he took his expertise with him: "Before long, other players from all around the baseball world saw what was going on with me and my buddies in Texas, how strong we all were and how our strength was helping us perform. And soon those players were coming up to me and asking me for advice about using steroids. . . . By then it was an open secret among players: If they wanted to know about steroids, they knew who to ask."

This turns out to be more than just idle boasting. In their paper "Learning Unethical Practices from a Co-worker: The Peer Effect of Jose Canseco," economists Eric D. Gould and Todd R. Kaplan attempted to measure the effect Canseco had on his teammates during his juicing years. They analyzed the power statistics of his teammates before and after Canseco's arrival on their team, and they found that for power position players, coming into contact with Canseco netted nearly two additional home runs and six

RBIs a year after exposure. "After checking 30 comparable players from the same era," they reported, "we find that no other baseball player produced a similar effect."

The other main known vector of drug penetration in the league was a trainer, bodybuilder, and former Mets clubhouse hand named Kirk Radomski. Radomski ran a steroid distribution circle for players, who would be referred by other players in the network. The monetary rewards were enormous: "I didn't help these players earn millions of dollars," he writes in his memoir. "I helped them earn hundreds of millions of dollars. In fact in 2001 I made up a twenty-five-man roster of players I was dealing with and added up their salaries. The total was staggering. My team, the Kirk Radomski team, was earning more than $300 million in salary that season. That was at least $100 million more than the entire Yankees payroll."

You'd have to have been a fool or uncommonly upright not to have wanted to join the Radomski team. Competitive pressures began to create a situation in which opting not to use steroids meant making an affirmative decision to put yourself at a disadvantage. "People who are not using them can't compete against people who do," Radomski says flatly. "They have no chance."

Even the league's best players were susceptible to this dynamic: Jealous of the attention lavished on Mark McGwire and Sammy Sosa in their 1998 home run race, Barry Bonds began using steroids in 1999, according to investigative reporters Mark Fainaru-Wada and Lance Williams's book *Game of Shadows*. That off-season, Bonds traveled to Las Vegas to compete in a charity home run derby along with, among others, Canseco. At this point, Canseco was in peak form. Sporting a comic-book physique, Canseco crushed the competition in the derby. Bonds approached Canseco: "Dude," he said. "Where did you get all that muscle?"

In addition to Radomski and Canseco there were others:

Roger Clemens's trainer Brian McNamee, who testified before a congressional committee about injecting Clemens with drugs, and the infamous Victor Conte, who ran the BALCO labs in Oakland that would ultimately lead to Barry Bonds's indictment. But in some senses the intense competition and ceaseless search for advantage that define life in the majors meant that, whoever introduced performance-enhancing drugs, once they had entered the bloodstream of the league, they were destined to spread.

"Talking to professional athletes about steroids," Radomski writes, "was like discussing investments with bankers." The drug use became so rampant it was no longer possible to maintain it as an open secret limited to the clubhouse. In 2002, *Sports Illustrated* published a blockbuster interview with former MVP and steroid user Ken Caminiti, who estimated that at least half the league was using.

In 2002, Selig and the players union finally agreed to a preliminary testing regime. During spring training the league would administer a completely anonymous test as a kind of diagnostic look at just how pervasive the drug use had become. If more than 5 percent of players tested positive, then automatically a more stringent (and not anonymous) testing regime would kick in.

At the time Kelly Wunsch was a middle reliever for the Chicago White Sox and, somewhat unusually for a relatively new player like himself, the team's union representative. Wunsch was a member of what might be called baseball's forgotten middle class. While stars get the most attention, the majority of a major-league roster is made up of players who will never make an all-star game. And though they're clearly well compensated, they tend to live their lives in a constant state of fear that their skills will diminish or they won't make the cut.

When he got to the big leagues, "what I was totally unprepared for," Wunsch recalls, "was the sheer terror every day that I was going to be sent down. . . . When you have a few bad moments, all of the sudden you start to think, What if I get sent down? How am I going to get my wife and kid to Charlotte, or wherever it is? What about the apartment I've leased?"

Wunsch says the clubhouse culture in the majors wasn't particularly welcoming to newcomers: "Being the new guy, you're immediately distrusted by everybody because they don't know they can count on you," he says. "Baseball's a little bit like being a cop: You protect your brothers. Once you get to the major-league level, the consequences of screwing up and the code of silence become that much more dire."

This code of secrecy was particularly acute because, as Wunsch explains, lots of players were engaged in extramarital affairs. In order to facilitate them, players would have secondary cell phones and be dodgy and noncommittal about their whereabouts. The unwritten rule of the clubhouse was that you didn't ask questions, and if confronted by, say, an angry wife or girlfriend, you never said a thing: you didn't throw other players under the bus. This code of conduct, Wunsch contends, helped allow the steroid culture to flourish.

Wunsch recalls that during his early years in the league, his steroid suspicions were largely focused on pitchers of comparable skill. "The people . . . that organizations are holding up as comparable to me in contract talks: Joe Blow makes this much money and you're 6 mph less than him, same number of appearances, smaller number of strikeouts. And when you begin to get a strong suspicion about those guys, it begins to dig at you."

So in the spring of 2003, as the first round of diagnostic testing was about to begin, Wunsch started discussing the drug testing policy with fellow players, and they happened upon a novel strategy. According to the rules set forth by the union and management, if a player refused to actually take the test, it would count as testing positive. Wunsch and a few teammates who weren't on performance-enhancing drugs realized that if enough of them refused the test, they'd push up the number of positive results and greatly increase the likelihood that the 5 percent threshold would be met and automatically kick in a testing regime.

The union strongly resisted drug testing and only agreed to the 2003 trial under intense public pressure. "The baseball union—to their credit—take kind of the NRA-type stance on just about anything that places any restrictions on players," said Wunsch. "Their ultimate position is zero restrictions. If you give [the owners] an inch, they'll take a mile. With some precedent. This game used to be run by the owners, and the players were like cattle."

The union leadership, Wunsch pointed out, tended to be dominated by veterans, often stars, who were most invested in the status quo. But Wunsch "was talking to first-year, second-, third-year guys. It seemed to most of us: Why the hell wouldn't we test?" The spread of steroids, Wunsch explained, "forces you to make that decision, do I want to compete and join 'em or do I want to stay away from it and stay clean and be fighting up a weight class. It just seemed like a no-brainer to us. . . . But I didn't feel like it was being communicated well to our representation to the players union.

"For those of us that just didn't feel like our voice was strong enough to prevail upon our union to police itself," Wunsch said, "I think it was just sort of a way to kind of get what we wanted." Wunsch's informal organizing among his fellow White Sox began to gain momentum, but being a dutiful union representative, Wunsch thought it would be a good idea to run his idea past the officials there. He called up Gene Orza, the union's number two official. It was, Wunsch recalls, "like walking into a buzz saw."

Orza argued that Wunsch and his co-conspirators' actions violated the entire democratic ethos of the union. "A handful of guys can't make a decision for a whole union," Wunsch recalls Orza arguing. "At the time I should have shot back [that] the guys who are doing the drugs are making the decision for the whole union." Wunsch got off the phone and dropped the idea. He and his fellow White Sox took the test. Of course, even with them taking it, and even with the advance warning of the test making it exceedingly easy to beat a positive, a full 7 percent, 103 players out of 1,438 tested, tested positive that spring. A new testing regime was triggered automatically.

Years later, when the steroids scandal broke completely out into the open, politicians, particularly Republicans, took great delight in savaging the players union for engineering the fraud. But management and the union were equally complicit in the entire undertaking. Nearly every single chronicle of the era is consistent on this point. "The owners had been smart enough not to chase steroid use out of the game," observed Canseco, "allowing guys like McGwire to make the most of steroids and growth hormone, turning themselves into larger than life heroes in more ways than one. The owners' attitude? As far as I could tell, Go ahead and do it."

The report on steroids commissioned by Major League Baseball, produced by former senator George Mitchell, concluded more or less the same thing: "There is validity to the assertion by the Players Association that, prior to 2002, the owners did not push hard for mandatory random drug testing because they were much more concerned about the serious economic issues facing baseball."

A 2003 postseason scouting assessment of Dodgers star pitcher Kevin Brown speculated about "what kind of medication he takes" and noted: "Steroids speculated by GM." Brown was never, apparently, confronted about this suspicion and was later traded to the Yankees, which continued to pay his annual salary of $15.7 million. One imagines there were quite a few similar memos written during that time.

The reason for the laissez-faire approach to drug use is blindingly clear: the steroids era was a lucrative time for baseball. In 2007, as the widespread steroid use was coming to the surface, MLB broke its attendance record for the fourth consecutive season. That same year, revenue for baseball's thirty teams went up by 7.7 percent, to $5.5 billion. In 2007, the average team was worth $472 million, up a whopping 143 percent since 1998. Players were making money, and so were the owners. The entire sport was caught up in a home run bubble. Like the peak years of the housing boom, the players and owners were all making far too much money to trouble themselves with the massive fraud that was driving the profits.

With the most powerful people in the league making staggering amounts of money off the enterprise, the more moderately compensated players, who almost certainly constituted a majority of the union membership, found themselves without a real representative of their interests. "It has to do with fairness among people in the business," Wunsch said. "It has to do with the haves and the have-nots. The haves are the ones getting all the drugs" and "the have-nots have a hard time cracking the rewards that accrued from them."

In twenty-first-century America we fetishize the athletic model of ceaseless competition and meritocratic ascent. Every two-minute biographical package during the Olympics tells the story of some hardworking athlete from the middle of nowhere who woke up early, trained late, and bested her peers to rise to be the best in the world. But what the baseball steroids scandal shows is that it's rather difficult to design a competitive system that heavily rewards performance and doesn't also reward cheating.

In one of the papers that made his reputation for ingenious economic analysis, *Freakonomics'* Steven Levitt used test score fluctuations in Chicago public schools to conclude that teachers were cheating in at least 4 percent of the classrooms. What prompted the outbreak of deception was an incentive structure put in place by Chicago Public Schools to push the system in a more merito- cratic direction and demand performance from its teachers.

"High-powered incentive schemes are designed to align the behavior of agents with the interests of the principal implement- ing the system," Levitt and his coauthor Brian Jacob wrote in their 2003 paper "Rotten Apples: An Investigation of the Prevalence and Predictors of Teacher Cheating."

> A shortcoming of such schemes, however, is that they are likely to induce behavior distortions along other dimen- sions as agents seek to game the rules.... As incentives for high test scores increase, unscrupulous teachers may be more likely to engage in a range of illicit activities, includ- ing changing student responses on answer sheets, providing correct answers to students, or obtaining copies of an exam illegitimately prior to the test date and teaching students using knowledge of the precise exam questions.

This isn't a strictly academic concern. Over the last decade, we've seen a wave of school reform measures across the country predicated on testing students and holding teachers accountable for their results. It is unsurprising to find that this has occasioned a series of scandals of teacher cheating and administrators' ma- nipulation of data. In Washington, DC, former school chancellor Michelle Rhee rose to prominence by appearing to delight in fir- ing incompetent teachers and championing a meritocratic model of "pay for performance," in which teachers would compete against one another to gain pay bonuses by producing the largest gains in standardized testing among their students. The DC school district that she ran is now under investigation by the Department of Edu- cation over allegations of widespread cheating.

At one Washington school that had been named a National Blue Ribbon award winner for its remarkable turnaround, seventh graders averaged 12.7 wrong-to-right erasures per test. The odds of winning the Powerball grand prize were better than that many wrong-to-right erasures, statisticians told investigators from *USA Today*. Rhee, who's gone on to found a national organization to champion "pay for performance"—and who once asked a crew from the PBS *NewsHour* to film her firing a principal and who appeared on the cover of *Time* magazine with a broom—refused to discuss the matter with the paper's reporters.

Atlanta, one of the national centers of school reform, is now mired in what might prove to be the biggest cheating scandal yet. An investigative report implicated more than 170 teachers. Cheating, it appears, was so fully normalized and routine, principals would actually host pizza parties where teachers would convene to sit and systematically change test answers of their students in order to boost scores.

OF COURSE, not every institution designed along competitive meritocratic lines devolves into widespread cheating and systemic fraud. Two main disincentives stop people from cheating, even under intense competitive pressure to do so. The first is the existence of ethical norms, whether social or individual. The second is fear of getting caught, and the sanction that might result.

Baseball players before 2003 had nothing to fear from regulation or league policing, since there was absolutely no testing in place. It was impossible to get caught, and the league sent the message from the very top that it would not only countenance but greatly reward those who cheated. This official license to cheat began to shift the norms in the league; as more players began using drugs, the moral condemnation that might once have attached to cheating dissipated. Cheating will always be present in any competitive environment to some degree, but systemic corruption comes about when it moves from anomaly to norm.

In the sixteenth century, in a very different context, a Tudor financier named Thomas Gresham identified and named the very process by which dishonest behavior crowds out honest exchange. Before there were modern nation-states with regulated currency, money was a somewhat freelance affair. Various entities—families, lords, the king—would coin precious metals, with the value determined by the weight and type of metal.

But without a system of state standardization, traders faced a problem. It was relatively easy to scrape or chip coins so that their nominal value was greater than their actual value. Kings and nobles would debase their own currency, issuing a coin that carried a nominal value of, say, 6 ounces of silver, but that actually only contained 5.5 ounces of silver and 0.5 ounce of a much cheaper alloy. The issuer was able to pocket the difference, managing a small profit on each coin.

In this wild, unregulated monetary world, you had two different types of coins floating in circulation: "good" money, which was pure and properly weighted, and "bad" money, which was debased and did not contain the amount of precious metal it purported to contain. In such a situation people got pretty good at identifying what was good money and what was bad; what they'd do was use bad money for exchange while saving the good money. Eventually, bad money became the only money in circulation.

Observing this phenomenon in a letter to his boss, Queen Elizabeth, Gresham concluded that such a result was unavoidable. Surveying the "unexampled state of badness" of England's coins, he proclaimed "that good and bad coin cannot circulate together."

Thus was born Gresham's law: bad money drives out good.

Or, in our modern incarnation, players on steroids push out those who don't juice.

In order for Gresham's law to kick in, it's crucial that there be a law requiring currency to be accepted by merchants; otherwise, savvy shopkeepers can simply refuse to accept the bad money and its circulation will cease. In our institutional settings there's an analog: fraudulent actors drive out the honest if the fraudulent actors receive no sanction for their actions. That's the key to understanding how Major League Baseball came to be so dominated by drug use: in the market for players, there was no distinction between juicers and non-juicers. And that's why the Chicago public school system's attempt to root out cheating by hiring Steven Levitt was crucial: it gave the institution the tools to spot cheaters and interrupt the vicious circle. It's why Michelle Rhee's apparent disinterest in doing the same was such a scandal.

There's another aspect of Gresham's law that has special bearing on baseball, Enron, and subprime finance. Most debasement of currency in Gresham's time came from the top. Kings, queens, and rulers of all kinds would routinely debase the coinage through alloys as a means of defrauding the populace and capturing the wealth gains. Gresham's law was most applicable when the fraud was being perpetrated by the ultimate authority. As the old German saying goes: "The fish rots from the head down."

I first heard of Gresham's law in this context from William Black, a lawyer, an economist, and a criminologist, who is an expert on precisely this dynamic. Black's area of expertise is white-collar crime and what he calls "criminogenic environments," institutional settings that produce systemic rule-breaking. Black had an opportunity to study financial fraud up close early in his career, during the savings and loan crisis, a financial implosion the contours of which years later look startlingly familiar: a major real-estate bubble, this one regionally based in Texas, and a massive escalation in loan volume and leverage, which went hand in hand with a systematic degradation of underwriting standards. Then: a huge crash, a panicked crisis, and a federal bailout.

Once Gresham's law kicks in, Black told me, it has the perverse consequence of turning reputation on its head. Those engaged in the most fraudulent activity, landing the largest deals and profits, creating the most dodgy and fictitious revenue, come to be the most highly regarded, while those who demur or, worse, blow the whistle come to be viewed suspiciously, even regarded with contempt.

"If you wanted a stellar reputation as a baseball player," observed Black, "you took steroids. That was the single thing you could do to boost your reputation. . . . Baseball then emphasized that by hyping home runs and the home run competition as a deliberate marketing strategy, so reputation becomes exceptionally perverse as an incentive structure."

Black pointed out to me that Gresham's law happens not just within institutions, but in the larger cultural landscape. Reading through the press coverage of Enron in the years before it imploded, one is immediately struck by its sycophantic, fawning tone, as if business reporters are competing with one another to heap the most superlatives on this hot-shit enterprise.

So it went in baseball. In August 1998, as McGwire and Sosa battled neck and neck for the home run title, amassing a press pool that rivaled the White House's, Associated Press reporter Steve Wilstein rained on the parade. After looking into McGwire's open locker and noticing a bottle of androstenedione ("andro" as it was known in gyms), he wrote an article questioning whether the drug, which was designed to mimic the bodily effects of anabolic steroids, was legit. What followed was a week of scandal: McGwire admitted to using the drug, but he and the Cardinals noted that it was both legal and did not appear on baseball's list of banned substances.

It was, however, banned in both the National Football League and the Olympics, which might have triggered the league and the players association to consider just what other substances players were putting in their bodies. Instead, baseball closed ranks around McGwire and ostracized Wilstein, who'd broken the story. Cardinals manager Tony LaRussa even tried to have the Associated Press kicked out of his locker room. Sure enough, a few weeks later the story was gone, eclipsed by the sluggers inching ever closer to Roger Maris's record.

CEOs received similar treatment during the housing bubble. Angelo Mozilo, the founder and CEO of Countrywide, was the subject of endless glowing profiles in the 1990s and early aughts as his company grew to become the largest mortgage lender in the country. As the housing bubble expanded, Countrywide maintained its competitive edge by pushing suicidally dangerous products like a mortgage that would—get this—allow borrowers to choose how much they would pay every month, adding the unpaid amount to their principal. Mozilo's reputation for integrity and entrepreneurial verve allowed him to oversee what according to an SEC complaint was a large-scale fraud, while also arranging for himself some of the most blatantly corrupt CEO compensation packages in the history of American capitalism. In 2007, the same year the national housing slump eviscerated his company, Mozilo earned $121.5 million by exercising stock options and $22.1 million in additional compensation.

The role of fraud in creating the conditions for the housing bubble is now generally recognized, but the extent to which it was the driving force behind the bubble remains poorly understood and rarely acknowledged. As fraudulent loans entered the marketplace, Gresham's law kicked in with violent force: Those willing to hand out faulty loans and engage in appraisal fraud were able to bag the fees and commissions, while those who wouldn't play ball found themselves with a shrinking pool of customers.

In the spring of 2010, Black was called to testify before the House Financial Services Committee during its hearing about the Lehman Brothers bankruptcy report. The report prepared by court-appointed bankruptcy examiner Anton Valukas showed that Lehman was knowingly manipulating its balance sheet to hide its losses from shareholders and the public. Enron redux. Black was called before the committee to offer his expertise on these kinds of transactions, and he sat before them, just a few feet from former Lehman CEO Dick Fuld. "Lehman's failure is a story," he said, "in large part, of fraud. . . . Lehman was the leading purveyor of liars' loans [loans that did not require documentation or proof of income] in the world for most of this decade . . . Lehman sold this to the world."

Neck and neck with Lehman in pushing liars' loans was Mozilo's own Countrywide. The company even managed to institutionalize Gresham's law in its own official corporate policy. Starting in 2003, Countrywide adopted what it called its "supermarket" or "matching" strategy: any loan a competitor offered, Countrywide itself would match. The SEC complaint filed against Mozilo and his deputy in 2009 explains how this worked in practice: "If Countrywide did not offer a product offered by a competitor, Countrywide's production division invoked the matching strategy to add the product to Countrywide's menu." This applied no matter how reckless or destructive the offered loan was.

The policy had the effect of breaching the firm's underwriting levee. Bad loans rushed into Countrywide until they had achieved equilibrium with the entire corrupt market outside the firm. By the time Countrywide was bought by Bank of America, fully 33 percent of its subprime loans were delinquent.

While the people who ran the company continued to represent to shareholders in their public quarterly reports that the firm had maintained the integrity of its underwriting standards, internal correspondence shows that Mozilo himself was increasingly horrified by the degradation of the underwriting standards that had taken place inside the firm. When, in 2006, Countrywide began offering a mortgage that required zero dollars down, Mozilo wrote to a few of his most trusted subordinates that it was "the most dangerous product in existence and there can be nothing more toxic." A month later he was still distressed, noting that while the company's CFO called these loans the "milk of the business . . . I consider the product line to be the poison of ours."

And yet even after these missives, Countrywide continued to push this poison. At a certain point, Mozilo reconciled himself to the fact that Countrywide was now making most of its money from subprime loans, and given the trepidation expressed in his e-mails, it doesn't seem to be too much of a leap to view the massive executive compensation he was awarding himself as his response to the impending blowup. Between 2001 and 2006, Mozilo managed to arrange for himself a staggering $470 million in total executive compensation. The most cynical interpretation of these actions, though also the most plausible, is that Mozilo was looting the company he'd built as fast as he could before the markets or regulators caught up to him.

The shift of Countrywide's focus from prime to subprime reverberated throughout the entire institution. Reputation, bonuses, and institutional status redounded increasingly to those parts of the business that were growing, and as the decade proceeded (and more or less everyone who wanted a prime loan had one), that meant all those rewards shifted to the subprime business. Adam Michaelson, a former advertising executive who worked in Countrywide's marketing division, recalls the atmosphere of the business this way: "Countrywide fashioned itself a meritocracy, that is, whoever generated the most value or profit for the firm would be granted the greatest rewards, growth and prestige." As happened in so many places over the past decade, the institutional definition of merit inside Countrywide became thoroughly perverse.

OPEN SECRETS

When cheating becomes an accepted norm within an institution, it produces a distinct and dangerous psychology in those who rise to the top. They come to view themselves as übermensches and begin to hold in contempt those not in on the secret. Enron, particularly in certain areas, like its trading desks, developed a culture of the open secret and the inside joke, two rhetorical tropes that are surefire tip-offs that an institution is in the midst of a Gresham's law–style devolution.

A somewhat infamous tape of two energy traders in the summer of 2003 revealed that counter to Enron's protestations that spiking energy prices and rolling brownouts in California that summer were the result of overwhelming demand, energy traders at the firm were deliberately shutting down power plants so as to artificially constrain supply and jack up prices. Here, two traders discuss a friend's proficiency at pulling off this particular fraud.

> "He just fucks California. He steals money from California
> to the tune of about a million."
> "Will you rephrase that?"
> "OK, he, um, he arbitrages the California market to the
> tune of a million bucks or two a day," replies the first.

Baseball had its own version of this kind of ironic, knowing euphemism, as Canseco describes:

[The use of steroids] was so open, the trainers would jokingly call the steroid injections "B12 shots," and soon the players had picked up on that little code name, too. You'd hear them saying it out loud in front of each other: "I need to go in and get a B12 shot," a player would say, and everyone would laugh.

Canseco notes that this was the kind of joke you only made around fellow users. Major League Baseball during the steroid years developed alternate languages and rituals for those who were hip to what was going on and those who were oblivious. Convicted felon and former superlobbyist Jack Abramoff says he and his fellow influence peddlers would say of a politician that he "got the joke," to describe the moment when a politician understood the terms of the implied bribe being offered: fund-raising money for a specific legislative favor for his clients. Black says this jokiness is common in white-collar fraud, and he calls it a "neutralization technique," a means of defusing one's own moral misgivings. One way to do this, Black told me, "is to make fun of the squares."

This impulse is evident nowhere more than in the internal communications of institutions involved in the subprime lending racket. Richard Michalek, who worked for the ratings agency Moody's, testified before a Senate committee in 2010 that the fee structure of investment bank deals created an incentive to rate securities positively, no matter the consequence. "The incentives for the . . . investment bank were clear," he testified before the Senate Permanent Subcommittee on Investigations, "get the deal closed, and if there's a problem later on, it was just another case of 'IBGYBG'—'I'll be gone, you'll be gone.'" It turns out IBGYBG was a commonplace shorthand among bankers during the boom, a bit of lingo that flaunted its own moral bankruptcy. Michalek says he first heard it from "an investment banker who was running out of patience with my insistence on a detailed review of the documentation."

Fabrice Tourre, a trader in the structured finance division of Goldman Sachs's London office and a named party in the SEC's civil suit against Goldman Sachs for fraud, was clearly internally conflicted about just what kind of work he was engaged in. In January 2007 he wrote to a girlfriend: "Anyway, not feeling too guilty about this, the real purpose of my job is to make capital markets more efficient and ultimately provide the US consumer with more efficient ways to leverage and finance himself, so there is a humble, noble and ethical reason for my job ;) amazing how good I am in convincing myself !!!" After touching down in Belgium for a business trip, he wrote, "I'm managed [*sic*] to sell a few abacus bonds to widow[s] and orphans that I ran into at the airport . . . " Abacus, of course, is the toxic security at issue in the suit that Goldman settled with the SEC, a security constructed, like an IED, with the sole purpose of blowing up.

While interviewing investment bankers for her ethnography of Wall Street, anthropologist Karen Ho encountered a sign in one office that laid out the steps in a deal. It featured two columns: on the left-hand side the official version of how a deal was put together and on the right-hand side the "real" version of what went down. So: "Build financial model: historical performance and projected earnings and leverage ratios" translated to "Manipulate projections so credit ratings are reasonable." And "Pitch Prospective Client" became "Lie, cheat, steal and bad mouth your competition to win the business."

In a complaint filed in federal court (and later settled), former Countrywide employee Mark Zachary said that this attitude was common at the nation's largest mortgage lender. From his position overseeing a joint enterprise with a local home builder in Houston, Zachary said he saw up close the systemic encouragement of fraud.

In one instance he e-mailed a supervisor to clarify just what would happen if a potential borrower mentioned that they were out of a job and didn't have any income. "If that case were to present itself, we'd have to deny it, huh?" Zachary asked.

"I wouldn't deny it," his supervisor wrote back, "because I didn't hear anything. I would definitely tell the [sales counselor] to shut up or shoot him!"

What ties together these internal communications is the lurking, nagging presence of a conscience. In each case and in dozens others, the perpetrator tips his hand that he knows what he's doing isn't quite on the up-and-up. The inside joke, and its close cousin the open secret, develop as a kind of moral defense, a way for the agents of a fraud to distance themselves from their own culpability: If it's worthy of a joke, it can't be so bad. Right?

From a forensic level these inside jokes show a state of mind, evidence that the people writing these e-mails, getting in on the joshing, knew what they were doing. And what they were doing wasn't simply making blindly incompetent decisions, but rather perpetrating intentional fraud. As Vincent Daniel, one of the very few investors who foresaw the implosion of the housing bubble, put it to author Michael Lewis: "There were more morons than crooks, but the crooks were higher up."

It is our suspicion that there are crooks at the top, that our elites are engaged in a con to which we are not privy, that makes a cruel joke out of our entire meritocratic social order. It is the predicate for Joe Stack's deranged rage, for Susan Southwick's radicalization. Our system is supposed to reward the virtuous and punish the vicious, and yet everywhere you turn, it seems the vicious are living high off the hog.

Like the fat-cat politicians depicted in the famous Gilded-era cartoon by Thomas Nast, each key authority plausibly responsible for the mess points to another in a circular game of buck passing, saying with a shrug: "'Twas him." Everyone else is left to clean up after the mess and suffer the misery the authorities' blundering and plundering has brought forth.

Along with all of the other rising inequalities we've become so familiar with—in income, in wealth, in access to politicians—we confront now a fundamental inequality of accountability. We can have a just society whose guiding ethos is accountability and punishment, where both black kids dealing weed in Harlem and investment bankers peddling fraudulent securities on Wall Street are forced to pay for their crimes, or we can have a just society whose guiding ethos is forgiveness and second chances, one in which both Wall Street banks and foreclosed households are bailed out, in which both inside traders and street felons are allowed to rejoin polite society with the full privileges of citizenship intact. But we cannot have a just society that applies the principle of accountability to the powerless and the principle of forgiveness to the powerful. This is the America in which we currently reside.

Chapter 4

WHO KNOWS?

*There are no more arbiters of truth. . . . We've crossed some
Rubicon into the unknown.*

—FORMER WHITE HOUSE PRESS SECRETARY
ROBERT GIBBS

A MONTH BEFORE HE TURNED ONE, MY BROTHER HAD his first asthma attack. My mom noticed Luke panting in his crib, his lungs laboring so hard she could see his tiny rib cage pulsing in and out of focus. At the time my parents basically knew nothing about asthma, but you can be damn sure that changed on a dime when their son was diagnosed. Though it was before the Internet, my mother doggedly tracked down as much research about treatment as she could get her hands on: reading books on asthma, clipping articles, talking with other parents of asthmatics, and swapping notes about treatment.

She soon grew skeptical of the doctor who was treating her youngest son: the doctor's answers contradicted those of other doctors, and her treatment suggestions departed pretty radically from some of the material my mom was reading. My mother's growing skepticism peaked after looking up the dosage of steroids the doctor had prescribed for my one-year-old brother, to find that it was sufficient for a three-hundred-pound adult. My parents decided to find another doctor, and though Luke got better, my mother always retained the same air of skepticism when talking to doctors.

She'd be so loaded up with questions that I thought the doctors must hate her. To my eyes at the time, she seemed like a real pain in the ass. "Mom!" I wanted to say, "they're the experts."

But that's precisely why the relationship between doctor and patient is so loaded. We confer significant amounts of money and status on doctors in exchange for access to their expensive and specialized knowledge. But doctors are also human: They make mistakes, they vary greatly in skill and acuity, and they can be disastrously wrong. A recent study of Medicare patients suggested that nationally about 180,000 people a year experienced an event during hospital stays, such as the improper administration of medication, that contributed to their deaths. That's sixteen times as many as are killed by drunk drivers.

So patients have to negotiate between two extreme poles. At the one end there is simple and absolute acceptance of doctors' pronouncements. History is littered with one horrifying story after another of where this can lead. In 1935, during the peak of the polio epidemic, a Philadelphia pathologist named John Kolmer tested a live-virus vaccine on ten thousand children, assuring their parents it was riskless. Ten children would later develop paralytic polio from the vaccine; five died. As recently as December 2004, Tenet Healthcare paid $395 million to settle litigation with 769 patients who had accused Redding Medical Center of performing unnecessary heart surgeries which led to paralysis, strokes, heart attacks, and at least ninety-four instances of wrongful death.

On the opposite pole, there is the total rejection of medical authority. This is a strain that runs through American history, connecting the spiritual visionary Mary Baker Eddy to the booming business of quackish fad diets, dietary supplements, and snake oils of various kinds. The Crisis of Authority has produced a particularly virulent strain of this kind of rejectionism, as millions of parents refuse to have their children vaccinated because they believe—against the evidence and a broad and durable medical consensus—that vaccines cause autism and other conditions.

Medical authority may have a specific and acute effect on our private lives, but our relationship to it is fundamentally similar to other kinds of social authority that structure our public life. The average citizen has no earthly way of knowing whether a foreign nation indeed possesses weapons of mass destruction. In order to form an opinion, a citizen turns to institutions that are sources of authority on the topic: government pronouncements and the media's reporting on the issue.

In all these cases, we think of trust (or its opposite) as dependent on knowledge. We compare what someone says to what we know to determine if they are truthful. If they are, we are inclined to trust them. We compare what the doctor says about a dosage to what the pharmacist and books on asthma recommend. When a mechanic tells us he's fixed our car, we listen to make sure the troubling rattle is, indeed, gone. It is through iterations of this process that we establish the bonds of trust in authority. When the doctor is proven right, we come to trust the doctor; when the mechanic gets it right, we can rely on him, and on and on.

But not only is it the case that trust is dependent on knowledge, the converse is also true: knowledge is dependent on trust. Let's return to the example of my mother and my brother's doctor. In order for her to evaluate the doctor's performance, my mom consulted a medical manual about drug dosages. Implicit in that was a fundamental trust in the book itself. Who's to say that the author of the book was any more trustworthy than the doctor? Perhaps the information in the book was outdated. Even more insidiously, perhaps the author had a major undisclosed contract with a drug company that skewed her advice. My mom could, instead, have consulted another doctor recommended by a friend, but then she would have been relying on her trust of her friend and her friend's judgment. Maybe she'd find that the books she reads and the other doctors she talks to suggest the dosage prescribed by her pediatrician is too high. This seems persuasive, but it simply means she's choosing to trust medical consensus over her son's doctor, and history has shown time and time again that the medical consensus at any given moment is far from infallible.

There is no way to extricate ourselves from this web of mediation. What we actually know firsthand is minuscule: the feel of the spring air on our skin, our own private daydreams and phobias. Outside of these tiny warrens of private knowledge, we have to depend on what others say. "The bulk of our knowledge—perhaps virtually all of it—depends on others in various ways," writes political philosopher Russell Hardin. "We take most knowledge on authority from others who presumably are in a position to know it." To know something is to have heard it from a trusted source. Trace the chain of knowledge a few links and you inevitably find it attached to some bedrock of institutional authority. Without these anchors, our basic knowledge structure threatens to drift away.

Imagine a weary sailor coming home to port in the midst of a brutal storm. Along the horizon he sees the burning lights of dozens of lighthouses. And yet he knows from experience that some are so old they've receded miles inland as the shore has grown. Others are simply fakes, put out by sadists and rivals. To be a citizen in these strange times is to perpetually find oneself in that poor sailor's perilous state. We know that danger lurks in the darkness, but we don't know if we have the means to avoid it.

Which brings us to the most destructive effect of the fail decade. The cascade of elite failure has discredited not only elites and our central institutions, but the very mental habits we use to form our beliefs about the world. At the same time, the Internet has produced an unprecedented amount of information to sort through and radically expanded the arduous task of figuring out just whom to trust.

Together, the discrediting of our old sources of authority and the exponential proliferation of new ones has almost completely annihilated our social ability to reach consensus on just what the facts of the matter are. When our most central institutions are no longer trusted, we each take refuge in smaller, balkanized epistemic encampments, aided by the unprecedented information technology at our disposal. As some of these encampments build higher and higher fences, walling themselves off from science and empiricism, we approach a terrifying prospect: a society that may no longer be capable of reaching the kind of basic agreement necessary for social progress. And this is happening at just the moment when we face the threat of catastrophic climate change, what is likely the single largest governing challenge that human beings have ever faced in the history of life on the planet.

At exactly the moment we most need solid ground beneath our feet, we find ourselves adrift, transported into a sinister, bewildering dreamscape, in which the simple act of orienting ourselves is impossible.

HOW DO WE KNOW?

Because we cannot investigate and verify the millions of bits of knowledge that float through our lives, we outsource the vast majority of the work of screening it all to others. The overwhelming majority of citizens are occupied primarily with earning a living and tending to their families. They attempt to squeeze in as much information as they can (or as much as they have an appetite for) during morning commutes, rushed lunch hours, and evening leisure time.

To stay informed, most of us have grown accustomed to using a few mental shortcuts, each of which has been discredited by the experience of the fail decade.

Consensus

A huge part of what we know rests on the foundation of consensus: if everyone agrees on something, it's probably true. This is how we "know" that gravity exists, that there are fifty states in the union, and that the earth orbits the sun and not the other way around.

But in our shared political and social life, consensus is far more elusive, if not impossible. Choose nearly any important public issue—the long-term solvency of Social Security, the effect of taxes on growth, the importance to student performance of merit pay for teachers—and you will find smart, well-credentialed, and energetic advocates arguing for mutually exclusive positions. In this way, the voter is asked to referee a series of contests for which he or she has absolutely no independent expertise.

That's why political parties are such a useful part of liberal democracy; they take on much of this informational burden. Citizens come to associate themselves with a party for myriad reasons—affiliation of worldview, agreement on a few vitally important issues, demographic and tribal association—and in turn the party grants back to those citizens a position on a whole host of issues that they otherwise would not have the inclination, resources, or time to develop independently. The party also constrains the set of people among whom one looks for consensus. As a Democrat, you can simply look to Democratic consensus on an issue and be relatively confident that it syncs up with your own opinion.

For all its flaws, this system allows citizens a rough-and-ready means of navigating the infinitely complex world of political disputes. But over the last several decades, partisan affiliation has generally weakened, with a large percentage of voters identifying as independents or moving back and forth between designations. Without an organized party platform to look to for guidance in forming opinions about complex issues, so-called independents are naturally inclined to seek out some form of general agreement to point the way: Which side of an issue do most of the experts and authorities come down on?

This is the reason that "bipartisanship"—at least as a concept— is so reliably popular among a polity increasingly alienated from political parties. People like bipartisanship not because they like the substance of what bipartisanship produces, but because it reduces the cognitive stress that partisan disagreement creates. If two sides are bitterly arguing over some major piece of public policy, this forces us to choose sides, and for those with weak mastery of the issue or tenuous connections to a specific worldview, it is easy to be stalked by the worry that you're choosing the wrong side: After all, there are a ton of people screaming in righteous indignation that the side you're on is about to destroy the country. Maybe they have a point.

Bipartisanship, on the other hand, sends a different signal: that the matter is settled. If everyone agrees, there's no need to seek out supplementary sources and authorities to adjudicate disputes. The public's consistent desire for bipartisanship as reported reliably in poll after poll is really a desire to off-load the burden of having to choose between competing narratives, arguments, and data points. This isn't laziness: it's entirely rational. Controversy is exhausting to our cognitive faculties.

But the experience of the last decade has shown us that bipartisan consensus can also produce disastrous policy outcomes. In the wake of 9/11 there was near unanimous support, across the two parties, for the authorization to use military force that led to the invasion of Afghanistan. The vote passed the House 420 to 1, and 98 to 0 in the Senate, and yet almost eleven years later that war rages on with little hope for a good outcome.

A little more than one year after Congress authorized the war with Afghanistan, it authorized war with Iraq. The resolution passed the Senate 77 to 22, with 29 Democrats (or 60 percent of the caucus) voting aye. Of course, it was the Republican administration and party that most aggressively pushed for the war, but even a casual observer of politics would have noticed that many high-profile Democrats, indeed the most high-profile Democrats, were saying things about Iraq that sounded more or less identical to what the Bush administration and congressional Republicans were saying. House Minority Leader Dick Gephardt said on *Face the Nation,* "What we're worried about is an A-bomb in a Ryder truck in New York, in Washington and St. Louis. It cannot happen. We have to prevent it from happening. And it was on that basis that I voted to do this." In a January 2003 speech Senator John Kerry said Saddam Hussein was "miscalculating America's response to his continued deceit and his consistent grasp for weapons of mass destruction." A few weeks later Al Gore warned that Iraq "represents a virulent threat in a class by itself." Even Massachusetts senator Ted Kennedy, a hero to liberals who called his vote against the Iraq War resolution the best he'd ever cast, echoed the bellicose rhetoric from the White House: "There is no doubt that Saddam Hussein's . . . pursuit of lethal weapons of mass destruction cannot be tolerated. He must be disarmed."

And it wasn't just elected officials. All kinds of sources normally thought of as "liberal" seemed to think the war was a good idea as well. *The New Republic,* which retained (wrongly) a reputation as a liberal publication, not only endorsed the war, it scolded the "abject pacifism" and "intellectual incoherence of the liberal war critics." The online muckraking blog *Talking Points Memo* featured an extended sympathetic interview with Kenneth Pollack, a former Clinton National Security Council staffer who authored a highly influential book, *The Threatening Storm*, which argued in favor of an invasion. *New Yorker* editor David Remnick penned a Comment in the front of the *New Yorker* in which he chastised George W. Bush for failing to make a persuasive case for war and then, invoking Pollack, warned that "history will not easily excuse us if . . . we defer a reckoning with an aggressive totalitarian leader who intends not only to develop weapons of mass destruction but also to use them," concluding that "a return to a hollow pursuit of containment will be the most dangerous option of all."

There were, of course, many voices of dissent: my own magazine, *The Nation,* the *New York Times* editorial board, prominent members of the foreign policy establishment, like Brent Scowcroft and Zbigniew Brzezinski, not to mention millions of people in the streets opposing the war, both in the United States and around the world. But they tended to be ignored or minimized by mainstream news coverage. A Syracuse University study looked at every single ABC and CBS news story in the run-up to the Iraq War and found that "Bush administration officials were the most frequently quoted sources, the voices of anti-war groups and opposition Democrats were barely audible, and the overall thrust of coverage favored a pro-war perspective."

If one were to come to one's opinion based on where the general agreement of elites stood—major media sources and the political class—there's no question that support for the war was the winning position. It wasn't quite consensus, but it was its nearest cousin.

Indeed, when it became clear that Iraq had no weapons of mass destruction and the war was a bloody disaster, many who'd reluctantly supported the invasion pointed toward precisely the breadth of this very same consensus as their rationale. "It wasn't just the

American intelligence community that said there were WMD in Iraq," said the *New Yorker*'s Remnick in a 2008 web video about the media's responsibility for the Iraq War. "The Israelis, the Germans, the French all said that there had been WMD."

Iraq was such a colossal failure of consensus it would be tempting to chalk it up to a once-in-a-generation screwup, but then along came the housing bubble, which was inflated by economists, policy-makers, and others who'd reached the consensus that housing prices had entered some new universe of asset appreciation in which prices would never come down.

In 2003, Federal Reserve chairman Alan Greenspan dismissed the very notion of a housing bubble, saying that while it was "of course, possible for home prices to fall as they did in a couple of quarters in 1990 . . . any analogy to stock market pricing behavior and bubbles is a rather large stretch." A year later, even as predatory lending exploded and underwriting standards degraded, Greenspan advised that as long as lenders "continue their prudent lending practices," households would be more likely to "weather future challenges." That same year the FDIC issued a report declaring flatly, "There Is No U.S. Housing Bubble," and the New York Federal Reserve Bank issued a report in December 2004 arguing there was "little evidence to support the existence of a national home price bubble. . . . Moreover, expectations of rapid price appreciation do not appear to be a major factor behind the strong housing market. Our observations also suggest that home prices are not likely to plunge in response to deteriorating fundamentals to the extent envisioned by some analysts."

In 2005, the man who would succeed Greenspan, Ben Bernanke, testified before Congress that the unprecedented increases in housing prices nationwide "largely reflect strong economic fundamentals." In March 2007, as the problems in the subprime markets first began to attract national press attention, Bernanke dismissed the possibility that the contagion could spread, telling Congress that "the impact on the broader economy and financial markets of the problems in the subprime market seems likely to be contained." As the housing bubble began to deflate, Patrick Lawler, chief economist for the Office of Federal Housing Enterprise Oversight, announced, "There is no evidence here of prices topping out. On the contrary, house price inflation continues to accelerate."

The housing bubble even became a kind of spectator sport, chronicled in reality shows like A&E's *Flip This House* and TLC's *Flip That House*. In 2005, an economist at the Federal Reserve told Greenspan in a meeting that he had seen an episode of *Flip That House* and it "was enough to put even the most ardent believer in market efficiency into existential crisis."

Sure enough, between early 2006 and 2011 housing prices declined by a third nationwide, and as much as 50 percent or more in particularly overheated markets, like Las Vegas and Miami. The popping of the bubble precipitated a financial crisis that produced the worst economic contraction in eighty years.

Summing up the consensus that led to this calamity, Alan Greenspan said, in 2010: "Everybody missed it: academia, the Federal Reserve, all regulators."

Once again, "everybody" was wrong.

Of course, we know consensus isn't foolproof. Whether it's the structure of the solar system or the morality of slavery, entire societies can achieve unanimity around deeply flawed beliefs. But translating knowledge of this possibility into daily life is a difficult task. All but the most resolutely contrarian mind will find itself drawn subtly, magnetically toward the view that "everybody" seems to hold. Which is why the rude reminder of the basic fallibility of consensus creates a long aftershock, a period in which we view consensus with justifiable suspicion. And yet discarding it does not leave us with any equivalently powerful alternative.

Proximity

After consensus, the next fundamental principle of knowledge acquisition is proximity: In order to find the truth, we have to get as close to the source as possible. The farther we get from the source, the more likely it is that the truth has been twisted through manipulation or error, a process gleefully reproduced in the child's game of telephone.

In our public life, proximity is nearly always impossible. If you're a high school teacher in East St. Louis, there's only so close you can get to the "newsmakers" in Washington who appear on Sunday shows and drive policy decisions. So you're forced to rely instead on the media, an institution that derives its name from its role in mediating between citizens and the powerful people who shape the world in which they live.

The media itself hews closely to the principle of proximity: When the 2011 uprising broke out on the streets of Cairo, all the networks rushed to send their anchors to the scene. For reporters, "being on the ground" and having "access" are points of pride precisely because they signal that the reporter is as close to the story as possible. Consumers of news seek out proximity for the same reasons. If you're choosing between getting your news about the CIA from a blogger in a basement in New Jersey or a reporter based in Virginia who spends half his time at Langley, you're almost certainly going to choose the latter.

And yet, just as consensus helped produce the Iraq debacle and the financial crisis, so, too, did our trust in proximity. Time and time again, those closest to the national security apparatus and the financial industry seemed most blinded to impending havoc.

The most notorious example of this is the *New York Times'* Judith Miller. Miller had unparalleled access to the big foreign policy players within the White House who were assembling intelligence and making the case for war on Iraq. She also had unparalleled access to defectors from Iraq who had previously worked inside the regime and claimed to have seen Hussein's weapons program firsthand. Short of being able to penetrate the current regime's weapons program, this was as close to firsthand evidence as one could hope for. So remarkable was her access that she was allowed to actually watch an interrogation of an Iraqi defector, who, she was told, described a vast nuclear weapons program.

Miller was particularly close to Ahmed Chalabi, the infamous Iraqi exile who worked tirelessly behind the scenes to push the United States into declaring war on Iraq. In an e-mail to her colleague John Burns, Miller wrote that Chalabi "has provided most of the front page exclusives on WMD to our paper."

The problem, of course, was that Chalabi was a huckster of the highest order. The defector whose interrogation Miller had witnessed, code-named Curveball, turned out to be not a "psychologically stable guy," as one German intelligence official put it. The vice president's office, to which she had unrivaled access, spoon-fed Miller exactly the information they wanted her to have, no matter how dodgy or poorly sourced. Then in a particularly masterful stroke, Cheney would go on TV to cite the *"New York Times"* to confirm exactly the information that he himself had planted there.

Miller helped facilitate one of the worst deceptions in the history of American foreign policy. On the eve of the invasion of Iraq, a full 85 percent of Americans believed, wrongly it would turn out, that Iraq had weapons of mass destruction. Years later the *New York Times* took the unusual step of apologizing for and retracting her reporting.

In the financial crisis, the role of Judith Miller was played by Jim Cramer, the notorious market analyst and CNBC host of *Mad Money* who became a financial star during the bubble years. Cramer's cachet came not just from his over-the-top antics but from his years spent managing a hedge fund and running TheStreet. com, which offered the general public a window into the world of Wall Street intel. NBC's promos for *Mad Money* used the audacious and slightly blasphemous tagline "In Cramer We Trust."

And yet, as *The Daily Show*'s Jon Stewart famously pointed out, this didn't prevent Cramer from missing the single most important story on Wall Street, the unsustainable securitization machine that pumped up the housing bubble and led to the crisis. In the spring of 2007, seven weeks before Bear Stearns began its slide toward oblivion, Cramer told his audience "to buy Bear Stearns." He continued:

CRAMER: I just think that this one has a very big upside, very limited downside. I think that that last quarter they've staunched the losses—they're very good at cutting their losses at Bear. But Bear I believe is for sale and there are many buyers.
INTERVIEWER: Could be a bidding war.
CRAMER: Yes. Buy Bear! I'm telling people to buy Bear.

On July 16, 2007, Cramer proclaimed that the subprime "lending thing" was "completely meaningless" and had "no relevance whatsoever." Less than three weeks later, Cramer would have an on-air meltdown in which he pleaded for the Federal Reserve to cut rates in order to save Wall Street. "Open the darn

Fed window," he yelled. "[Bernanke] has no idea how bad it is out there. None! . . . My people have been in this game for twenty-five years. . . . They are losing their jobs—these firms are going out of business. . . . They [the Fed] know nothing. The Fed is asleep. . . . We have Armageddon!"

Cramer is a particularly colorful example of a much bigger problem. Many of the most connected business journalists didn't do any better than Cramer in understanding what was happening. "We committed journalistic malpractice on a grand scale," wrote *Seattle Times* economics columnist Jon Talton in a March 2009 blog post. "We wrote glowing accounts of the heroic masters of the universe, epitomized by endless reverential profiles of the likes of Jack Welch of General Electric, and, until the roof fell in, Ken Lay of Enron. We asked far too few questions about derivatives and risky changes to the banking system, instead following mergers and slick new securities like star-struck sportswriters."

Former *Wall Street Journal* business reporter Dean Starkman undertook the most comprehensive analysis of the business press's coverage of the housing and financial sectors before the crash, combing through more than two thousand articles. "Business journalists as a rule are as smart, sophisticated, and plugged-in as they seem," he wrote. "And yet that army of professional business reporters—an estimated 9,000 or so nationwide in print alone—for all practical purposes missed the biggest story on the beat." He concluded that while there were many excellent articles about the underlying problems in mortgage markets, the business press was "a watchdog that didn't bark."

While proximity grants access to information others do not have, it also has a tendency to produce cognitive capture: reporters who spend all their time covering and talking to investment bankers come to see the world through their eyes and begin to think like investment bankers. There's nothing nefarious about this tendency—it's an inevitable outcome of sustained immersion—but what it meant was that when all the investment bankers were seeing a bull market and a securitization bonanza that would last forever, so were many reporters on the beat.

More perniciously, access is not something reporters can achieve unilaterally. In the highest circles of politics and finance, it must be granted by those who hold the power, and they are, for obvious reasons, more inclined to grant that access to those reporters they feel are sympathetic.

In practice this means that access and proximity don't simply confer superior insight or knowledge. They provide both benefits and costs that can be difficult to untangle. The rise of independent publishing on the Internet allowed those frustrated with the shortcomings of access journalism to develop a pointed and unsparing critique. But it wasn't just the rise of technology that produced the explosion of the blogosphere; it was the perceived failings of the mainstream media. It turned out that, to return to the hypothetical above, someone sitting in a basement in New Jersey, using the Internet, reading from a diverse set of sources about WMD intelligence, could actually get closer to the truth than the beat reporter with the inside sources at Langley.

Good Faith

The third fundamental rule of thumb we use in deciding what to believe is a default assumption of good faith. We know people lie; we don't simply take everything we hear at face value. But on the whole we assume, until given reason not to, that those we engage with are not in the midst of some systemic effort to deceive or defraud us. We know that various tribunes of officialdom spin and dissemble, but we are not, as a rule, disposed to think they are engaged in a comprehensive, systematic cover-up of some monstrously destructive hidden agenda.

Because revelations of systemic deception erode our most basic, default expectation of good faith, they play an outsize role in producing a crisis of authority. Each exposure of previously secret misdeeds—steroid use, Ponzi schemes, rigged intelligence—produces an acute and debilitating psychological effect. Vertigo sets in, similar to that experienced by a spouse who, after decades of what he thought was a happy, loyal marriage, discovers his wife has been cheating all along. Suddenly we realize we live in a world entirely more depraved than the one we thought we inhabited.

This was the defining experience of many Americans during the mid-1970s, the last period in which the nation suffered through a crisis of authority. "One of the frightening effects of watching the Watergate hearings," a New Jersey man wrote in a letter to the *New York Times* in 1973, "is the feeling that we can no longer trust in the reality of our experience. We have witnessed so much facade, contrivance, and deception in our political and economic processes . . . that one has the sensation of living in a kind of movie-set society where the people and the buildings look real but are actually hollow. In considering the damage Watergate has done to so many of our accepted values, perhaps the one that has been most dangerously undermined is face value—that reality is what we perceive it to be. Our common acceptance of this principle is essentially the cement that holds society together."

While the systemic deception around weapons of mass destruction comes closest to reproducing that same sensation in our own time, the Iraq debacle happened three decades after Watergate and Vietnam had already done a lot to rid people of their previous innocence about the American president and his war-making powers.

But the scandal in the Catholic Church is another story. To the devout, the lapsed, and even the non-Catholic observer, the depths of ruthlessness and depravity among church officials, as they covered up the crimes of the child predators in their ranks, induced a sickening vertigo that exceeded even Watergate's.

The broad outlines of the scandal are familiar. For decades priests sexually molested children, using their clerical status as protection. When church authorities were alerted, they simply moved the predators to new parishes, where the abuse would continue. This didn't just happen a few times: it was, it appears, a policy. In 2007, when the Irish Church dealt with its own burgeoning crisis by crafting a policy that would require bishops to report suspected abusers to civil authorities, the Vatican sent a letter expressing its reservations about "mandatory reporting" and instructing the bishops that the Code of Canon Law (as opposed to secular law) "must be meticulously followed." The command, in other words, was for bishops to shield their wayward priests from prosecution, to administer whatever justice would be administered in secret, within the fold of the church.

It wasn't the Church's attempt at a cover-up that separated it from other large, powerful institutions, but rather its success. According to a report from John Jay College on incidents of abuse within the Church (the most comprehensive that exists), the peak year for alleged abuse was 1970. Yet two-thirds of the total accusations of abuse were only reported after 1993. That's an entire generation of silence. Fully a third of the allegations surfaced in the year 2002–2003, when Boston's notorious Father John Geoghan dominated the news. The Church's elaborate bureaucratic mechanisms of scandal troubleshooting managed to keep thousands of individual cases more or less entirely obscured from both the press and the police for as much as three or four decades; a success that Nixon could only dream of.

In hindsight, this method of control looks like miscalculation of epic proportions. Now that it's all come to light, each letter directing subordinates to keep things quiet, each attempt to convince distraught parents to keep their pain to themselves, seems impossibly depraved. While it was happening, however, it must have looked to many within the Church as though they were putting out the fires with impressive efficiency.

Jeff Anderson, a Minneapolis lawyer who has become the foremost legal pursuer of the Church, remembers his first case, which came to him by accident in 1983. A couple came to his office to report that their son had been abused by their priest. They had spoken to their bishop, but he had refused to act, and when Anderson went to the police, they told him the statute of limitations had already passed. So Anderson decided to sue.

The suit got the diocese's attention, and after some back-and-forth the Church's lawyers offered Anderson's clients $1 million to settle. Of course, they told Anderson, as part of the settlement there would have to be "the usual confidentiality agreement."

"The usual?" he asked.

"We always do that," they replied.

Anderson was incredulous. "You mean this has happened before?"

Barbara Blaine, a survivor and an activist herself, said she was equally blind to the scope of the crime at first. "When I first started dealing with my abuse, I was this gullible Catholic," Blaine said. Molested by a priest in the Toledo parish where she grew up, Blaine is now the Church's single biggest scourge, having founded the Survivors Network of Those Abused by Priests (SNAP) in 1988. It is to the Church's sex abuse scandal what ACT UP was to the AIDS crisis. "I thought there were two dozen of us across the United States," she says. By reaching out to reporters who were covering early reports of abuse, and lawyers representing survivors, she started to put together small meetings of survivors in different cities. At one meeting, she was sharing her story and said that when she met with the bishop of Toledo he told her that she was the first case of abuse in the whole diocese. Next, a woman from Oakland shared her story and said when she'd raised her abuse with church authorities in Oakland, they told her she was the first victim in all of Oakland. A third woman started laughing. "Don't you get it?" she said to the group. "We can't all be the first one."

The Church was attempting to shoot the moon. It employed bullying, threats, and theological entreaties to keep its horrifying secrets secret. It was a high-stakes strategy, with high rewards in the decades of success, and brutal costs in the one decade in which the truth was ripped free. Rather than relieving through disclosure the institutional pressure created by the crimes of the pedophiles within its ranks, the Church created a kind of secrecy bubble. Each gruesome infraction that was successfully kept out of the headlines and away from the police pushed in more air. As with the housing bubble that would collapse at the end of the decade, it was really only a matter of time until the Catholic Church could no longer contain the force of what it had repressed.

This is how we learn of an institution's bad faith: when its secrets are revealed. And it is the experience of that revelation, the slow untangling of the messy, ugly truth that is so profoundly destabilizing.

For much of the past decade, Terry McKiernan has been painstakingly documenting the havoc the Church's secrets have wrought. Like nearly all of the Irish American boys of his generation, McKiernan was raised in the Roman Catholic Church: altar boy, confirmation, a lifetime of Sundays. His uncle was a priest. But the reports of the Church's protection of serial child rapists shook his faith. "I was here in Boston in 2002 when the shit hit the fan," McKiernan told me. "I had little kids and the whole thing honestly hit me kind of hard. I was trying to raise them Catholic. One of the worst offenders [Paul Shanley] was connected with our parish." McKiernan had also lost a good friend on 9/11 and says it changed his outlook. "That left me vulnerable in a way that I had never been before to what the Church was doing."

McKiernan quit his job as a management consultant and started BishopAccountability.org. At first, he worked for free, with his family barely getting by, but eventually BishopAccountability .org raised enough money to pay salaries for a staff of three, and they set about collecting, indexing, and posting the millions of documents that had been released in Church legal proceedings. For the last five years McKiernan has probably spent more time than anyone in the country wading through them. "To be honest it is pretty mind-boggling what is suddenly available. At no time before in the history of the institution could you look inside and see how they work. It's not pretty, but it's pretty interesting."

Secrecy is the dominant theme. "In every single case the perpetrator himself enforces secrecy, sometimes by threats," says McKiernan. "Then, even the families of the victims honor it because the priest has a kind of status that trumps all other concerns. They don't go to the cops; they contact the bishop instead. When the priest is transferred out of the parish, the statement made to parishioners is that Father was a little tired. There are so many moments when lies are chosen over honesty. When you look at the panoply of secret moments, it does seem like it's the nature of the institution."

In uncovering the inner workings of the Church, McKiernan highlights another component of the Crisis of Authority, distinct from the ways in which it has discredited our mental habits. Unlike the Iraq War and the financial crisis, the event that precipitated McKiernan's (and so many others') loss of faith in the Church didn't happen during the past decade; that's just when it was finally uncovered. But as cathartic and necessary as uncovering the awful truth was, the revelation itself precipitated only more doubt.

The abuse scandal forever made it impossible for millions of Catholics to impute good faith to the Church. But it also made many of those closest to the scandal wonder just how many other secrets were lurking everywhere they looked: the new knowledge they gained made all their old knowledge suspect.

As I spent time talking to people at SNAP's 2010 conference, I found that many would darkly intimate collusion and conspiracy on a scale that didn't seem quite plausible: that local police, prosecutors, politicians, and the press were all in on the grand effort to hide the abuse from the public. My instinct was to view these claims skeptically, since in many cases they beggared belief. The Church was one thing, but why would police help the Church cover up its crimes?

But just a little cursory research showed these suspicions weren't quite as far-fetched as I had assumed. To cite just one example, in 1969, after several young boys alleged they had been sexually abused by Gonzaga University president Rev. John P. Leary, local police reportedly issued an ultimatum that Leary leave town within twenty-four hours rather than arresting and prosecuting him.

The more you learn about the documented instances of active, coordinated conspiracy and collusion, the harder it is to dismiss even the most seemingly far-fetched allegations of wrongdoing. This applies far more broadly than to the Church. On one hand, we can view scandal and revelation as fundamental proof that ultimately the truth will out. That is how an institutionalist is disposed to interpret things. But we can just as easily take a more cynical view: If, say, Bernie Madoff was allowed to pull off his $50 billion heist for decades with no sanction, if the SEC ignored a detailed letter from a knowledgeable whistle-blower titled simply "The World's Largest Hedge Fund Is a Fraud," then what's to say they're not ignoring the next Madoff as I write this?

In this way, more information and more openness can, perversely, feed more mistrust and more wild speculation: The more we know, the more we realize just how in the dark we truly are.

For someone like myself, professionally tasked with reporting facts about the world, this experience has a special paralyzing force. Like Susan Southwick, the Tea Party organizer who helped oust Senator Bob Bennett, I have an instinct to, in her words, "kind of trust authority." (This is a strange disposition for a journalist, I'll admit, but there it is.) And like Southwick, I've also been traumatized and radicalized by the experience of seeing that trust repaid with catastrophe.

I've seen firsthand that you can't trust consensus, because consensus can be horribly and violently wrong. You can't trust those people with the greatest proximity to the issue in question, because proximity can blind them as much if not more than distance. And you certainly cannot simply assume good faith, particularly from our pillar institutions and the powerful elites who run them.

The old methods of figuring out the world have failed us. So we turn to the new, and find they can do everything imaginable except restore to us the faith we've lost.

IT WOULD be disorienting enough to experience this past decade in which our mental habits have been discredited, but we are also simultaneously adapting to an entirely new informational environment, one which provides us with more information, and, also, bewilderingly, more secrecy than ever before.

To take but one important example: the Freedom of Information Act, passed in 1966 and strengthened considerably over a presidential veto in 1974, completely revolutionized citizens' access to their government's records. "A private individual can force a national security agency to disgorge information it does not want to release," says Steve Aftergood, an open government activist who's spent decades wrenching classified documents out of the federal bureaucracy and into the public sphere. Since 1995, approximately 1.5 billion pages of historical records have been declassified, largely because of the pressure of outside advocates wielding the law. Thanks to FOIA we know everything from the contents of the infamous Office of Legal Counsel memos that sanctioned torture during the Bush administration, to the individual recipients of federal farm subsidies.

As important as the raw number of documents now made public is the technology that now makes official data accessible. You can pull up your neighbor's political contributions, or just about any court filing in the country, in a matter of minutes, if not seconds. Thirty years ago it would have been totally inconceivable for the average citizen to read the full text of a bill Congress was about to debate and vote on. Today it's available to anyone with an Internet connection.

Of course, the usefulness of this access is limited. Anyone with an Internet connection could have read the entirety of the Patient Protection and Affordable Care Act, but at two thousand pages, almost no one did. In fact, the possibility of access to information that we can't possibly process induces a constant thrum of anxiety among conscientious citizens, one for which there is no obvious remedy.

The combination of disclosure and technology allows us to know more than we've ever known about just about every one of our pillar institutions—the latest SEC filings, last night's cable news ratings, and the latest bits of rumor and gossip circulating through Wall Street circles and posted to insider financial blogs.

But in surveying this explosion of information and access thereto, we also tend to overlook the other side of the coin: the simultaneous explosion of secrecy. "While we have the most open government in the world, we also have the most prodigiously secret government in the world," says Aftergood. "No one is generating as many secrets as we are."

Stanford history professor Robert Proctor studied what he calls the world of "secret knowledge," and was shocked to discover just how massive it is. "The world of secret knowledge is larger than the world of public knowledge," he told me. "In the U.S. there are four thousand censors who just work on censoring nuclear secrets. We live in this world where the public knowledge is just a tiny fraction of secret military knowledge."

The trend accelerated in the wake of 9/11, when the government began constructing a whole new, largely privatized national security apparatus atop the already-massive national security apparatus built up over forty years of cold war.

Roughly 850,000 people hold top secret security clearances. In an extensive investigation into what they called "Top Secret America," the *Washington Post*'s Dana Priest and William Arkin found a secret national security state so large and sprawling that almost no one could actually account for what its individual component parts did.

It is the alternating waves of secrecy and disclosure that characterize our present epistemic crisis in realms far beyond just national security. We may have more financial data at our fingertips than ever before, but during the last several decades, the hidden universe of financial dark matter has dramatically expanded.

The private equity industry, which takes companies private, outside the view of the SEC and public filings, more than tripled in size between 2001 and 2007. Between 2004 and 2007, the market for over-the-counter derivatives grew 74 percent. These derivatives, usually highly specialized, are traded one-to-one, away from the prying eyes of an organized exchange. It was this market in a specific kind of derivatives, credit default swaps, that converted a collapsed housing bubble into a global financial cataclysm. Because credit default swaps weren't traded on a public exchange, no one knew what anyone else's outstanding liability was. An institution that looked solvent on Tuesday could turn out to be bankrupt by Wednesday morning. And yet, astonishingly, in the wake of the crisis, the market for over-the-counter derivatives had grown 122 percent, to $25 trillion by 2011.

While the OTC market metastasized, so, too, did the so-called shadow banking system, a market for capital that operated outside of existing banking regulation. Because it was hidden from view of the public and regulators, it wasn't until the crash that everyone realized just how massive the shadow banking sector had become. A 2010 report from the Federal Reserve Bank of New York found that on the eve of the crisis the shadow banking system was almost twice as large as the regulated, visible, traditional banking system.

So we find ourselves in the paradoxical situation of knowing more than we need to and yet still not enough. We know the latest whereabouts of Britney Spears, but not how much money we spend on spy satellites; we have access to every single one of the two thousand pages that make up the Patient Protection and Affordable Care Act, but we don't definitively know what kind of deal the White House struck with the big pharmaceutical companies to get it passed. We can read and instantly translate any newspaper from around the world but don't know which of our major financial institutions are insolvent.

We live in an informational interregnum. The old gatekeepers have been discredited but not discarded. Their challengers are capable of subverting consensus and authority but not reconstituting it. And into the breach comes Julian Assange bearing a single, simple radical promise: total information can provide our salvation. If Julian Assange did not exist, we would have to invent him. With his white hair and lip that curls into something between a smirk and a snarl, his playful but vaguely sinister affect, Assange seems almost too cinematic to be real, as if our collective skepticism and distrust managed to conjure him into being.

Founded in 2006 as a secure means by which international whistle-blowers and hackers could anonymously publish secret documents, WikiLeaks' ethos was grounded in Assange's worldview, one distrustful, to the point of near paranoia, of any source of authority. "He had come to understand the defining human struggle not as left versus right, but as individual versus institution," the *New Yorker* wrote in a 2010 profile. "As a student of Kafka, Koestler, and Solzhenitsyn, he believed that truth, creativity, love and compassion are corrupted by institutional hierarchies 'that contort the human spirit.'" He is, in other words, the ultimate insurrectionist.

In the first five years of its existence, WikiLeaks made headlines for disclosing everything from official corruption in Kenya to a manual describing daily operations at the Guantánamo Bay detention facility. But it only really gained notoriety in 2010, when it came into possession of nearly a quarter million classified U.S. documents. On April 5, 2010, the site uploaded a video it provocatively titled "Collateral Murder," which recorded an Apache helicopter in Iraq as it (mistakenly) gunned down two Reuters journalists and a dozen Iraqi civilians, most of whom were unarmed. The video precipitated outcries from across the globe and intense coverage in the foreign press. At home, it prompted an explosion of commentary and debate in the blogosphere and, after WikiLeaks produced seventy thousand classified documents on the Afghanistan war, a harsh condemnation from the Department of Defense: "We deplore WikiLeaks for inducing individuals to break the law, leak classified documents, and then cavalierly share that secret information with the world, including our enemies."

But those were just the first tremors. In December 2010, WikiLeaks sent shock waves through governments around the globe when it posted 6,000 secret U.S. diplomatic cables (out of a total of 150,000 in its possession) revealing, among other embarrassing details of U.S. statecraft, that the United States was waging a more or less secret war in Yemen and that Hillary Clinton had directed diplomatic staff abroad to spy on foreign officials (in contravention of the UN charter). In Tunisia, anti-regime activists read with interest U.S. diplomats' description of the egregious corruption and self-dealing by the country's ruling strongman Ben Ali (he would be dislodged by a popular uprising one month later).

Republican congressman Peter King called for WikiLeaks to be designated a foreign terrorist organization and for Assange to be criminally prosecuted. Bill O'Reilly fantasized on air about Assange being killed by a U.S. predator drone. Vice President Joe Biden called WikiLeaks "terrorists," and reports surfaced that Attorney General Eric Holder had commissioned an inquiry to see if Assange could be tried under the 1917 Espionage Act.

WikiLeaks' defenders pointed to a simple, powerful principle: Citizens of a democratic republic have a right to know what their government is doing. Daniel Ellsberg, who struck his own blow for openness during the Vietnam War by leaking the infamous Pentagon Papers to the *New York Times,* defended Assange in precisely these terms. "The founding of this country was based on the principle that the government should not have a say as to what we hear, what we think, and what we read," he told Stephen Colbert in December 2010. "We're not in the mess we're in, in the world, because of too many leaks."

Assange himself once explained WikiLeaks' philosophy this way: "What we want people to do is fight with the truth. If people shoot truth at each other, then after the bodies are cleared away all that remains are the bullets of truth and the historical record, then we can get somewhere."

Assange's piercing faith that the truth will out seems almost quaint in a postmodern universe of manipulation, distortion, and selective leaking. In the wake of the failure of so many of our methods of knowing, in the wake of the malfeasance of many of our mediating institutions, what Assange seems to be attempting to do is to get rid of mediation altogether.

But there is an infinite amount of truth in the world, and only a tiny bit of it will ever make its way to us. Someone or some group of people or some set of institutions is going to be involved in the process of deciding what we know and what we don't. What is important and what is not. In other words: Fidelity to "the Truth" is meaningless, because not all truths, not all facts, are created equal. A publication could devote itself entirely to reporting truthfully on, say, the allegations and charges of sexual assault against Assange, and yet it's hard to imagine Assange would simply tip his cap to them for being "truthful."

If WikiLeaks' exposure of the American security state shows the possibilities of Assange's vision, its decision to post a massive trove of e-mails and documents from climate scientists at the University of East Anglia's Climate Research Unit shows its limitation.

The ten years' worth of private e-mail correspondence between climate scientists within UEA and elsewhere revealed a group of academics who viewed themselves as under siege from well-funded and disingenuous critics, not to mention a group contemptuous and defensive toward their outside skeptics—not necessarily a flattering picture. But according to critics of global warming, the e-mails also showed the scientists to be guilty of genuine scientific fraud, plotting secretly to manipulate data to strengthen their case that the earth is warming as a result of increased carbon emissions.

Confronted by a questioner about his decision to leak e-mails that were the product of an illegal hack targeted at private citizens, Assange contended that WikiLeaks had no choice but to post them. "It doesn't matter what we think," he said. "We had no choice."

The disclosures precipitated a full-fledged media frenzy, particularly among the right-wing press in both the UK and the United States. Glenn Beck, Sean Hannity, and professional conspiracy theorist Alex Jones, along with many others, pointed to these e-mails as a smoking gun, evidence in black-and-white that scientists were engaged in a massive global conspiracy to hoodwink the world into believing global temperatures have been rising, presumably as a pretext for more taxes, bigger government, and less freedom. "If your gut said, 'Wait a minute, this global warming thing sounds like a scam,'" Beck told his audience, "well, I think you're seeing it now. We told you this was going on, without proof, because we listened to our gut."

The frenzy in the conservative media occasioned mainstream outlets to also pick up the story, culminating with all three nightly network newscasts reporting the most damning snippets of the stolen e-mails. That attention then prompted no less than six official inquiries into the scientists' conduct. The University of East Anglia, Penn State, the British House of Commons' Science and Technology Committee, the British Royal Society, and even the U.S. Department of Commerce's inspector general all sifted through the e-mails looking for evidence of malfeasance, deception, and misconduct. Every single one of the inquiries cleared the scientists of any scientific malpractice. Every one. All concluded that nothing revealed in the e-mails called into question either the conclusions of their published work or, more broadly, the robust consensus on anthropogenic global warming. The "rigour and honesty" of the scientists in question, concluded the East Anglia investigators, "are not in doubt." Perhaps not surprisingly, the reports clearing the scientists received nowhere near the attention of the initial titillating leaks that hinted at possible misconduct. "The story followed a depressingly familiar trajectory," wrote environmental writer David Roberts, "hyped relentlessly by right-wing media, bullied into the mainstream press as he-said she-said, and later, long after the damage is done, revealed as utterly bereft of substance."

It's all part of a larger concerted effort on the part of incumbent energy interests and the conservative media to sow doubt in the minds of the public, an effort that has been staggeringly effective. In the UK, a quarter of the population is "unconvinced" that the planet's temperatures are warming—a figure that has doubled in the past four years. In the United States, roughly two-thirds of the population is unconvinced that global warming is "a very serious problem."

This trend is a direct challenge to Assange's faith that the truth will win out. The climate scientists are fighting back with the truth and they are losing, badly.

In their Pulitzer Prize–winning history, *The Race Beat,* Gene Roberts and Hank Klibanoff show how in a bygone era a functioning, if risk-averse and cautious, press was able to effect a nearly unprecedented shift in public opinion by faithfully reporting the story of segregation and the challenge it faced from the Civil Rights Movement. "At no other time in U.S. history were the news media more influential than they were in the 1950s and 1960s," the authors contend, and the organizers of the Civil Rights Movement understood this. One of their chief strategic goals was to convince the pillar institutions of the mainstream media, the

New York Times and the broadcast evening news, to see the struggle for Civil Rights as they did, as a battle of the forces for justice and progress against those for reaction and hatred. Once the Northern white establishment was won over and began to use its considerable power to document the violence, hatred, and cruelty of the Jim Crow establishment's reaction to Civil Rights protesters, public opinion began to turn.

The concentration of the media at that moment, in other words, provided activists with an Archimedean point of leverage: They could focus their energies on a relative handful of press outlets and through these outlets broadcast their message to almost every last member of the voting public.

In some ways, the story told in *The Race Beat* bears out Julian Assange's simple vision: The truth of the nature of segregation was exposed and the truth won. Roberts and Klibanoff quote Swedish economist Gunnar Myrdal, who prophetically observed in his 1944 book that "there is no doubt that a great majority of white people in America would be prepared to give the Negro a substantially better deal if they knew the facts."

But key to this "truth" getting out was the concentrated authority that the establishment press at the time, particularly the *New York Times,* possessed. Imagine how the Civil Rights Movement would be received were it to happen today. Fox News would work ceaselessly to convince Northern audiences that the protesters were in fact Marxists and subversives and posed a violent threat to the American way. Sleazy interviews with King's various mistresses would appear on segregationist blogs, while right-wing activists would gleefully videotape and disseminate embarrassing interviews with bewildered protesters.

This isn't an idle thought experiment. The challenge of climate change forces us to stare into the dark void left by the collapse of traditional institutional authority. One democratic political operative I know calls this feature of modern public life "post-truth politics." Without some central institutions that have the inclination, resources, and reputational capital to patrol the boundaries of truth, we really do risk a kind of Hobbesian chaos, in which truth is overtaken by sheer will-to-power.

You don't have to be a defender of the status quo to fear this outcome. Even the most unrelentingly critical observers of our current elites and institutions are terrified by it. "We're marching over the cliff for institutional reasons that are pretty hard to dismantle," Noam Chomsky said in a 2011 video about climate change. "The anger and fear and hostility in the country about everything carries over to this. If you look at polls, everyone hates Congress, they hate the Democrats, they hate the Republicans even more, they hate big business; they hate banks and they distrust scientists, so why should we believe what these pointy-headed elitists are telling us? We don't trust anything else, we don't trust them."

Even Assange himself has come, I think, to recognize this central problem. An early manifesto he wrote about WikiLeaks activities in 2006 called "State and Terrorist Conspiracies" laid out a truly radical vision in which the goal of WikiLeaks was to destroy the "authoritarian conspiracy" that lay behind what he called "unjust regimes." By leaking information from within, WikiLeaks would lead these institutions to grow paranoid and no longer able to communicate with themselves, spelling their demise.

But by 2011, Assange's views had evolved. Rather than wanting to use leaks as a means of destroying institutions from the inside, he told interviewer David Frost he was trying to save them from themselves. "You're not automatically opposed to authority?" Frost asked Assange.

"You know, having run an organization, I understand the difficulties in building institutions, having a good institution," Assange said.

Institutions are very important. I mean anyone who's worked in Africa, as I have, knows that successful civil institutions don't just come from nowhere.... Clean roads and so on don't just come from nowhere. There is an institutional infrastructure behind this. But secret institutions start to become corrupted in their purpose. They're able to engage in secret plans which would be opposed by the population and carry them out for their own internal purposes. So they're not performing the function that people demand that they perform.

In other words: Progress is dependent upon a productive and dynamic tension between institutionalism and insurrectionism. Insurrectionists keep our institutions honest. Institutionalists are stewards of our collective public life. The most important social project we must undertake in the wake of the fail decade is reconstructing our institutions so that we once again feel comfortable trusting them. Because without the social cohesion that trusted institutions provide, we cannot produce the level of consensus necessary to confront our greatest challenges. I believe the most important of these is climate change. Public opinion in the United States is nowhere near where it would have to be to produce the kinds of dramatic policy changes we must make if we are to cap carbon at a level scientists say is sustainable. In 2001, 75 percent of Americans believed in anthropogenic global warming; as of 2012, that number is 44 percent. The fundamental problem is that too many Americans simply don't trust the various forms of scientific and elite authority through which information about the threat of climate change is transmitted.

And this is the crux of the problem. As unreliable as elite authority has been over the past decade, we can't fix what needs fixing without it.

Chapter 5

WINNERS

We are the 1%

— Sign in the window of the Chicago
Board of Trade

NEXT TO "FREEDOM" THERE IS PROBABLY NO MORE contested word in the American political vocabulary than "elite." Each side of the political spectrum has its own definition, but in our contemporary politics it is the right that has most assiduously cultivated anti-elite animus. In the right's imagination it is not the owners of the means of production that compose the elite, but rather intellectuals, academics, members of the media and government. "Washington and the media elite," Sarah Palin thundered at a Republican fund-raiser in March 2010, "quit disrespecting the wisdom of the American people!"

Pressed by Brian Williams during the 2008 campaign to define just who the elite were, Palin alluded to a state of mind. "Anyone, who thinks that they are—I guess—better than anyone else, that's—that's my definition of elitism." As soon as she was finished with her answer, her ticket mate John McCain piped up. "I know where a lot of 'em live," McCain said with a snide laugh. "In our nation's capital and New York City. I've seen it. I've lived there. I know the town. Know what a lot of these elitists are. The ones that she never went to a cocktail party with in Georgetown." (Needless to say, McCain, son of naval royalty, owner of ten homes, and husband of a beer heiress worth millions, knew whereof he spoke.)

Conservative populism of this sort has a fairly long history. William F. Buckley Jr., son of an oil baron and graduate of Yale, famously pronounced in 1963: "I should sooner live in a society governed by the first two thousand names in the Boston telephone directory than in a society governed by the two thousand faculty members of Harvard University." Segregationist George Wallace attacked those pushing for Civil Rights as "pointy-headed intellectuals." Spiro Agnew unloaded on the "effete corps of impudent snobs" who made up the "media elite," a construct he ceaselessly presented as a nefarious foil. (Many of Agnew's speeches were written by William Safire, who'd previously been a well-compensated Madison Avenue flack and ad man.) Today, references on Fox News to the "media elite" outnumber references to the corporate or business elite by forty to one.

What makes people part of the elite, according to the right, isn't their degree of power or political influence, but rather their condescension, their worldview, their tastes, preferences, and cultural diet: they watch *Mad Men* and listen to NPR while the simple masses listen to talk radio and watch *American Idol*. They have, in the words of linguist Geoff Nunberg, "seditious taste in cheese and beverages." They are snobby cosmopolitans who look down on the ordinary Americans who unpretentiously and earnestly devote themselves to the bedrock virtues of faith, family, and flag.

That's why Dick Armey, a multimillionaire former House majority leader and erstwhile lobbyist at DLA Piper, one of Washington's premier influence-peddling firms, can castigate "elites" and the "establishment" as if he were a scruffy newsie with his nose pressed up against the glass watching the plutocrats from outside.

Through sheer overdeployment, conservatives have rendered the word "elite" nearly unusable. We now find ourselves in agreement that "the elite" have been discredited, but we can't quite figure out exactly who they are. We've seen how the contagion of distrust spreads out to infect any and all institutions and people that are plausibly associated with the elite. So if "pointy-headed intellectuals" who spend their days in quiet anonymity running climate models count as members of the elite, we end up with the perverse situation of the world's most powerful energy companies marshaling anti-elitist sentiment to keep their profits intact and the atmosphere polluted.

So then: What makes the elite the elite?

"From the hour of their birth," Aristotle once observed, "some are marked for subjection and some for command." For nearly all of human history the former have vastly outnumbered the latter, and while modern democracy represents the single most durable challenge to this immutable logic, our own history shows that democracy does not necessarily foreclose the possibility of rule by an elite.

So long as the franchise is granted to a small enough group of people, or the layers of representation between the masses and political leaders are sufficiently attenuated and mediated by powerful interests, a democracy in name can still feature rule by the few over the many. During the late nineteenth century and into the twentieth, as democratic experiments spread throughout Europe, a group of theorists set themselves to the task of analyzing how it was that a small subset of citizens could retain de facto control over a society despite the downward pressures of democratization. One of those theorists was Robert Michels, whose Iron Law of Oligarchy offered a model for how to think about our own meritocracy.

Michels's fellow theorists of the elite—Vilfredo Pareto, Gaetano Mosca, and José Ortega y Gasset—shared a similar descriptive analysis, though because they were hostile to egalitarianism, they viewed this as a feature rather than a bug. To them the "elite" was made up of both those with the most power and also those who deserved the most power. Central to their theories was a kind of proto-meritocratic vision of cream rising to the top, a conception of rule by the best, brightest, and noblest that stretches all the way back to the vision of the Greeks. "As one advances in life," Ortega y Gasset wrote in his 1930 book *The Revolt of the Masses,* "one realizes more and more that the majority of men—and of women— are incapable of any other effort than that strictly imposed on them as a reaction to external compulsion. And for that reason, the few individuals we have come across who are capable of a spontaneous and joyous effort stand out isolated, monumentalized, so to speak, in our experience. These are select men, the nobles, the only ones who are active and not merely reactive, for whom life is a perpetual striving, an incessant course of training." Ortega y Gasset was horrified by the way in which democracy as it spread across Europe was empowering what he called the Mass Man, an industrial brute, prone to ideological extremism, over those special best and brightest nobles whose prudential guidance was necessary for proper social order.

A few decades later, the most famous American elite theorist, C. Wright Mills, turned the elite theories of his predecessors on their head. Whereas Ortega y Gasset and his cohort argued that society was threatened by too much power in the hands of the Mass Man, Mills surveyed a postwar landscape in which Mass Man had been successfully alienated from the actual levers of power in the society. As institutions grew larger, and war and governance more complex, a subclass of men that Mills dubbed the "Power Elite" exerted more and more control over the nation's pillar institutions. "Insofar as national events are decided," Mills wrote, "the Power Elite are those who decide them."

It's this basic sense of "elite" that I want to recapture here. For generations, scholars and thinkers of both left and right who have taken to analyzing the elite have recognized that the most salient features of its members isn't their consumer preferences, aesthetic tastes, or some vague notion of "snobbishness," but rather their relatively small number, their power relative to the power of the wide swath of their fellow citizens, and their interconnectedness.

Which is not to say those in the "elite" aren't different and distinct in many of the ways conservatives ridicule. During any given era, elites tend to have consumer choices, religious beliefs, tastes, preferences, and worldviews quite distinct from those of the masses. But these distinguishing features are best understood as symptoms of their elite status, not the cause. Elite tastes are the emanations of high levels of power, status, and wealth. An English chimney sweep in nineteenth-century London would not have been a member of the elite simply because he nurtured a love of opera and foxhunting. He would still have been a chimney sweep. Conversely Warren Buffett may still drive a beat-up old American sedan, live in a modest house in Omaha, and like unpretentious heartland food, but that doesn't mean he's not a member of the elite. When the world economy looked as if it were about to plunge into the abyss, Buffett fielded frantic calls from some of the most powerful and wealthy men in the world begging for his aid. If he doesn't count as a member of the elite, then no one does.

But if the "elite" is, as a group, small, powerful, and connected, the main definitional challenge is figuring out just how small: A majority of Americans don't have four-year college degrees, but does that mean the 64 million who do constitute "the elite"? How about the 20 million with graduate degrees? The *New York Times* is widely understood to be an elite institution with an elite readership, but that "elite readership" includes my father, who works as a civil servant for the New York City Department of Health in East Harlem, and Henry Kissinger. What sociological generalizations can productively be offered about these two? Likewise, "elite" can

describe both a tenure-track anthropology professor at Columbia University and multibillionaire JPMorgan Chase CEO Jamie
Dimon. And while our anthropologist may have more influence
than, say, the bodega owner on her corner, when she's compared to
Jamie Dimon, that small difference vanishes from view.

In its simple formulation of the 99 percent on one side and
the 1 percent on the other, Occupy Wall Street offered the entire
culture a way of drawing precisely this dividing line, the one that
runs between the young, highly educated, but relatively powerless
anthropologist and Jamie Dimon. OWS defined just how big the
elite is, and it did it based on what is the most significant feature
of the development of the American political economy during the
meritocratic age: the 1 percent now lay claim to nearly a quarter of
the total economic pie. The last time their share was this high was
on the eve of the 1929 stock market crash.

In fact, one could argue that even the 1 percent doesn't capture
just how extreme inequality has grown at the highest reaches. In
2007, according to the IRS, the richest four hundred taxpayers
had an average income of more than ten thousand times the average income of the bottom 90 percent of taxpayers. Hedge fund
billionaire John Paulson made $2.4 million per hour in the year
2010. That's as much as a worker making $50,000 a year would
make over the course of her entire forty-seven-year working career.

In 1981, a University of Chicago economist named Sherwin
Rosen described markets that produce these kinds of distributions
as exhibiting what he called the economics of superstars. "In certain kinds of economic activity," he wrote, "there is concentration
of output among a few individuals, marked skewness in the associated distributions of income, and very large rewards at the top."

Rosen argued that certain technological trends had radically
expanded the demand for services for those who were the best in
their field: in 1950, a top basketball player could only monetize his

talent with an endorsement deal that would sell sneakers to Americans; today, LeBron James is featured on billboards from Florida to Turkey to China. The same goes in a whole host of domains: the best opera soprano can, with the advent of MP3s and the Internet, sell to anyone in the world with an iPod, which spells trouble for the fifth best soprano. If you can buy the best, why settle? In 1982, the top 1 percent of pop stars, in terms of pay, raked in 26 percent of concert ticket revenue. In 2003, that top 1 percent—names like Justin Timberlake, Christina Aguilera, or 50 Cent—took 56 percent of the concert pie.

But superstars don't just exist in the celebrity arenas of basketball and pop music. They are increasingly the norm across professional domains. In the law, the top rainmakers at major firms have pulled away from both their fellow partners and the associates below them. Top legal stars can now expect to "earn $10 million or more a year," the *Wall Street Journal* reported in 2011, "compared with $640,000 for the average partner at a U.S. firm. . . . Star partners are routinely earning 8 to 10 times the amount given to other partners—roughly double the usual compensation spread of a decade ago."

The same trend goes for CEOs. Between the 1970s and early 2000, the ratio of the pay of the top 10 percent of CEOs to those in the middle doubled from two to four. Not only that, but CEOs even pulled away from their own deputies. A 2006 study found that the ratio of CEO pay to the average of the next two most highly compensated employees of the firm also almost doubled during the period between 1980 and 2005.

In attempting to get a handle on the elite, income serves as a useful proxy for power more broadly because it allows us to quantify what is otherwise abstract. But it would be a mistake simply to conclude that power and money are equivalent. While the two more often than not go together, power is greater than just material wealth. Aside from the formal political power vested in those elected and appointed to government, twenty-first-century America features three main sources of power: money, platform, and networks.

MONEY

In most cases, of course, money does confer power: the ability to make decisions about which products will be made, what innovations will be nurtured or abandoned. Those with capital to lend exert tremendous dominion in their capacity as creditors (as we've seen during the foreclosure crisis): the International Monetary Fund's role as lender of last resort to developing countries has empowered it to issue decrees that completely remake a nation's social contract and domestic policy as a condition of its extension of credit.

But in a society as fully monetized as ours, money is also crucial because it can readily be exchanged for all other kinds of power. Money can purchase platform: When Fox News mogul Roger Ailes bought an expansive estate in the Hudson Valley, he also purchased two local newspapers, which he used to crusade for changes to local zoning laws. ("Freedom of the press," *New Yorker* writer A. J. Liebling famously quipped, "belongs to those who own one.")

Likewise, money can grant you access to powerful social networks, whether on Park Avenue or in country clubs, because people with money tend to socialize with other wealthy people. These bonds of association lower coordination costs and make organizing toward some mutually beneficial goal easier and more effective.

Money can also buy political power: it pays for lobbyists, PACs, political donations, and the all-important access. In his book *Oligarchy,* political scientist Jeffrey Winters focuses on what he calls the income defense industry, made up of "lawyers, accountants, lobbyists, wealth management agencies" who "have highly specialized knowledge and can navigate a complex system of taxation and regulations, generating a range of tax 'products,' 'instruments,' and 'advice' that enable oligarchs to keep scores of billions in income annually that would otherwise have to be surrendered to the state."

Over the last decade, the political arm of the income defense industry has been wildly successful. The tax cuts passed by Bush and extended by Obama represent a total of $81.5 billion transferred from the state into the hands of the richest 1 percent. Meanwhile, hedge fund managers and their surrogates have deployed millions of dollars to lobbyists to maintain the so-called carried interest loophole, a provision of tax law that allows fund managers to classify much of their income drawn from investing gains as "carried interest" so that it is taxed at the low capital gains rate of 15 percent, rather than the marginal income rate, which would in most cases be more than twice that. It was this wrinkle in the law that helped Mitt Romney, a man worth an estimated quarter of a billion dollars, pay an effective tax rate of just under 14 percent in 2010. In 2008, 2009, and 2010, the House of Representatives passed a bill closing the loophole, only to see it beaten back by an intense wave of lobbying in the Senate.

This is a crass example of money purchasing direct political results, but there is mounting empirical evidence that our system of democratic representation as a whole heavily weights the preferences of the wealthy. In a 2005 paper, "Economic Inequality and Political Representation," Princeton political scientist Larry Bartels looked at how senatorial voting records tracked with the positions of constituents in different parts of the income distribution. "In almost every instance," Bartels found, "senators appear to be considerably more responsive to the opinions of affluent constituents than to the opinions of middle-class constituents, while the opinions of constituents in the bottom third of the income distribution have no apparent statistical effect on their senators' roll call votes."

A few years later, Bartels's Princeton colleague Martin Gilens offered further evidence of this phenomenon. Gilens studied a large survey library of answers to questions about "proposed policy changes" between 1981 and 2002 and then matched them with legislative outcomes. When he looked at how the preferences of different income groups affected legislative outcomes, the results were striking. First he looked at issues where the wealthy (top 10 percent) and poor (bottom 10 percent) diverged and found that legislative outcomes "are fairly strongly related to the preferences of the well-to-do . . . but wholly unrelated to the preferences of the poor."

That might not be totally shocking, of course, but Gilens also looked at issues where middle-class voters (50th percentile of income) and wealthy voters diverged and found again that legislative outcomes closely tracked the preferences of the wealthy and nearly *totally ignored* the desires of the middle class. He concludes that "government policy appears to be fairly responsive to the well off and virtually unrelated to the desires of low and middle income citizens."

While the basic logic of democracy is one person, one vote, our entire system of representation heavily weights the preferences and interests of those with the most money, reliably aiding those with the most money in their efforts to get richer.

PLATFORM

Platform is a term I first learned from the publishing industry, where the sales potential of a given author is judged largely as a function of how many people (and how many People Who Matter) a given author can reach. With nearly 15 million weekly listeners, Rush Limbaugh has about as big a platform as you can get. Bill O'Reilly, who commands a nightly audience of 3 million (the largest on cable news), also has a huge platform. And perhaps not surprisingly, both men reliably turn out books that do, indeed, dominate the *New York Times* bestseller list: yet another example of the rich getting richer.

That said, what's distinct about platform is that unlike both money and political power, which I mentioned above, the trend over the past decade has been toward less concentration, rather than more. While media companies have merged and concentrated at a frightening rate, audience share has gone in the exact opposite direction. Walter Cronkite routinely spoke to 20 million people a night; now the top nightly newscast, NBC *Nightly News,* gets about 9 million viewers. The same goes for nearly every aspect of media. As audiences fracture, everyone now has a smaller share of the total than the largest players, like *Time* and the *Washington Post,* had in their heyday.

The reason that audiences are fracturing is that outlets and sources of media are wildly proliferating. Instead of one Walter Cronkite with 20 million viewers, we now have 800 million Facebook users each broadcasting thoughts and activities to a small, interconnected audience. So though the distribution of platform power in America in the twenty-first century is still radically unequal, it is far more equal than it was just a decade earlier. Of no other form of power can this be said. Twenty-five years ago, if you had something you wanted to say, a cause you believed in, maybe you'd call a few friends or talk to them over dinner. Someone truly motivated and with enough time and energy could sit down for a few hours and mimeograph letters or make a bunch of phone calls, hoping to reach a few dozen people. It's now the case that you can post a link on Facebook and instantly reach 250 people. What's more, the nature of Internet correspondence, in which enthusiasm can spread like contagion, means that even people with an extremely limited platform can find themselves caught in a fierce updraft that propels their letter or YouTube video or blog post out to millions of people. All of which means the average teenager now has a platform far greater than your average well-regarded professional adult only two decades earlier. This potentially represents a radical, historic shift in the distribution of power in the country.

NETWORKS

The earliest elite theorists recognized that social networks are profoundly powerful and irregularly distributed. So much of elite power, C. Wright Mills observed, stems from the tight social connections between different members of the Power Elite in different spheres: the CEO who goes to work at the Treasury Department, the retired general who sits on the CEO's corporate board. The social capital of the elite, the dense connections of familiarity exhibited by its members, gave Mills a more nuanced theory of elite power than Marx's concept of a ruling class. "The American government is not, in any simple way nor as a structural fact, a committee of 'the ruling class,'" Mills wrote. "It is a network of 'committees,' and other men from other hierarchies besides the corporate rich sit in these committees."

Grover Norquist, a man we've met before, is a perfect example of a member of the elite whose chief source of power is network power. One of the central organizers of the conservative movement, Norquist has an ability to get Republican lawmakers to oppose any and all tax increases that comes not from his own fortune or his political office, but rather from his dense tangle of connections to donors and activists he can marshal to punish wayward Republicans. "To the extent that there is a conservative network," one political scientist who specializes in modern conservatism observed, "Grover is at the switchboard."

Occupying the right "switchboard" can, in certain cases, confer even more power than access to riches might. But it should also come as no surprise that Norquist happens to be a very rich man with access to a large platform.

That's because while money, political power, platform, and network power may be distinct conceptually, they are tightly correlated in practice. Mills recognized this, noting the tendency of hierarchies of different kinds of power to converge at the top. Today, that tendency is even more pronounced. The sophisticated and extensive system of meritocratic sorting manages to draw from a wider swath of society than in Mills's time but distills the elite down to an even smaller and more potent number. While the Power Elite of Mills's day was more homogeneous—white, male, Protestants almost to the last man—it was also more geographically diffuse. Cleveland had its members of the Power Elite, as did Detroit and Milwaukee. Today, the Power Elite is more geographically concentrated in specific areas. Economist Jamie Galbraith found that if you measured inequality across counties in the United States in the 1990s, half the rise occurred in 5 counties out of 3,150: New York, New York; King County, Washington; and San Francisco, Santa Clara, and San Mateo in Northern California.

The members of today's elite have never been farther from the median worker and closer, in the literal sense, to their fellow meritocrats. And because of the primacy of money in our post-meritocratic culture, there is a ready path by which one can trade certain kinds of power for others: money can purchase influence, and influence can later be cashed out.

Just look at our elected officials. Getting elected to office requires such a large sum of money that you more or less have to be rich yourself so you can both fund your own campaign and know enough fellow rich people who can raise money for you. When recruiting candidates for the House of Representatives, the Democratic Congressional Campaign Committee (DCCC) looks for aspirants to raise so much money, so early—$250,000 in the first quarter the candidate has declared—that it's almost impossible to do without a massive personal or family bank account. "They'll say to you, you gotta be hitting 250," says one former congressional candidate. "And I was struggling to hit 100,000. You have to think out the actual economics of it. If you don't have a big bank account, then raising money has to be your full-time job," which means forfeiting your actual job and the income from that, "and if it's not going to be your full-time job, you better know a huge, huge number of rich people."

The results of this funneling process are clear in the composition of the country's least-trusted institution, the United States Congress: nearly half of all members of Congress have a net worth north of a million dollars, compared to just one in twenty-two households nationwide. Between 1984 and 2009, while the median net worth of American households remained essentially unchanged, the median net worth of members of the House of Representatives rose by 260 percent. Not only did the rich get richer, so did Congress.

While money can get you access to networks and political power, those who have lots of power and influence but not much money can, when the time is right, sell their networks, influence, and access for a very high price. This is such a common occurrence in Washington, DC, that it has its own name: "moving downtown." That's what happens when a relatively modestly paid Capitol Hill staffer leaves his job working for a legislator to join a lobbying firm where he can make two to three times his salary. More than one-third of congressional staffers turn to a career in lobbying after leaving Capitol Hill. It's clear the staffer-turned-lobbyist's value to special interests depends on the robustness of his or her network on Capitol Hill. According to an August 2010 study, when a lobbyist's former boss on Capitol Hill left office, the lobbyist's salary declined by an average of 50 percent in the six months following the departure.

Moving from Capitol Hill to K Street isn't limited to staffers: In 2010, 37 percent of the newly out-of-office members of Congress went to work for lobbying firms or clients. After losing his run for Senate in 2006, Tennessee Democrat Harold Ford Jr. moved to New York to take a job with Merrill Lynch with a guaranteed annual compensation of $2 million. At the time he had no experience in finance. What he was paid for were his networks: "A telegenic young lawmaker with a wide network of relationships around the country, Mr. Ford was courted by several Wall Street firms after he lost his bid for the Senate in Tennessee four years ago," noted the *Times*. When Peter Orszag, the forty-two-year-old director of the Office of Management and Budget for the first two years of the Obama administration, resigned his post in July 2010, he quickly announced he'd be joining Citigroup as a vice chairman for a salary that Wall Street insiders estimated was between $2 million and $3 million.

Sarah Palin took a different, but even more lucrative approach than Orszag. When she emerged onto the national scene, Palin and her husband were making $250,000 a year, which put them in a very high portion of the income distribution but outside the inner ring of superstars. As an Alaskan politician, Palin also didn't necessarily possess a tremendous amount of network power, and her political power as governor of Alaska was similarly circumscribed because it is a small state, detached from the social networks of the mainland power elite. What she did have, though, was platform.

People wanted to hear her, the media loved to cover her, and after abruptly leaving the office of governor in 2009, she directly monetized that platform through book contracts, cable deals, speaking fees, and even her own cable show on the Discovery Channel. In her first year out of the governor's office she made a reported $12 million and she is now worth an estimated $20 million. It is, in a very real way, the twenty-first-century postmodern capitalist version of the American dream.

Once a member of the elite has sufficiently monetized his or her power, that money can be traded for other kinds of power, which in turn can be invested and reap its own kinds of rewards. Harold Ford Jr.'s political and media networks made him an attractive hire for Citigroup, where he was, in turn, able to expand both his Rolodex and his earning potential. As this positive feedback loop plays out, the elite increasingly becomes an entirely distinct group, moving effortlessly between public and private life, alternating between access to state power and market power.

As a snapshot of what this looks like in practice, consider the routine staffing changes in the Obama administration as it reached the midway point of its first term. Chief of Staff Rahm Emanuel left his position to run for mayor of Chicago. Emanuel got his start as a fund-raiser for Mayor Daley, moved to the Clinton White House, where he lasted nearly the entire eight years, eventually becoming a senior adviser to the President. After serving in the Clinton administration, at the age of thirty-nine he left to become an investment banker, spending two and a half years at Wasserstein Perella, where he amassed a fortune of more than $18 million. He then ran for Congress, became White House Chief of Staff, and left to run successfully for mayor of Chicago.

To replace the multimillionaire Rahm Emanuel, the multimillionaire President Obama (net worth $5 million) named multimillionaire William Daley, the brother of the mayor that Emanuel was hoping to replace. Daley's résumé included stints as commerce secretary in the Clinton administration and as campaign manager for Al Gore's 2000 campaign, but at the time he was named chief of staff, he was Midwest chairman at JPMorgan Chase, making $8.7 million a year. His net worth was estimated at more than $50 million. When Bill Daley later left his post as chief of staff in January 2012, he was replaced by Jack Lew, who spent four years at Citigroup and received a bonus of $950,000 in 2009, even after it was disclosed that his division made high-stakes bets on the housing market.

Around the same time Emanuel departed, the White House faced the loss of another key team member when National Economic Council director Larry Summers announced his intention to return to Harvard. Summers, who had served as a deputy Treasury secretary and president of Harvard University, also spent a spell as a consultant at the hedge fund D. E. Shaw: that gig paid him $5.2 million a year, or more than $100,000 per week, for one day of work a week. According to his disclosure forms, his net worth at the time he left the White House was between $17 million and $39 million. To replace the multimillionaire Summers, the White House faced a choice between two other millionaires: Roger Altman, a founder and chairman at Evercore Partners who'd served as deputy secretary of the Treasury in the Clinton administration, and Gene Sperling, the counselor to the Treasury secretary who'd served as deputy director of the National Economic Council under Clinton. Altman's 2010 total compensation was nearly $6.5 million. (Not to mention the fact he owns a private jet.) While Sperling had spent most of his adult life in public service and policy jobs, he managed to make $2.2 million in 2008 alone from consulting fees from financial institutions like Goldman Sachs and hedge funds.

In February 2011, presidential adviser David Axelrod announced he was leaving the White House to return to Chicago and advise the President's reelection campaign. Axelrod reported income of $1.5 million the year of Obama's election, and his net worth is much more thanks to more than two decades of running the highly lucrative and successful political consulting firm Axelrod and Associates (later AKPD Media). Staying behind as one of the only remaining members of the President's original White House inner circle was his longtime friend from Chicago Valerie Jarrett. Before coming to the White House, Jarrett had been CEO of the property management firm Habitat Co., which had earned millions off government contracts developing low-income housing to replace the dismantled Chicago Housing Authority projects. When entering office, she reported a money market fund that held between $1 million and $5 million.

The point is this: The 1 percent and the nation's governing class are more or less one and the same. If you are a member of the governing elite and aren't a millionaire, you're doing something wrong. And if the divide between the 1 percent and the 99 percent really is a defining feature of our politics, how can the 99 percent trust that same wealthy, governing elite to zealously pursue its interests?

1 PERCENT PATHOLOGIES

Nearly all of the commentary on America's growing inequality focuses on the ways in which skewed distribution of income and wealth is bad for those on the bottom of the pyramid: the way it leads to stagnating wages and competition for scarce positional goods, how it alienates the middle and working classes and the poor. But we largely ignore the effect of extreme inequality that may, in the long run, prove to be the most destructive: the way it makes those at the top of the social pyramid worse.

Desmond Tutu, the heroic archbishop who helped lead the triumphant battle against South African apartheid, made a similar observation about the effects of the apartheid system on the white ruling class. "Even the supporters of apartheid were victims of the vicious system which they implemented and which they supported so enthusiastically," he wrote in his book *No Future Without Forgiveness*. "In the process of dehumanizing another, in inflicting untold harm and suffering, inexorably the perpetrator was being dehumanized as well."

What Tutu was referring to was the moral and spiritual damage that extreme inequality inflicted on even those who dominated the apartheid system. But there are actual cognitive, organizational, and social costs to such systems as well. The slave economy of the antebellum South conferred massive material gains on a very small number of extremely wealthy white plantation owners. But it also severely stunted the development of the region. With a steady supply of low-cost human labor, there was no incentive to invent and industrialize, so that by the time of the Civil War the North was far richer than the South, though the South contained far more of the nation's richest men.

Though it's obviously a far cry from the antebellum South, extreme inequality of the particular kind that we have produces its own particular kind of elite pathology: it makes elites less accountable, more prone to corruption and self-dealing, more status-obsessed and less empathic, more blinkered and removed from informational feedback crucial to effective decision-making. For this reason, extreme inequality produces elites who are less competent and more corrupt than those in a more egalitarian social order would. This is the fundamental paradoxical outcome that several decades of failed meritocratic production has revealed: As American society grows more elitist, it produces a worse caliber of elites.

The kind of inequality that's at the core of the problem is what we might call "fractal inequality." Fractals are nifty shapes rendered by computers based on recursive mathematical formulas that exhibit the characteristics of self-similarity. They have a psychedelic look and are often characterized by a series of spirals of tentacle-looking cornices. If you look closely at a fractal and zoom in on one of those tentacles, you'll see that it, too, features a set of smaller, identical tentacles, arranged in the exact same way as the larger ones off of which it shoots. Zoom in again and the pattern repeats. You could, theoretically, zoom in infinitely and keep seeing the same images over and over, each tentacle sprouting smaller identical copies, and on and on.

Fractal inequality functions the same way, with the same vast inequality reinscribing itself at every level of analysis. If you look at the broad distribution of income gains, you'll see that the distance between the top 1 percent and bottom 99 percent is similar to the distance between the top 0.01 percent and the top 0.99 percent, which is similar to the gap between the top 0.0001 percent and the top 0.0099 percent.

You can think of it as a strange, surreal M. C. Escher–style tower, the top of which recedes ever upward the higher you climb. Such a distributional structure reliably induces a dizzying vertigo among those ambitious souls who aim to scale it. The successful overachiever can only enjoy the perks of his relatively exalted status long enough to realize that there's an entire world of heretofore unseen perks, power, and status that's suddenly come within view and yet remains out of reach.

I caught a glimpse of this in 2011 when I attended the Davos World Economic Forum, the annual gathering of the global ruling class that takes place each January in Switzerland. When you arrive in the Zurich airport, your first instinct is to feel a bit of satisfaction that you are one of the elect few chosen to hobnob with the most powerful people on earth. Airport signs welcome and direct you to a special booth where exceedingly polite staff give you a ticket for a free shuttle bus that will drive you the two hours to the small ski-resort town in the Alps.

But you can't help but notice that other guests, the ones who landed on the same plane but who were sitting in first class, are being greeted by an army of attractive red-coated escorts who help them with their bags before whisking them off in gleaming black Mercedes S-Class sedans for the two-hour drive.

Suddenly your perspective shifts. At first you had viewed yourself as special and distinct from all those poor saps who would never be allowed into the inner sanctum of global power that is the World Economic Forum. But now you realize that, in the context of Davos attendees, you are a member of the unwashed masses, crammed into a bus like so much coach chattel.

And while you're having this realization, those same special VIPs whom you've quickly come to envy are enjoying their ride inside their plush leather confines. But later that night they will find out over cocktails that those who are the true insiders don't fly on commercial flights into Zurich, they take private jets and then transfer to helicopters, which make the trip from Zurich in about thirty minutes and feature breathtaking views of the Alps.

This constant envy is the dominant experience of the Davos conference, an obsessive looking over the shoulder instilled by the participants' knowledge that the reality of fractal inequality means there are infinite receding layers of networking happening that one doesn't even know about! "The point about Davos is that it makes everyone feel wildly insecure," observed Anya Schiffrin, the wife of Nobel Prize–winning economist and frequent Davos attendee Joseph Stiglitz. "Billionaires and heads of state alike are all convinced that they have been given the worst hotel rooms, put on the least interesting panels, and excluded from the most important events/most interesting private dinners. The genius of World Economic founder Klaus Schwab is that he has been able to persuade hundreds of accomplished businessmen to pay thousands of dollars to attend an event which is largely based on mass humiliation and paranoia."

The irony here is that if you didn't attend Davos, you wouldn't know what you were missing, but it is the nature of the endless meritocratic scramble that each success brings into view some new higher status level to envy.

Davos is fractal inequality in its purest form, but so much of American life, particularly in elite circles, is similarly structured. A social hierarchy that extends ever upward instills a potent combination of egomania and insecurity. The experience of being just outside the place where we think real success is creates an even more intense desire to ascend and cultivates a dangerous willingness to do anything to pass each successive checkpoint, scale each next flight of stairs, always hoping that you'll finally arrive at the penthouse or somewhere you can call home.

In a far different time and place, C. S. Lewis articulated the emotional structure of such a hierarchy and the moral stakes of succumbing to it. Speaking to the students of the University of London in 1944, he warned them of the siren call of what he called "The Inner Ring." "You have met the phenomenon of an Inner Ring," he told them. "You discovered one in your house at school before the end of the first term. And when you had climbed up to somewhere near it by the end of your second year, perhaps you discovered that within the Ring there was a Ring yet more inner.... You were beginning, in fact, to pierce through the skins of the onion."

Lewis recognized that as we learn of inner rings, that knowledge provides a welcome bed into which the seeds of corruption might fall. For the experience of being just outside the elusive "inner ring" produces such a keen sense of self-doubt that it makes one disposed to do evil just to achieve entrance. "In the whole of your life as you now remember it," Lewis asked the students before him, "has the desire to be on the right side of that invisible line ever prompted you to any act or word on which, in the cold small hours of a wakeful night, you can look back with satisfaction? If so, your case is more fortunate than most."

So forceful is the pull of the inner ring that Lewis contends that "unless you take measures to prevent it, this desire is going to be one of the chief motives of your life, from the first day on which you enter your profession until the day when you are too old to care."

The hierarchies of postwar England were different in many crucial ways from the hierarchies of twenty-first-century America, but what is the meritocracy if not an endless series of inner rings? It is quite consciously designed not only to funnel "the right people" into successively smaller inner rings, but also to stoke in them an insatiable desire for achievement, the need to penetrate farther and farther into the elusive center. But Lewis saw decades ago that a system that requires passing through a near endless series of such inner rings will also provide a near endless series of opportunities for moral corrosion.

Societies whose upper class is marked by birth, title, and lineage do not tend to cultivate a voracious appetite for competition in the same way ours does. There is a certain security that comes from being at the top, but in a society of fractal inequality there is no top. There is always another height to which to ascend, more competitors to vanquish, more money to obtain. Which is why our elites display a destructive and combustible combination of egomania and entitlement on the one hand and insecurity on the other.

A 2011 poll of millionaires commissioned by Fidelity found that fully 42 percent of the more than one thousand who were surveyed did not feel rich. Those who qualified for the survey had at least a million dollars in investable assets, excluding retirement funds and real estate, which placed them in the top 1 percentage of wealth. But in order to truly feel wealthy, those surveyed said they would need, on average, $7.5 million. The reason, according to Sanjiv Mirchandani, who oversaw the poll for Fidelity, was that "they compare themselves to their peer group."

Keeping up the with Joneses has been a staple of postwar American life, but the current generation has seen what was once implicit made explicit: competition is now the model for American life, and "winning" the model of success. Because competition is the central engine in the model of both meritocratic and capitalist achievement, affection for it and acclimation to its spiritual and psychological demands are inculcated from a young age. To be successful, one must never be satisfied, and so no one ever is. Our elites are conditioned to fight for every last inch of beach, to parry and thrust their way forward no matter how much they have already achieved, all of which produces two rather nasty psychological side effects.

One is that it tends to make people believe they have absolutely earned what they have achieved. A legacy student at an Ivy League university certainly doesn't feel as if she has coasted in on her father's coattails. She feels instead that she's killed herself for four years at her prestigious high school to earn her grades, her internships, and her postgraduate job opportunities. As was said of George W. Bush, it is tempting for those born on third base to believe they've hit a triple.

This means we are cursed with an overclass convinced it is composed of scrappy underdogs, individuals who are obsessed with the relative disadvantages they may have faced rather than the privilege they enjoyed. It is remarkable how under siege and victimized even the most powerful members of society feel, how much they tout their own up-by-their-bootstraps story. In fact, a basic ritual associated with entrance into the circle of winners is constructing a personal story about how it was through grit, talent, and determination that you fought your way into it.

Mitt Romney, the multimillionaire son of a car company CEO and governor of Michigan, told an audience at a 2012 Republican debate that if you squinted hard enough, he looked like a figure right out of a Horatio Alger tale. "And I—I mean—you know, my dad, as you know—born in Mexico, poor, didn't get a college degree—became head of a car company. I could have stayed in Detroit, like him, and gotten pulled up in the car company. I went off on my own. I didn't inherit money from my parents. What I have, I earned. I worked hard, the American way."

Or look at Roger Ailes. One could say, without hyperbole, that Ailes is one of the most powerful men in America. He's been a close confidant and adviser to several presidents. He earns upward of $20 million a year. He runs Fox News, the most watched and politically powerful cable news network in the country.

And yet Ailes seems to genuinely view himself as a persecuted underdog, a man surrounded by elitist snobs who look down at him. The son of a factory worker who taught him to distrust "college boys," Ailes has a persona entirely constructed around evidently sincere populism. "He really believes that he is an average American," observed journalist Tom Junod in a long 2011 *Esquire* profile. "He really believes that he is looked down upon by those who admire and fear him."

In midtown Manhattan, the hottest lunch spot for the media elite is a restaurant called Michael's. Ailes of course has his own table there, in the most prime location, reserved for him every day. Yet it is not enough. "You'll be sitting at his table at Michael's," one of his guests told Junod, "and he'll grouse about not getting any respect and being an outsider while everybody is lining up to kiss his ring. And you'll be like, Roger, you're at Michael's, you're at the best table—what more do you want?"

This is a recurring trope of meritocratic elites. Here's Bernie Madoff whining to a *New York* magazine reporter about the injustices of Wall Street he had to overcome: "It was always a business where you had to have an edge, and the little guy never got a break. The institutions controlled everything. . . . I realized from a very early stage that the market is a whole rigged job. There's no chance that investors have in this market."

This penchant to view oneself as an outsider is coupled with the other psychological side effect produced by ceaseless competition, which is a kind of compulsive self-obsession. One of the most interesting psychological trends over the last four or five decades is a marked increased in the population's self-esteem. According to psychologist Jean Twenge, who studies longitudinal trends in Americans' mental dispositions, in 1950 12 percent of teenagers agreed that "I am an important person." Three decades later, that percentage was 80 percent.

But among those who assert their own self-worth, psychologists found two distinct personality types. One group are those who report high self-esteem and also high levels of happiness, fulfilling friendships, and social relations. The other group report high self-esteem but also display a host of antisocial tendencies, including violence, racism, and lack of empathy. In their book *The Spirit Level*, authors Richard Wilkinson and Kate Pickett describe this latter kind of self-esteem as "primarily defensive, a kind of internal attempt to talk oneself up":

> People with insecure high self-esteem tend to be insensitive to others and to show an excessive preoccupation with themselves, with success, and with their image and appearance in the eyes of others. This unhealthy high self-esteem is often

called "threatened egotism," "insecure high self-esteem," or narcissism.

At its most extreme, the constant perception of competition rather than privilege, the need to insulate one's psyche from the possibility of failure, produces a tendency toward this kind of threatened egotism. Fractal inequality means that status is never fixed, no success ever final. It means always looking at the next rung up on the social ladder, a posture that makes it very difficult to empathize with those on the rungs below. Twenge's long-term data show a marked increase in precisely this psychological profile.

Ralph Waldo Emerson once observed that "each man carries in his eye the exact indication of his rank in the immense scale of men, and we are always learning to read it." In twenty-first-century America, this basic human instinct has been cultivated into a guiding ethos. Our culture is overrun with lists and rankings: the most beautiful people, the most influential politicians, the top 500 wealthiest moguls. Anyone who's ever worked as an editor at a magazine website knows that such stories are what is called in the business "click bait": readers cannot get enough of them. The obsession with rank reflects deep cultural anxiety over and simultaneous addiction to the ceaseless war for top status, the never-ending treadmill of competition and achievement that we've set as our ideal. What was once sublimated is now very public. We have jettisoned any vestigial affection for civic equality in exchange for the false promise of a hierarchy of merit.

CULT OF SMARTNESS

Of all the status obsessions that preoccupy our elites, none is quite so prominent as the obsession with smartness. Intelligence is the core value of the meritocracy, one which stretches back to the early years of standardized testing, when the modern-day SAT descended from early IQ tests. To call a member of the elite "brilliant" is to pay that person the highest compliment.

Intelligence is a vitally necessary characteristic for those with powerful positions. But it isn't just a celebration of smartness that characterizes the culture of meritocracy. It's something more pernicious: a Cult of Smartness in which intelligence is the chief virtue, along with a conviction that smartness is rankable and that the hierarchy of intelligence, like the hierarchy of wealth, never plateaus. In a society as stratified as our own, this is a seductively natural conclusion to reach. Since there are people who make $500,000, $5 million, and $5 billion all within the elite, perhaps there are leaps equal to such orders of magnitude in cognitive ability as well.

Having spent a lot of time around lawyers, I can say this belief is particularly widespread among them. When Barack Obama faced an opening on the Supreme Court in the spring of 2009, *The New Republic*'s legal correspondent Jeffrey Rosen began writing a series of articles evaluating the prospective candidates rumored to be on the President's short list. His first article appeared on May 4, 2009, and offered an evaluation of appeals court judge Sonia Sotomayor with the headline THE CASE AGAINST SOTOMAYOR. Loaded with blind quotes from former clerks of judges who'd served on the Second Circuit with Sotomayor, the case amounted to a single central indictment: She wasn't smart enough. "The most consistent concern was that Sotomayor, although an able lawyer," was "not that smart and kind of a bully on the bench." It went on from there: "Her opinions, although competent, are viewed by former prosecutors as not especially clean or tight, and sometimes miss the forest for the trees."

Even Sotomayor's defenders, as quoted in the piece, seemed

to echo Rosen's point. One former clerk said, "I know the word on the street is that she's not the brainiest of people, but I didn't have that experience." Another says, "She's a fine Second Circuit judge—maybe not the smartest ever, but how often are Supreme Court nominees the smartest ever?" Keep in mind the person under discussion is someone who, from humble beginnings in the Bronx, had gained entrance to Princeton, graduated summa cum laude, and gone on to Yale Law, where she edited the *Yale Law Journal.* She had checked off every box on the to-do list of meritocratic achievement. Apparently, it wasn't enough.

It's not just Rosen and his sources who think this way. The same month Rosen published his article, famed liberal Harvard law professor Laurence Tribe penned a memo to President Barack Obama with some thoughts about how the President should think about filling the Supreme Court vacancy created by Justice David Souter's retirement. At the time, three candidates were widely viewed as making up the short list: Sonia Sotomayor, Elena Kagan, and Seventh Circuit Appeals Court judge Diane Wood. The thrust of Tribe's memo was to warn Obama off nominating Sotomayor (advice he ultimately ignored). "Bluntly put," Tribe wrote to the President, "she's not as smart as she seems to think she is." Tribe's preferred candidate was Kagan. "I can't think of anyone nearly as strong as Elena Kagan, whose combination of intellectual brilliance and political skill would make her a 10-strike, if you'll forgive my reference to bowling." The final candidate, Diane Wood, Tribe placed in between Kagan and Sotomayor on the brains spectrum. Wood, he wrote, was "more powerful intellectually than Sonia Sotomayor or any of the others mentioned as plausible prospects at the moment with the sole exception of Kagan, who is even smarter."

What, exactly does it mean to say that Elena Kagan is "even smarter" than Diane Wood, who is, in turn, "more powerful intellectually" than Sotoymayor? It's a judgment that sounds definitive. But underlying Tribe and Rosen's analyses are some dubious assumptions about how intelligence works. The first is that intelligence is a single ordinal quality, like height. In the same way that Yao Ming is taller than Michael Jordan, who is taller than Danny DeVito, Elena Kagan is smarter than Diane Wood, who is smarter than Sonia Sotomayor. And yet this very notion of a single, clear, and discernible ranking of intelligence has been undermined by decades of research in the field of cognitive psychology. Additionally, Rosen and Tribe assume not only that this ordinal ranking exists, but that it is readily apparent to anyone who reads a few writing samples or talks to a few ex-colleagues.

These two assumptions about the evaluation and ranking of smartness aren't limited to highly credentialed lawyers. They're widely and deeply held by the superstar class produced by meritocratic institutions. In *Liquidated,* Karen Ho shows how the obsession with smartness produces "a meritocratic feedback loop," in which bankers' growing influence itself becomes further evidence that they are, in fact, "the smartest."

According to one Morgan Stanley analyst Ho interviewed, those being recruited by the firm "are typically told they will be working with 'the brightest people in the world. These are the greatest minds of the century.'" Robert Hopkins, a vice president of mergers and acquisitions at Lehman Brothers, tells her of those who inhabit Wall Street: "We are talking about the smartest people in the world. We are! They are the smartest people in the world."

And just as one would suspect, given the fractal inequality at the top, hovering above those who work at big Wall Street firms is an entire world of hedge fund hot shots, who see themselves as far smarter than the grunts on Wall Street. "There's 100 percent no question that most people on Wall Street, even if they have nice credentials, are generally developmentally disabled," a hedge fund analyst I'll call Eli told me, only somewhat jokingly, one night over dinner. "By '06 and '07, the very good ones had left to form hedge funds. And maybe I'm being self-congratulatory because I work at a hedge fund, but I interact many times on a daily basis with people at banks, and they're not nearly the caliber of people who are not at banks." For Eli and his colleagues, Wall Street may have pretended to be a meritocracy, filled with the "smartest ever," but it was really just a parking lot for the overcredentialed and underequipped. "The banks in general are populated by second-class intellects," Eli said. "What's amazing is how much money they make."

Hedge funds, however, according to Eli and his colleagues, are the real deal; the innermost of inner rings. "I was surrounded my whole life by people who took intelligence very seriously," Eli told me. "I went to good schools, I worked at places surrounded by smart people. And until now I've never been at a place that prides itself on having the smartest people and where it's actually true. . . . So that's why we feel self-congratulatory."

That confidence of course projects outward, and from it emanates the authority that the financial sector as a whole enjoyed (and in certain circles still enjoys). "At the end of the day," Eli says with a laugh, "America does what Wall Street tells it to do. And whether that's because Wall Street knows best, whether Wall Street is intelligently self-dealing, or whether it has no idea and talks out of its ass, that is the culture in America."

This is the cult of smartness at its most pernicious: Listen to Wall Street. They've got the smartest minds on the planet.

While smartness is necessary for competent elites, it is far from sufficient: wisdom, judgment, empathy, and ethical rigor are all as important, even if those traits are far less valued. "Could it be at all possible," Harvard undergraduate Matthew Siegel wondered in the *Crimson* in 2003, "that the culture of success at Harvard drives people to skip right over the most important part of cognition—

getting to know themselves and what they want and need—and instead, sends them straight into the outstretched arms of J.P. Morgan's H.R. department?"

Extreme intelligence without the other qualities I mentioned above can be extremely destructive. But empathy does not impress the same way smartness does. Smartness dazzles and mesmerizes. More importantly, it intimidates. When a group of powerful people get together to make a group decision, conflict and argumentation ensue, and more often than not the decision that emerges is that which is articulated most forcefully by those parties perceived to be the "smartest."

It is under these conditions that destructive intelligence flourishes. Behind many of the Bush administration's most disastrous and destructive decisions was one man: David Addington, counsel and then chief of staff to Dick Cheney. Addington was called "Cheney's Cheney" and a "hidden power." *U.S. News and World Report* called him "the most powerful man you've never heard of." A former Bush White House lawyer told the *New Yorker*'s Jane Mayer that the administration's legal framework for the war on terror—from indefinite detention, to torture, to rejection of the 1949 Geneva Accords, to denial of habeas corpus—was "all Addington."

Addington's defining trait, as portrayed in numerous profiles and articles, is his hard-edged, ideologically focused intelligence. "The boy seemed terribly, terribly bright," Addington's high school history teacher told Mayer. "He wrote well, and he was very verbal, not at all reluctant to express his opinions. . . . He was scornful of anyone who said anything that was naïve, or less than bright. His sneers were almost palpable." A *U.S. News and World Report* profile of Addington observed that "his capacity to absorb complex information is legendary." Coworkers referred to him as "extremely smart" and "sublimely brilliant."

What emerges in these accounts is a figure who used his daz-zling recall, razor-sharp logical ability, and copious knowledge to implacably push administration policy in a rogue direction. Be-cause he knew the law so well, because he possessed such a gifted mind, he was able to make legal arguments that, executed by any-one else, would have been regarded as insane. He would edit briefs so that they always reflected a maximalist interpretation of presi-dential power, and his sheer ferocity and analytic horsepower en-abled him to steamroll anyone who raised objections in meetings. During a meeting just after 9/11, Pentagon lawyer Richard Schif-frin described Addington's posture to Mayer this way: "He'd sit, listen, and then say, 'No, that's not right.' . . . He didn't recognize the wisdom of the other lawyers. He was always right. He didn't listen. He knew the answers."

This dynamic, in which the smart, sneering, self-assured hawk steamrolls his ideological opponents, should be well familiar to anyone who watched the run-up to the Iraq War. One of the great mysteries of the last decade is how so many smart people could end up endorsing an idea as stupidly destructive as the Bush adminis-tration's war on Iraq. There are a multitude of reasons, of course, but postwar reflections by intellectuals reveal how important a role the Cult of Smartness played in getting them to go along. Many smart writers came to be convinced of the merits of war because it seemed to them that the war's proponents were "smarter" than its opponents. The opponents were the silly knee-jerk lefties and kooks, the daffy Code Pink, whereas its supporters were the bril-liant Christopher Hitchens, the incomparable Andrew Sullivan, and perhaps most influential, Kenneth Pollack.

Pollack was a former CIA analyst and NSC official under Clinton, whose book *The Threatening Storm* laid out an argument for U.S. military confrontation with Saddam Hussein's regime. The book became the bible of the so-called liberal hawks, prominent center-left writers and intellectuals who supported the Bush administration's push for war.

In a review of *The Threatening Storm*, *Talking Points Memo*'s Josh Marshall wrote: "Pollack manages to eschew the cant, stupidity, and obfuscation which are the common currency of much of the current public debate over Iraq policy and has produced one of the key books—probably the key book—for anyone trying to grapple with the Iraq question." Marshall tips his hand: there were too many dumb arguments, he says, about the war from both the Bush administration and knee-jerk lefty opponents. Pollack provided the smart version of the pro-war argument, the one that ultimately made converts of the influential opinion leaders like Marshall, the *New Yorker*'s David Remnick, and *Slate*'s Jacob Weisberg.

New York Times columnist and future editor Bill Keller said Pollack's "argument for invading Iraq is surely the most influential book of this season," and noted that it "has provided intellectual cover for every liberal who finds himself inclining toward war but uneasy about Mr. Bush." Blogger and author Matthew Yglesias cited Pollack as well in a blog post about why, as a senior at Harvard, he supported the war, before admitting a deeper psychological motivation:

> I was 21 years old and kind of a jerk. Being for the war was a way to simultaneously be a free-thinking dissident in the context of a college campus and also be on the side of the country's power elite. . . . The point is that this wasn't really a series of erroneous judgments about Iraq, it was a series of erroneous judgments about how to think about the world and who deserves to be taken seriously and under which circumstances.

This is a potent articulation of the dark emotional roots of the Cult of Smartness: the desire to differentiate and dominate that the meritocracy encourages. Ironically, in seeking to stand apart, the Cult of Smartness can kill independent thought by subtly training people to defer to others whom one should "take seriously." This has a particular allure if the views of the serious, smart folks are contrary to those of the public at large or one's particular peer group. The contrarian position then takes on the aura of prophecy and works as a kind of social signaling; it displays just how smart the possessor of the contrary view is. It shows that person is on the right side of the line that marks off the inner ring.

And this is the same message Wall Street continues to have for America at large. As one investment bank VP told Ho: "If you [the average investor or the average corporation] don't know anything, why wouldn't you invest with the smartest people in the world? They must know what they are doing." "Everyone on Wall Street thinks that everyone else is smart," says Eli. "'If so-and-so made that decision, then he must know what he's doing.' So there are very smart people on Wall Street who saw through the mess, but there are also a lot of people, whether they're smart or not, who've been trained by the banks to just follow the leader."

Fractal inequality doesn't just produce errors of judgment like those we saw during the run-up to Iraq, it also creates a system of incentives that produces an insidious form of corruption. This kind of corruption isn't the obvious quid pro quo kind of the Gilded Age or the old Chicago machine—there are precious few cases in which politicians are taking satchels of cash in exchange for votes. What's far more common is what the Harvard law professor Lawrence Lessig calls "institutional corruption," in which, in Lessig's words, an institution develops an "improper dependency," one that "conflicts with the dependence intended."

This kind of corruption is everywhere you look. Consider a doctor who receives gifts and honoraria from a prescription drug company. The doctor insists plausibly that this has no effect on his medical decisions, which remain independent and guided by his training, instincts, and the best available data. And he is not lying or being disingenuous when he says this: he absolutely believes it to be the case. But we know from a series of studies of prescribing behavior that there is a strong correlation between gifts from pharmaceutical companies and doctors' willingness to prescribe their drugs. And this knowledge bothers us because we recognize that it represents an improper dependence: we want the doctor to be dependent on the best available medical evidence and the needs of her patient, not on booty from Big Pharma.

This basic dynamic infects some of our most important institutions. Key to facilitating both the monumental housing bubble and its collapse was ratings agencies' habit of giving even extremely leveraged, toxic securities a triple-A rating. The institutional purpose of the ratings agencies (and their market purpose as well) is to add value to investors by using their expertise to make judgments about the creditworthiness of securities. Originally, the ratings agencies made their money from investors who paid subscription fees in exchange for access to their ratings. But over time the largest agencies shifted to a model in which the banks and financial entities issuing the securities would pay the agencies for a rating. Obviously these new clients wanted the highest rating possible, and often would bring pressure to bear on the agencies to make sure they secured the needed triple A. And so the ratings agencies developed an improper dependence on their clients, one that pulled them away from fulfilling their original institutional purpose of serving investors. They became corrupt, and the result was trillions of dollars in supposedly triple-A securities that became worthless once the housing bubble burst.

Lawrence Lessig argues that we see a similar and singularly destructive example of this dynamic at work in the United States Congress. Nearly every single legislator will insist, vigorously and plausibly, that he or she has never changed a vote in exchange for a donation. But rather than a complete dependence on the voters, Congress also now has a dependence on the funders. And it is obvious that this powerful dependence on check-writers is, from the perspective of the Constitution, an improper one. It pulls Congress away from its true purpose, which is to turn the conflicting, complicated wishes of the people into laws with which they can govern themselves.

There are certain institutional functions and professional roles—like, say, member of Congress—that we want to see insulated from crass commercial concerns. And yet during our era of fractal inequality, the noncommercial sphere has shrunk, leaving noncommercial institutions increasingly dependent on commercial interests. What we're left with is a blurring of the boundaries between what Jane Jacobs described as the Guardian Syndrome on the one hand and the Commercial Syndrome on the other. According to Jacobs, the Guardian Syndrome ("shun trading," "be loyal," "treasure honor") regulates the behavior of the soldier, the politician, and the policeman among others, while the Commercial Syndrome ("compete," "respect contracts," "promote comfort and convenience") guides the behavior of the banker, the baker, and the businessman. This basic division captures something essential about our expectations of many "authority" figures, particularly elite authority figures in positions of great social and financial esteem. We want them to be Guardians first; we don't think they should be for sale.

Yet our current system of fractal inequality creates the conditions in which everything is inexorably drawn into the realm of commerce. The absolute size of the payouts available to the suc-

cessful politician, doctor, or regulator is so large that those filling these jobs are drawn into the orbit of improper dependencies.
Nearly everyone has a price, and the higher the potential payout,
the more likely that price will find you. The greater the gap between compensation among those who adhere to the Guardian
code and those whose adhere to the Commercial one, the more the
latter will come to corrupt the former.

In a paper about the financial crisis, Rob Johnson and Thomas
Ferguson tracked the salary trends for those working in finance
and those federal guardians in the agencies tasked with regulat-
ing them and found a striking divergence between the two. The
authors note:

> At some point after incomes in the financial sector took off,
> lifetime earnings of the regulated far outstripped what any
> regulator could ever hope to earn. Rising economic inequal-
> ity was translating into a crippling institutional weakness in
> regulatory structure. Not surprisingly, as one former mem-
> ber of a U.S. regulatory agency expressed it to us, regulatory
> agencies turned into barely disguised employment agencies,
> as staff increasingly focused on making themselves attrac-
> tive hires to the firms they were supposed to be regulating.

The same problem bedevils Capitol Hill, where salaries for
lobbyists have exploded while those for staffers have not, and numerous areas of academic inquiry such as biotech and economics,
where knowledge can be very lucrative. In his film *Inside Job,* Charles
Ferguson documents the insidious ways in which consulting fees
and moonlighting gigs with financial companies created systematic conflicts of interest for some of the nation's most prominent
economists. Ferguson's film parades through some of the most ad-
mired names in the field, from Larry Summers to Martin Feld-

stein to Frederic Mishkin, who all had lucrative sidelines working for business interests with stakes in their academic work. Mishkin even took $124,000 from the Iceland Chamber of Commerce to write a paper endorsing the country's economic model, just a few years before it collapsed.

What we are left with is confusion that arises from an ambiguity of roles: Are our regulators attempting to rein in the excesses of those they regulate or are they auditioning for a lucrative future job? Are economists who publish papers praising financial deregulation giving us an honest assessment of the facts and trends or courting extremely lucrative consulting fees from banks?

In her book about the new global elite, Janine Wedel recalls visiting the newly liberated Eastern Europe after the fall of the Berlin Wall and finding the elites she met there, those at the center of building the new capitalist societies, toting an array of different business cards that represented their various roles: one for their job as a member of parliament, another for the start-up business they were running (which was making its money off government contracts), and yet another for the NGO on the board of which they sat. Wedel writes that those "who adapted to the new environment with the most agility and creativity, who tried out novel ways of operating and got away with them, and sometimes were the most ethically challenged, were most rewarded with influence."

This has an eerie resonance with our predicament. We can never be sure just which other business cards are in the pocket of pundit, politician, or professor. We can't be sure, in short, just who our elites are working for.

But we suspect it is not us.

Chapter 6

OUT OF TOUCH

An imbalance between rich and poor is the oldest and most fatal
ailment of all republics.

—PLUTARCH

NOTHING IS MORE FATAL TO A POLITICIAN THAN
the perception that he or she is "out of touch." In 1992,
at the National Grocers Association conference in Orlando, reporters watched President George H. W. Bush marvel at
a convention exhibit that showed an ordinary supermarket scanner. The front-page *New York Times* article, based on a pool report,
painted the picture of an aristocrat expressing wonderment at the
most mundane aspects of daily life among the masses. "Today . . .
[Bush] emerged from 11 years in Washington's choicest executive
mansions to confront the modern supermarket," observed *Times*
reporter Andrew Rosenthal:

> He grabbed a quart of milk, a light bulb and a bag of candy
> and ran them over an electronic scanner. The look of won-
> der flickered across his face again as he saw the item and
> price registered on the cash register screen.
>   "This is for checking out?" asked Mr. Bush. "I just took
> a tour through the exhibits here," he told grocers later.
> "Amazed by some of the technology."

Upon further investigation, it appeared the story wasn't quite fair: Bush was being shown a cutting-edge, new model of supermarket scanner, and other witnesses to the encounter say he displayed nothing more than the dutiful polite acknowledgment that politicians practice in their sleep. Nonetheless, the image stuck. One Bush commentator wrote that "the story resonated because there was a perception that Bush had no idea how 'Joe Six-Pack' lived." In the months leading up to the 1992 presidential election, only 18 percent of respondents in a CBS News/New York Times poll said that Bush "cares 'a great deal' about the needs and problems" of people like themselves. He would, of course, go on to lose to Bill Clinton that fall.

Twelve years later, Republicans gleefully circulated a picture of John Kerry windsurfing off Martha's Vineyard during a break from the 2004 presidential campaign. The Bush campaign even cut a campaign ad with the photo, asking "Which way would Kerry lead on Iraq?" while flipping the windsurfing image back and forth. Despite the near identical class profiles of Kerry and his opponent (they were both products of prep schools and Skull and Bones members at Yale), conservative commentators gleefully pounced on the photo to demonstrate just how out of touch the effete, snobbish Kerry was compared to the down-to-earth man of the people Dubya. It was a recurring theme. Married to Teresa Heinz Kerry, whose net worth was over $1 billion, Kerry wasn't too difficult to paint as a caricature of ruling class affectation. The *New York Times* even ran a front-page story about a personal aide of Kerry named Marvin Nicholson Jr., whom the headline described as "Part Butler Part Buddy." Kerry—the guy with the butler!—lost to Bush 51 percent to 48 percent.

In the 2008 presidential campaign, a reporter asked John McCain how many homes he owned. McCain's wife Cindy is the heiress to a sizable fortune from her beer distributor father, and the couple's combined net worth is somewhere in the ballpark of $140 million. But this didn't take center stage until McCain drew a blank in response to the question: "I think—I'll have my staff get to you," he told *Politico.* "It's condominiums where—I'll have them get to you." Again, opponents pounced. The DNC sent out an itemized list of McCain's seven homes, noting the value of each. The Obama campaign connected McCain's flub to their argument about his general "out-of-touchness" on economic matters. "The fact that John McCain can't keep track of how many houses he owns is a telling moment that helps explain why he thinks 'the fundamentals of our economy are strong,'" one Obama spokesman said.

Like George H. W. Bush and John Kerry before him, John McCain lost the election, with exit polls showing that a majority of voters thought that Barack Obama, the black man with the foreign name, was more likely to "care about people like me." Among those who ranked "cares about people like me" as their most important presidential quality, Obama beat McCain 73–19.

At one level, this makes sense: Voters are more likely to vote for politicians they feel they can relate to. But on another level it's preposterous: every elected official, certainly at the national level, cannot but be wildly out of touch. Being a professional politician is a bizarre, consuming, and alienating life, deeply abnormal in nearly all of its particulars. You spend hours a day begging wealthy people for money; you are constantly traveling, constantly in the presence of staff. Almost every interaction you have is with someone who wants something from you, and even during the most mundane moments, a trip to an ice cream shop with your son, say, you must be "on." In the same way an NBA star lives a life that is profoundly removed from the reality of the vast majority of Americans, so, too, does any politician successful enough to make a credible run for president of the United States.

If this is such an obvious truth, why does the charge of being out of touch prove so fatal? I think it's precisely because we know, somewhere deep down, that our political leaders are out of touch that we feel a compensatory desire to construct a mythology in which this is not the case. Because the performance of "in-touchness" requires an effortful suspension of disbelief on the part of all involved—politicians, their staffs, the media, and the voters— when politicians fail to faithfully hold up their end of the bargain by maintaining the myth, the media and the voters punish them harshly.

THE ORIGINAL PROBLEM
OF SOCIAL DISTANCE

Our obsession with "out-of-touchness" reaches back centuries; you could even say the nation was founded out of frustration with it. The Declaration of Independence fulminates against not just King George's tyranny, but his maddening inattentiveness and disengagement: "He has forbidden his Governors to pass Laws of immediate and pressing importance," the revolutionaries charge, "unless suspended in their operation till his Assent should be obtained; and when so suspended, he has utterly neglected to attend to them."

The fundamental problem America's revolutionary generation confronted was distance. England was ruled by a king who lived an ocean away, in a land distant and different from the colonies in too many ways to count. Letters took several weeks back and forth, which meant it was technologically difficult if not impossible for the Crown to govern the colonies in a responsive manner. Local colonial administrators had the best sense of the mood of the colonies, of which policies would be met with anger and disfavor, but their authority was, of course, subject to the royal administration across the ocean. In *Common Sense,* Thomas Paine took this stark geographic fact as an indicator of divine preference: "Even the distance at which the Almighty hath placed England and America," he wrote, "is a strong and natural proof, that the authority of the one, over the other, was never the design of Heaven." The king was not only physically distant, but socially distant as well—distant even from the affluent gentry in the colonies, who comprised the revolutionary class.

Eventually the social distance between those who ruled the colonies and those who inhabited them proved untenable. Because the effects of ruling fiats were not felt by those who promulgated them, the gulf between ruler and ruled manifested itself to the colonies' revolutionaries as a crisis of representation: hence the phrase "No taxation without representation." That phrase captures the sense that the distance of the Crown had produced a fundamentally one-sided social contract, a vector of oppression rather than a closed loop of feedback. What was lacking was basic proximity between governors and governed.

In reflecting on a model form of governance in *Common Sense,* Thomas Paine stresses the importance of the proximity of politicians, and their habitual and continued "mixing" with those who elect them:

That the ELECTED might never form to themselves an interest separate from the ELECTORS, prudence will point out the propriety of having elections often; because as the ELECTED might by that means return and mix again with the general body of the ELECTORS in a few months, their fidelity to the public will be secured.... On this ... depends the STRENGTH OF GOVERNMENT, AND THE HAPPINESS OF THE GOVERNED.

In considering ideal proportions of representation in the republic, colonial farmer John Dickinson of Pennsylvania echoed the same concerns: "A small representation can never be well informed as to the circumstances of the people," he wrote, "the members of it must be too far removed from the people, in general, to sympathize with them, and too few to communicate with them." If the proportion between constituents and representatives is too vast, Dickinson argued in his private correspondences with contemporaries, then the politician "can only mix, and be acquainted with a few respectable characters among his constituents," which would lead to "a very great distance between the representatives and the people in general represented."

For self-government to function well, in other words, the people near the top of the system need to be embedded in the system itself. They should be connected or proximate to the results of their decisions; otherwise, it will be impossible for them to make course corrections, to respond dynamically to the preferences and interests of those they represent.

What's needed, in other words, is feedback. In order to produce a reliable system in everything from a fighter jet to a nuclear reaction, a controlled system must produce feedback—a constant stream of information about its own performance that operators and controllers can see and use to adjust if necessary. Feedback is how governors govern a system and how they are able to maintain its equilibrium. A thermostat is a type of governor, and feedback is transmitted through the metal coil that shrinks or expands depending on the temperature.

When a computer programmer is working on a long and complicated program, she will often insert little flags and error messages into portions of the code as ways of knowing just where something goes wrong inside the black box of the software: if a certain message then appears while the program is running—"Hey:

that section you just coded isn't working, doofus!"—she knows exactly what portion of the code has produced it. Successful companies create and manage extensive and costly programs to elicit feedback from their customers prior to investing in and launching a new product. After launch, businesses have clear and direct feedback in the form of sales. In fact, a well-functioning price system functions precisely because of the feedback that market prices give to market participants.

In the absence of reliable feedback, a system will veer dramatically off course, and there is a corollary in the sphere of human governance. A wide distance between the governors and the governed will produce a state that is predatory toward its own citizens, indifferent to their desires, and subject to the inbred whims and compulsions of its ruling class. It will produce crisis.

Countering this, in some ways, is the original genius of self-governance. Democracy can be viewed as a human right, a system of human coordination that pays proper deference to the dignity of individuals, but it is also a system of government that solves the feedback problem that bedeviled the colonial-era English Crown.

In non-democratic settings, this central problem of the absence of feedback occupies much of the state's energies. When I spent two weeks in China in 2009, I was struck by how obsessed Chinese officials are with public opinion: they closely monitor online message boards, not just to stifle dissent but also to keep attuned to developing grievances. They have begun to create myriad channels for citizens to lodge their complaints, without resorting to questioning the fundamental legitimacy of the ruling clique. It is an article of faith among the Chinese ruling class that they can only manage their monopoly on power if they don't grow excessively "out of touch."

In Afghanistan and Iraq, American commanders have wrestled with the intractable problem of what amounts to imperial administration: they must rule over a population without inspiring precisely the kind of frustration and rage that led our own founders to take up arms in revolt. Through a long, bloody decade they have developed an entire organizational strategy—counterinsurgency— that trains soldiers to be solicitous and attentive to grievances from the local population.

The founders, who were obsessed with accountability, put in place mechanisms to mitigate against "out-of-touchness." Enshrining a right to petition the government is an extremely powerful means of ensuring a constant stream of feedback and information to the system's governors about the effects of their decisions. More recently, in the era of modern polling and electronic communication, elected officials have a nearly inexhaustible supply of data on the preferences, beliefs, and prejudices of their constituents at any given moment in time.

In a democracy, elections are the ultimate feedback mechanism, which is why it's not surprising to find that some of the worst abuses happen in policy aimed toward those populations— undocumented immigrants, prisoners—who don't have access to the ballot. And yet at the moment the marginalized and mainstream alike, immigrants and Tea Party activists, college professors and inner-city adolescents, all feel alienated from the system, all somehow feel that representation has been successfully monopolized by some small set of self-dealing elites: the special interests, the lobbyists, the big money. That the feedback mechanisms are no longer working.

To talk to members of MoveOn or Occupy Wall Street or the Tea Party is to see a system that has radicalized those who under normal circumstances should feel most represented. The activist ranks on both left and right are largely drawn from demographic groups whose concerns are the most reflected in our national political culture. And yet their chief complaint echoes that of the colonists: that those in power are irredeemably distant. The problem we now face is that there is a very real sense in which the winners of twenty-first-century America live on a different continent than everyone else. And as they recede away from the rest of the country, we are faced with a crisis of representation.

Societies can exhibit two kinds of social distance: horizontal and vertical.

Horizontal social distance occurs between members of a society of roughly equivalent station. We might imagine a country that contains two different religious sects: they have roughly comparable levels of education and income, but they have different Sabbath days, worship at different temples, live in different neighborhoods, and dominate different professions. They may live in the same city, but they live, in a very real sense, in different worlds.

We know well the problems that increasing and extreme social distance pose for a pluralistic democracy: In the extreme case of a different language, such as in Quebec, or a different religion, such as in Northern Ireland, the result is often an attack on the very foundation of the unified state and a call for separatism and national self-determination.

A far less extreme version of this kind of social distance is familiar to us here in the United States. I lived for six years in Chicago, one of the best cities in the world, but one whose most fatal flaw is its persistent and extreme racial residential segregation. If you stood on an el platform in the Loop at the end of the workday, you would see that nearly everyone on the northbound side of the platform was white or Latino, while the southbound platform's commuters were almost exclusively black. Obviously there is a powerful vertical dimension to racial segregation in Chicago or anywhere else in the United States, but what's striking about Chicago is how geographically and socially separate even upper-middle-class black Chicago and upper-middle-class white Chicago are from each other. According to the most recent census data, Chicago has the fourth highest level of black-white segregation in the entire nation.

Segregation of this kind presents all kinds of problems for social cohesion, even when people are segregated along lines that are less loaded than race. In his book *The Big Sort,* Bill Bishop presents a persuasive case that Americans have begun to geographically segregate themselves according to political ideology and worldview. In 1976, the year Jimmy Carter won the presidency, 26 percent of Americans lived in what Bishop calls "landslide counties," counties where a single political party won or lost by at least twenty points. By the 2004 election that number had almost doubled. Bishop contends that this kind of clustering and the social distance it creates are among the driving forces behind the increasing polarization of American politics, but it's not the kind of social distance I'm occupied with.

Vertical social distance—whose reach and effects are far greater than horizontal distance—refers to the gap between decision-makers and the people those decisions affect. Its growth is what presents the most acute existential threat to our project of self-governance. It is the experience of extreme vertical social distance, of feeling alienated from a shadowy and unresponsive set of incumbent elites, that constitutes the single shared grievance across lines of party and ideology.

Some level of vertical social distance is unavoidable in a representative democracy such as ours. The lowest level of vertical social distance is exhibited in kibbutzes, communes, or the General Assembly of the Occupy Wall Street movement, where decisions are reached collectively and the work and life of the community are more or less evenly shared. Such communities are often fraught in their own ways (a lot of conflict, intrigue, jockeying, etc.) and difficult to scale. Low levels of vertical social distance might also be found in a small town, with a volunteer mayor and a few prominent local businessmen and lawyers tending to make the most important local decisions. The richest man in the town lives in close proximity to his fellow townspeople, attends the same church, sends his children to the same schools, eats at the same diner, etc. The same goes for the mayor, whose house sits among the homes of the people who elect him.

This is not to romanticize small-town life or small-town politics, but simply to sketch one extreme. At the other extreme is an empire with a distant potentate ruling over a foreign land. At a more micro level, we might think of the ways a CEO, boss, or manager chooses to embed himself in an organization. Mayor Michael Bloomberg famously imposed an open-air plan both at his eponymous company and in city hall, ridding managers of their corner offices and spatial sequestration from their employees. This is one means of shrinking vertical social distance within an organization. Lehman Brothers CEO Dick Fuld, on the other hand, had a separate elevator that was commandeered just for him every time he arrived at work, so that he would not have to mix with employees on his way into the office.

As a general principle the more vertical distance there is in an institution, the greater the threat that its leaders will grow out of touch and lose the ability to govern the institution for the maximal benefit of all. As an illustration, imagine two office buildings operating side by side in Chicago's Loop. It is the middle of a brutally cold January day, when the heat in both buildings, through a sheer freak coincidence, goes out. In one building, the manager has an on-site office, so he finds out the heat is broken when he, himself, reaches for the thermostat only to find that it no longer works. The other building is managed remotely from a suburban office park where the heat continues to function. If you had to bet on who would restore heat the soonest, you'd likely choose those who were experiencing the cold themselves.

The basic intuition here is that the closer those in charge are to the consequences of their actions, the more responsive they'll be, and the better decisions they will make. It's not ironclad, of course, but all things being equal one would rather have one's mayor live in the city he administers, rather than halfway around the globe. It's the logic upon which our constitutional protection to be tried by a "jury of one's peers" is grounded. It's the same notion behind our sometimes messy system of federalism, which allows for decisions to be made at the level closest to those who are affected.

In practice, the many layers of representation mean that decision-makers can be quite remote from the citizenry, something the White House of Barack Obama seems particularly attuned to. Every weeknight, before he goes to bed, the President reads ten letters from ordinary citizens carefully screened by his correspondence outfit. They often feature people in distress, family members out of work, in the midst of foreclosure or losing their health insurance. The President's advisers say Obama views it as one small way to make sure that he does not get too out of touch. "They help him focus on the real problems people are facing," the President's adviser David Axelrod said. "He really absorbs these letters, and often shares them with us. . . . He did it because his greatest concern is getting isolated in the White House, away from the experiences of the American people. . . . The letters impact him greatly."

There is ample psychological evidence to suggest the President is right to worry about the ability of those in power to empathize with those over whom they exercise that power. In recent years a group of psychologists have begun looking systematically at the psychological effects of power and finding robust evidence to back up Lord Acton's dictum that "power tends to corrupt, and absolute power corrupts absolutely." It turns out that the experience of being powerful, even if that experience is fleetingly induced in a lab, has quite profound effects on the psyche. And many of the pathologies of power uncovered in recent experimental psychology track, with eerie precision, some of the signature excesses of our era.

Experimental psychologists use the technique of "priming" to induce the feeling of high or low power in experimental settings. Subjects are placed in positions that subconsciously signal status and power—one at a large desk and one forced to stand, or a role-playing situation in which one party tells the other what to do, or asked to do a word puzzle in which scrambled words are associated with high or low power.

Once primed, psychologists can then observe how "high power" and "low power" subjects respond to a variety of tasks. The results of the literature are mind-blowing. Psychologists find that those in high-power situations are more abstract in their thinking and pay less attention to details; they are more inclined to stereotype and to form snap judgments. They display a larger appetite for risk and are more inclined to be optimistic and think that things will work out. They are also more inclined to take decisive action when faced with stimuli or uncertainty. Perhaps least surprising of all, the research finds that those in high-power situations are more self-justifying.

But the most meaningful finding is that power narrows the vision of the powerful. According to the literature, those in power pay less attention to the characteristics, views of, and details about the low-power people they encounter, and are less empathetic overall. In one study, psychologists separated subjects into groups primed for either low power or high power, and then instructed subjects to draw the letter "E" on their foreheads with a black Magic Marker, as quickly as possible. The high-power group were far more likely to draw an "E" as if they were reading it themselves (meaning it would be backward to anyone else), while the low-power subjects were more likely to adopt the viewer's viewpoint and draw the "E" backward so that it would be legible to others. In other words, those primed for high power automatically projected their own view outward, while those primed for low power automatically adopted the viewpoint of others.

Other experiments yield similar results. In the article "Social Class, Contextualism, and Empathic Accuracy," psychologists report on a test in which they devised a set of tasks to measure empathic ability and found that "lower-class individuals (compared with upper-class individuals) received higher scores on a test of empathic accuracy . . . judged the emotions of an interaction partner more accurately" and even "made more accurate inferences about emotion from static images of muscle movements in the eyes." There's a logical reason for this higher empathic acuity among those of lower social status: Their lives, fortunes, and fates are far more dependent on the whims of those with power, as well as their neighbors and community members. And as a natural result they develop a more sophisticated set of tools to deduce how others are feeling and what their motivations might be.

Those in positions of power and high status, on the other hand, are relatively less dependent on others, and so those skills never develop, or as these people attain more and more power and status, the skills atrophy. Which means that those members of the elite who occupy the high offices of our pillar institutions and organizations are already psychologically disposed to close themselves off to the perspectives of others. If those of lower status are going to be represented in the decisions made by those of higher status, it's not going to just happen naturally. There have to be some mechanisms in place that make it happen.

And if there is one throughline uniting the disparate scandals and catastrophes of the fail decade it is the devastating effect of excessive social distance. Time and again, in radically different contexts, we saw those in charge be so blind to the interests of those outside their small circle that they pursued a course of action that would ultimately bring ruin and disgrace.

THE CHURCH

The most vexing and incomprehensible aspect of the Catholic Church abuse scandal isn't the fact that there were priests who were pedophiles: any sufficiently large pool of men will contain a certain number of perverts and predators. Nor was it necessarily that the Church attempted to cover up the crimes committed by its representatives: an ancient and deep-pocketed institution will act ruthlessly to preserve its reputation and legal sovereignty at all costs.

But what is nearly impossible to understand is why Church authorities kept putting priests they knew to be child abusers in positions where they could prey on more children. Why not just exile the pedophiles somewhere away from children permanently? Or quietly kick them out of the priesthood and disown the scandal? "Not only did they cover up sexual abuse," says SNAP founder Barbara Blaine, "but they transferred the predators. It wasn't just allowing it to go on: they fostered the crime so that the predators could have access to more kids."

The most comprehensive study of priest abuse found that 3.5 percent of priests accused of sexual abuse had allegedly molested more than ten victims. This tiny group of repeat offenders make up a staggering 26 percent of the allegations against Catholic priests. What this means is that hundreds, possibly thousands of children could have been saved from abuse if the most incorrigible serial offenders had simply been exiled to posts in which children were not present. Why didn't the cardinals and bishops take this obvious step?

The short answer is social distance. What you find time and time again in church documents is that when a bishop, cardinal, or fellow priest was confronted with an abused child and abuser priest, he extended unfathomable compassion toward his fellow man of the cloth, generating a laundry list of excuses or exculpatory details, while treating the victim with stony officiousness.

Here, to pick just one instance, is the letter Cardinal Law wrote to serial child rapist John Geoghan upon his retirement from the priesthood.

> Yours has been an effective life of ministry, sadly impaired by illness. On behalf of those you have served well, and in my own name, I would like to thank you. I understand yours is a painful situation. The passion we share can indeed seem unbearable and unrelenting. We are our best selves when we respond in honesty and trust. God bless you, Jack.

Law wrote that letter in 1996. At that point, Geoghan had already been shuttled through five parishes. In each one, his MO was the same. From the outset he'd go about ingratiating himself into the lives of harried single mothers with several young boys. Geoghan would act as a kind of surrogate father and use his proximity to the children to systematically abuse them. From time to time he would be caught: The boys would break down in panic and tell their mothers, or a parent or relative would actually walk in on Geoghan in the midst of some vile deed, and there would be reports up the chain of command within the church hierarchy. Several times Geoghan was sent to "treatment," but then soon allowed back into parishes where he had ready access to children. In every single instance for more than two decades, secular law enforcement was not notified. The victims were guilted into keeping quiet or, when they sued, paid off and required to sign confidentiality agreements as a condition of their settlement.

Law knew all this when he wrote that letter. Now here's the same Cardinal Law, this time writing in response to a concerned parishioner at St. Brendan's in Dorchester who raised red flags in 1984 about the number of evenings Geoghan was spending with young boys: "The matter of your concern is being investigated and appropriate pastoral decision will be made both for the priest and God's people." Notice the priest comes first in that sentence.

Even years into this scandal, that same instinct of bishops and cardinals to side with priests over victims remained intact. When the former head of the Catholic Church in Belgium, Cardinal Godfried Danneels, met with a victim of an abusive bishop named Roger Vangheluwe in April 2010, he urged the victim to keep quiet, saying, "The bishop will resign next year, so actually it would be better for you to wait." He then urged the man not to drag the bishop's "name through the mud."

The victim was incredulous: "Why do you feel sorry for him and not for me?"

When you burrow into the Church's scandal, digging past the shocking nature of the crimes themselves, down past the institutional roots of the Church's fetish for secrecy and desire to retain jurisdiction over its own, you end up hitting bedrock at this question. Why did the bishops feel sorry for the predators and not the preyed upon? Why did they side with the wolf over the lamb? If you can answer that simple question, you can understand why what happened happened.

The answer lies in the fundamental social distance between bishops and the parishioners whose children were being victimized. The mark of ordination and the vow of celibacy create a fundamental gap between the parishioner and the priest, the latter of which has, by definition, no subjective access to the protective instinct of a parent for his or her child. Bishops exist in an even more rarified world, both spiritually and materially. They are driven in chauffeured cars, their meals cooked and served to them, an entourage of staff attending to their every need. Blaine recalls how intimidated she and her fellow SNAP members were when they first were invited into a bishop's conference to share their stories. "[The bishops] were well polished and they really used it against us," she recalls. "We were angry and hurting and crying and we'd been standing out in the rain. They had their hair fixed perfect and their cuff-link shirts."

Bishops are the very archetype of a cosseted elite, remote and diffident and hermetically sealed. This remoteness was the key enabling factor: it misformed the allegiances of the bishops as loyalty first to their institution, followed by compassion for their brother priests, with very little left over for their actual flock.

Bishops may be an extreme example, but this same kind of social distance is a reliable theme in the biggest disasters of the decade. Take, for instance the case of New Orleans and the thousands of its citizens stranded in the drowning city.

EVACUATING NEW ORLEANS

Nineteen hours before Hurricane Katrina made landfall, at 11 A.M. on the morning of Sunday, August 28, 2005, New Orleans mayor Ray Nagin called a press conference. After several days of increasingly urgent warnings from him and the governor of the state for residents of the Crescent City to leave, Nagin finally issued a "mandatory evacuation." He announced that the city was "facing a storm that most of us have feared," that the "storm system most likely will topple our levee system," and that it was a "once in probably a lifetime event."

Because what followed this warning was such a disaster, it's a little known fact that the private, vehicular evacuation of the city initiated by Nagin and then governor Kathleen Blanco went fairly smoothly. Due to massive traffic jams along main highways caused by earlier hurricane evacuations, local authorities had adopted an orderly plan for highway evacuation, staggering departure times of the various surrounding counties and reversing the flow of major highways to accommodate increased outward traffic. The results were impressive: no large traffic jams and smooth, rapid evacuation of those residents with access to cars and the means and wherewithal to evacuate.

The problem was those left behind. As would be tragically revealed, hundreds of thousands of the city's residents did not evacuate. When the hurricane hit, as many as three hundred thousand people were holed up in their homes, or left to the deprivations of the overwhelmed Superdome. In the Katrina aftermath, some critics took this as a sign that those who had stayed behind, largely black and poor, deserved what they got or, at least, shouldn't have had quite the purchase on our sympathies that some had assumed. In 2007, Newt Gingrich, speaking at a large conservative conference, spoke of "the failure of citizenship in the Ninth Ward, where twenty-two thousand people were so uneducated and so unprepared, they literally couldn't get out of the way of a hurricane."

There's no question that some portion of the city's residents, hardened by a lifetime of warnings that came to nil, simply chose to ride out the storm with their belongings. But many, if not most, of those who didn't evacuate stayed behind for an obvious reason: They had no way to leave. One study found that 39 percent stayed simply because they had nowhere to go and no means to get there. "Where can you go if you don't have a car?" Catina Miller, a thirty-two-year-old grocery deli worker who lived in the Ninth Ward, asked a reporter. "Not everyone can just pick up and take off." "I've only got like $80 to my name," another woman told a public radio reporter, explaining why she stayed behind. "My job and my bank and everything like that is all in New Orleans."

Mobility is something that the majority of Americans take for granted, and that's even more the case for members of the elite. A variety of social science studies show that those with money and high levels of social capital are far more mobile in the most literal sense: they have cars, are able to pay for travel, and are more able to move to pursue job opportunities. In fact this mobility confers a very significant economic advantage as it is very often the case in large metro areas that the geographic locations of desirable housing with good school districts are far from the place where there are the best job opportunities.

Meanwhile, lack of access to a car is one of the most debilitating aspects of modern poverty, particularly for those in places where public transportation is scarce and unsteady. According to the 2000 census, 8 percent of Americans resided in a household without access to a car, but that number varies widely depending on class and location. Among the poor nationwide, 20 percent live in households that don't have access to a car, and among the poor in the city of New Orleans that number was 47 percent. What's more, the city was home to tens of thousands with disabilities, according to the 2000 U.S. census: fully 50 percent of residents over sixty-five had some kind of disability.

Further compounding the problem was that the storm hit at the very end of the month, a time when those on fixed income, and Temporary Assistance for Needy Families, were at their most cash strapped. During congressional hearings devoted to untangling what went wrong during Katrina, Representative Gene Taylor pointed this out to FEMA head Michael Brown: "In all these scenarios that I'm sure you've thought out, did FEMA bother to realize that it is the 28th of the month, a lot of people live on fixed income, be it a Social Security check or a retirement check, they've already made their necessary purchase for the month. What they couldn't envision is having to fill up their gas tank one more time, at almost 3 bucks a gallon just to get the heck out of there." Brown responded that making such arrangements was simply not FEMA's job. "It is not the role of the federal government to supply five gallons of gas for every individual to put in a car to go somewhere."

Whether or not FEMA should have been doing precisely this kind of thing, what was clear in the aftermath was that nobody did. If policy-makers truly believed people needed to be completely evacuated from the city and did not want to resort to forcible expulsion, one could imagine they might have created a system of monetary incentives, along with a fleet of buses and use of Amtrak to make sure those of very limited means and mobility were able to get out. It would have cost money, of course, but less than the cost of rescue post-hurricane.

With his announcement of a mandatory evacuation, Nagin had the power, according to the text of the New Orleans Evacuation Plan, to "direct and compel, by any necessary and reasonable force, the evacuation of all or part of the population from any stricken or threatened area within the City," noting that "special arrangements will be made to evacuate persons unable to transport themselves or who require special life saving assistance." But rather than actively facilitating the evacuation of the indigent, the carless, and the disabled, the city directed those stranded without a way out of the city to the centrally located football stadium, the Superdome. (This was done, it should be noted, in contravention of established evacuation best practices and the city's own written plan, but likely necessary given how late the mandatory evacuation order was issued and the scarcity of bus drivers by that late point.)

It soon became clear, as people streamed toward the Super-dome, that planners had vastly underestimated just how many people would end up there: eventually as many as twenty thousand people were massed in the Superdome, which had lost electricity, had a hole in the roof, and the plumbing of which was soon over-whelmed and filling the entire structure with the odor of raw sew-age. Another several thousand people massed at the Convention Center, though it's unclear whether officials ever issued a direc-tive for people to head there or it was simply another central loca-tion on high ground. At the Convention Center, conditions were even worse. All in all, as numerous social autopsies and what-went-wrong reports show, planners simply did not properly anticipate the raw number of people who, having been left behind in the city, would need to make use of the shelters of last resort.

Given that the poverty and immobility of the urban popula-tion was well known prior to the storm, the failure to plan for it cannot be chalked up to ignorance. Rather, it was a planning fail-ure enabled by social distance. The population of New Orleanians who constituted the bulk of those left behind were a subsection of the city—poor, old, and infirm—that was nearly entirely alienated from the circle of those policy-makers who crafted the evacuation. Whatever objective information was available about rates of mo-bility, carlessness, and poverty, it did not resonate with and affect elite judgment in the same way it would have had the social experi-ence of the New Orleans elite included at least some of the same maladies that afflicted those left behind.

Katrina wasn't the first time social distance helped turn natu-ral disaster into social catastrophe. In July 1995, Chicago expe-rienced a week of record heat that resulted in the deaths of more than seven hundred of the city's residents. In his landmark study of the disaster, sociologist Eric Klinenberg highlighted the ways in which the tragedy was fundamentally one born of social distance:

Those who were the most alienated, primarily poor senior citizens who lived by themselves, were invisible to both policy-makers and neighbors, so much so it cost them their lives. While Mayor Daley was telling reporters, "It's hot, but let's not blow it out of proportion," the Cook County morgue was filling up past capacity.

FIGHTING THE "LONG WAR"

If there is one constant to the last decade of American life, it is war. From moments after the attacks of 9/11, to the time of this writing, the United States has been on war footing without pause or respite. It is, in the words of former Defense Secretary Robert Gates, "the longest sustained combat in American history." We have sent hundreds of thousands of troops to Afghanistan and Iraq, and dozens of Special Forces units into Yemen, Pakistan, and likely many other countries as well. We have increased total defense expenditures by 83 percent from 2000 to 2010, and our war in Afghanistan is now longer than World War II.

In a way unseen since Vietnam, a shooting war has become the de facto norm for the country over an entire decade, and shooting war of the intensity and duration that we have undertaken for the last decade requires a fantastic amount of resources and human labor. This has taken its toll. The cost of wars in Iraq, Afghanistan, and inside Pakistan total more than a trillion dollars over the past decade, which would be enough money to pay the inflation-adjusted cost of Roosevelt's New Deal twice over—or ten times the amount of the Marshall Plan. But more brutal are the human costs: more than 6,000 Americans have been killed in action, and another 2,000 have taken their own lives while serving or after completing service. More than 47,000 troops have been wounded, and 1,400 have had a limb amputated.

Even those who have escaped injury have been pressed into levels of service unseen in generations: During the Vietnam War, servicemen were typically deployed once, for an average of six months. During the Gulf War, service members were also typically deployed only once, for an average of 153 days. Today, average deployments last thirteen months, and more than one-third of service members are deployed more than once. This has taken a huge mental and emotional toll on those Americans who've been asked to bear the burden. A 2007 study by the Brookings Institution found that 27 percent of soldiers who'd done three or more tours of duty in Iraq showed signs of post-traumatic stress disorder, while for those with just one tour it was 12 percent. A 2008 survey of 3,400 officers reported that 88 percent believed Iraq had "stretched the U.S. military dangerously thin" while nearly half thought Iraq had "broken" the military.

These costs are by no means broadly shared. First, unlike previous wars, which imposed some level of civilian sacrifice through rationing, higher taxes, or both, this last decade of war has been financed through government debt at the same time that total federal revenue from individual income taxes has declined by 30 percent in real terms. For current taxpayers who aren't in the military, the wars are, quite literally, costless. In his comprehensive study of American war funding, Bob Hormats notes that "by supporting and signing expensive spending and tax legislation, President George W. Bush broke with a tradition that had extended from Madison through Lincoln, Wilson, Franklin Roosevelt, Truman, and, eventually, Johnson and Reagan" of "wartime tax increases, cuts in civilian programs, and sometimes both" to pay for larger military engagements.

Then there's the fact that in a nation of 90 million fighting-age adults, less than 2 percent are serving in the armed forces. As a percentage of the population that's at the lowest level since before

World War II. Any reporter who's even dipped his toe in reporting on the military during this past decade of constant war is immediately struck by the degree to which a very small percentage of the American population—1.4 million active duty soldiers, with 3.1 million immediate family members—bear the burden of waging the war.

What's even more striking is the degree to which the class of people serving in the military and their families is distant from the class of meritocratic overachievers who run the country. In her 2008 paper "Who Joins the Military?: A Look at Race, Class, and Immigration Status" Amy Lutz concluded that "as family income increases, the likelihood of having ever served in the military decreases." Further, she found "low representation of the children of the very rich" within the armed forces and that "the highest income quartile was significantly less likely to have served than the lowest." She concludes that "the economic elite are very unlikely to serve in the military" and that the "all-volunteer force continues to see over-representation of the working and middle classes, with fewer incentives for upper class participation."

It's not just the economic elite, but the political elite as well. Prior to 1995, the percentage of veterans in Congress was generally greater than the population at large; since then it's been lower. "There's a disconnect," says Walter Jones (R-NC).

Jones, a conservative, Southern Republican, voted for the Iraq War before a crisis of conscience turned him into one of Congress's leading antiwar voices. Recently he has devoted himself to bridging the gulf that separates the policy-makers making the war and those fighting. Though he's never served himself, in his district alone there are three bases and sixty thousand active duty service members. The walls outside his office are plastered with photos of all those from his district who have died in Iraq and Afghanistan, and he makes frequent pilgrimages to Walter Reed and to funerals for soldiers from his district who were killed in action. He offers eulogies to the fallen nearly every time he takes to the House floor, carrying with him pictures of the children who no longer have fathers. His single-minded focus on the casualties of war feels almost as if he is attempting to will himself past the social distance that separates him, a non-veteran member of Congress, from his constituents who must pay the cost firsthand.

This remove isn't just between Congress and soldiers, but between soldiers and everyone else. As former Secretary of Defense Robert Gates put it in a 2010 speech at Duke, "Whatever their fond sentiments for men and women in uniform, for most Americans the wars remain an abstraction. A distant and unpleasant series of news items that does not affect them personally."

This phenomenon, the "civilian-military gap," is, to a certain degree, an enduring feature of American life, but the particularly acute class division we see now is of fairly recent vintage. Donald Downs, a political scientist at the University of Wisconsin, Madison, who's written about the relationship between the military and top universities through the ROTC system, says the cost of the civilian-military gap is "alienation that impoverishes citizenship on both sides." The vast and increasing social distance between the overwhelming majority of current elite decision-makers and the warrior class amounts, he says, to a "corrosive civic scandal: Elites wash their hands of this burden. It's out of sight, out of mind." People on "both the right and the left," Downs says, "can agree that this is problematic."

The Reserve Officer Training Corps was originally conceived as a means of closing the gap between civilians and the military. "There's this immense worry that [military officers trained at West Point] are basically separating themselves from American society," Downs told me, "and they're not going to reflect broad American values." But in the 1990s, in order to make most efficient use of its resources, ROTC began to withdraw from the Northeast and the coasts and focus nearly all of its energies on the South and the Midwest, the regions with the highest yield of recruits. Around the same time, the implementation of Don't Ask, Don't Tell policies led to nearly every elite university expelling ROTC off campus, although in most cases it had already been absent since the Vietnam era. The result is that for nearly the entirety of the meritocratic era, the prime institutions of elite formation have had no military presence: In 1956, the Stanford ROTC program trained one thousand cadets. But by the early 1970s, the program had been phased out, only returning to campus in 2011 after the repeal of Don't Ask, Don't Tell.

Writing in the *Chronicle of Higher Education,* political scientist Michael Nelson argues that the expulsion of ROTC from elite campuses, combined with the implementation of the all-volunteer military, has produced a dangerous estrangement of meritocratic elites from the armed services, one that has "made the nation's inclination to war and other military action greater than at any time in its already war-saturated history."

It was, after all, the implementation of the draft that so energized the antiwar movement during Vietnam, and it was the continued use of that draft and the widespread experience of the horror of the war and the stalking fear of being forced to serve in it that made the costs of the war real to an American public that then turned decisively against it. "The college campuses in 1969 were hotbeds of activism," says Nate Fick, a graduate of the University of Pennsylvania and a marine who fought in Iraq and Afghanistan. "In 2009, they were islands of apathy because no one was affected."

In January 2003, decorated Korean War veteran and opponent of the Iraq War Charlie Rangel sponsored a bill to reinstate a draft, citing more or less precisely this rationale. "There's no question in my mind," he said at the time, "that this president and this administration would ever have invaded Iraq if indeed we had a draft and members of Congress knew that their kids from their communities would be placed in harm's way."

The most sustained and comprehensive study of the effects of military service on the judgment about use of force confirms Rangel's core intuition: those who have served and seen war firsthand are more reticent about initiating wars and deploying force. "There's a long-standing debate in American foreign policy circles about how the civil-military relationships shape the use of force," says Peter Feaver, a professor of political science and public policy at Duke who coauthored *Choosing Your Battles: American Civil-Military Relations and the Use of Force.* "Some people subscribe to the militarism school: The military is like kids with a hammer and everything looks like a nail. Most of the historians, though, say that's not how it played out. Sure there are occasions where you've seen more hawkish positions taken by the military, but very often it was the military being a little more reluctant."

The decision by policy-makers to go to war, to use the bodies of their citizens as instruments in waging that violence, is the most consequential and solemn elected representatives can make. If it is the case that politicians who have not experienced war are more disposed to advocate force, then there is a very real and dangerous cost to the social distance we now have between our civilian elite and our soldiers. And this is precisely what Feaver and his coauthor found. They looked at the voting records of politicians who were veterans, going all the way back to 1816. They found that those with military experience were less likely to favor force than their non-veteran peers. "If you aggregate across the cases," says Feaver, "you get a pattern that looks like what would happen if you multiplied the famous interaction between Albright and Colin Powell in the Clinton years." That interaction, as reported in both Madeleine Albright's and Colin Powell's memoirs, was a heated debate between the two over U.S. military intervention in the Balkans, with Albright arguing for it and Powell against it. At one point Albright said to Powell, "What's the point of you saving this superb military you're always talking about if we can't use it?" Powell wrote in his memoir that when he heard this he thought he would have an "aneurysm."

Feaver and his coauthor, Christopher Gelpi, found that military elites and veterans also tended to share the belief that in cases where force is used it should be overwhelming and done with a clear exit strategy in mind, a principle laid out in the infamous Powell Doctrine. "The general view of the guys I was with," says Nate Fick, "was that the U.S. should go to war very rarely and we should win uncompromisingly when we do."

The causes of the Iraq War, and the escalation in Afghanistan, are multifaceted. They have much to do with a long legacy of American militarism, the growth of the military-industrial complex, the reaction to 9/11, and the ruthless effectiveness of war-happy ideologues in pushing the country into an ever-widening circle of violent engagements. But what has enabled these conflicts to proliferate and drag on for a decade is the social distance between those same war-happy ideologues, along with those at the highest levels of political and economic power, and those who must, at tremendous personal cost, carry out the "long war" on the ground.

THE FINANCIAL CRISIS

Michael Lewis's masterful chronicle of the crisis, *The Big Short,* contains a remarkable, though largely unremarked upon, anecdote that gives a glimpse of just how social distance facilitated the greatest financial disaster of our age. One of Lewis's protagonists, a hedge fund manager, had an epiphany in a chance conversation with a domestic worker he employed to provide child care. An immigrant from the Caribbean, she mentioned to him that she and a sister owned six townhomes in Queens. At first it seemed to make no sense; he knew exactly how much she made and it was hardly enough to afford so much property. Eventually he unraveled the mystery: It turned out that mortgage brokers had been targeting immigrants for large mortgages on purpose. Since immigrants often didn't have much of a credit history, brokers could exploit a loophole in how creditworthiness was analyzed and more or less invent a credit score for them. This, in turn, made them look like much better credit risks than they actually were and facilitated feeding the mortgages into the securitization machine that would then produce mortgage-backed securities that conferred a wellspring of money on everyone involved in the process.

Within the immigrant communities in New York, the ready availability of massive mortgages was common knowledge, but those same communities were entirely removed from the inner circles of Wall Street where these mortgages were transubstantiated into the asset-backed securities that generated trillions of dollars of revenue for it. So it took a chance encounter between a multimillionaire hedge fund manager and his baby nurse to connect the dots.

Like a disease at first confined to paupers, the plague of bad lending practices and fraud spread among working-class "subprime" borrowers, while the economic mainstream largely ignored their plight and forged ahead, either in ignorance or with unearned confidence that the disease couldn't ever reach them. Community groups working with subprime borrowers saw this story play out in grim slow motion. They recognized, probably before anyone else, that the entire mortgage industry had taken a very dark turn, and they sounded early and consistent warnings that went unheeded.

One of the most vocal of these groups was the Center for Responsible Lending (CRL) in Durham, North Carolina. CRL's parent organization is Self-Help, a nonprofit lender that runs a credit union and makes loans for small businesses and local development projects. Its relationship to its customers is the kind of face-to-face connection of the bygone *It's a Wonderful Life* era. It's this social proximity that allowed Self-Help to build a business targeted at low-income, "subprime" borrowers that did not implode when the crisis hit. "When we talk about Self-Help's success," says Mary Moore, who works as senior communications associate at CRL, "part of it is spending time with the borrowers. It's what we call 'high touch.'" The opposite, in other words, of out of touch.

It was this social proximity that first alerted Self-Help's CEO Martin Eakes to the changes in the mortgage market that would spell doom, first for borrowers, then for the entire global economy. Moore recounts the story of a Self-Help customer who came into their offices one day in 1998 absolutely distraught. The man's lender, Associates, had put him through a familiar cycle of predatory loans. First they pushed him into a refinance with a teaser rate, promising to lower his monthly payment. After a short while, when the rate exploded, they came back again with another refinance offer. Each time they refinanced, the lender took a fee, stripping out equity until there was none left. The borrower appeared in person in Self-Help's offices with a look of desperation in his eyes: he'd run out of room to refinance, had fallen behind on his payments, and was now going to lose his home. "He went to talk to Martin about it and basically broke down and said he couldn't lose that home," recalls Mary Moore. "He was a single father with a little girl and that home was the last tie to his child's mother and he wasn't going to lose it."

So Martin Eakes called up the lender, Associates, himself and asked how much the gentleman owed on his loan. "They wouldn't tell him," says Moore. "They wouldn't tell the borrower either. Basically they were determined just to let the guy fail; they had made their money on him." The experience precipitated an epiphany for Eakes, who now realized just how abusive lender practices had become.

Self-Help spun off the Center for Responsible Lending to focus on research and policy advocacy, and they became among the closest observers and critics of the burgeoning market in subprime finance, from payday lending to shady mortgages with bait-and-switch terms. As the housing bubble expanded, securitization accelerated, and underwriting standards eroded, CRL's research staff started sounding the alarms. "We published a paper in 2006," says CRL analyst Wei Lee, that concluded "for the next 5 years we will see 2.2 million foreclosures a year in the subprime market. At that time when we released the report people just laughed at us."

That report now seems clairvoyant. Between 2006 and 2010, there were, in fact, more than 10 million subprime foreclosures. Wei and his colleagues also predicted in 2006 that a shockingly high percentage of subprime loans—one out of five—would lead to foreclosure in the next two years. They ticked through the worrying trends in the industry that were leading toward a disaster: "loose underwriting," "predatory lending," "third party originators/lack of accountability," and "inadequate oversight." "From 2003 to 2006, the market was just crazy," says Wei, "and nobody cared!"

During the same time that CRL was predicting a coming catastrophe in housing, Ben Bernanke, then a Federal Reserve governor nominated to become chair, was assuring anyone who would listen that the housing market was fine. In July 2005, he said that the "fundamentals" of the housing market were "very strong." In February 2006: "We expect the housing market to cool, but not to change very sharply. . . . The weakness in housing market activity and the slower appreciation of house prices do not seem to have spilled over to any significant extent to other sectors of the economy." And he was doing this despite the fact that representatives from CRL and other similarly situated groups were actually meeting with members of the Fed to warn them of what was coming. "I don't think people realize how much information the regulators had," says CRL chief operating officer Debbie Goldstein. "They had plenty of complaints, they had plenty of research. They had standards they could have put in place. It took them a very long time to put in standards. The Fed was slow, it was really slow."

Goldstein says CRL found state governments far more responsive than the federal government to their concerns because, crucially, there was less social distance between the victims of predatory lending and their state representatives. "I think legislators had constituents who were getting bad loans and they heard about them," says Goldstein. "At the state level you had more legislators who were in the business, were Realtors or they'd been screwed by somebody. They understood much more personally what these products meant."

The Fed, however, the one entity with the most authority and power to crack down on the abuses, looked the other way, while the Office of Comptroller of the Currency set about gutting tougher state-based regulations by preempting state regulations. "It wasn't until it started happening on blocks where people didn't expect it to happen," one CRL staffer told me, "that it became a national problem."

In *Inside Job,* director Charles Ferguson confronts former Federal Reserve governor Frederic Mishkin, who served on the Fed committee charged with oversight of consumer abuses. Speaking of Robert Gnaizda of the Greenlining Institute, an ally of CRL and someone who met several times with the Fed, Ferguson says:

CHARLES FERGUSON: [Gnaizda] warned, in an extremely explicit manner, about what was going on, and he came to the Federal Reserve Board with loan documentation of the kind of loans that were frequently being made. And he was listened to politely, and nothing was done.
FREDERIC MISHKIN: Yeah. So, uh, again, I, I don't know the details, in terms of, of, uh, of, um—uh, in fact, I, I just don't—I, I—eh, eh, whatever information he provided, I'm not sure exactly, I, eh, uh—it's, it's actually, to be honest with you, I can't remember the, the, this kind of discussion. But certainly, uh, there, there were issues that were, uh, uh, coming up.

Part of the issue was that the institutional setup of the Federal Reserve is designed to produce a very narrow kind of feedback. Wary of too much concentration of geographical powers, the Federal Reserve Act created twelve different banks spread throughout the country, with the idea that they would be responsive to different local concerns. But the profiles of the local bank boards are all bankers, and they're the only people who get a vote when selecting those who will serve on the Federal Reserve Board. What this means is that the people running the single most powerful economic institution in the country are mostly chosen by bankers. And as we've learned the hard way over this past decade, bankers' information about the economy isn't necessarily the only information there is, and their interests don't necessarily align with those of the public's at large.

But imagine for a moment if the board were constituted so that it had to include consumer advocates or even bank customers themselves. Or imagine if Ben Bernanke and Frederic Mishkin lived in the neighborhoods in which foreclosures had become a widespread scourge. Now imagine if they had to walk past the foreclosure signs or counsel distraught neighbors through the trauma of being expelled from their homes. Think of the difference between the mnemonic salience of a meeting in an airless boardroom, with a bunch of anonymous do-gooders waving charts in your face, and just one conversation with a terrified and desperate single father who's about to have his home taken right out from under him.

Here's where the distinction between information presented through official channels and the subconscious experiential force of your daily observations matters: the difference between being in the freezing building and simply seeing a temperature display in your warm office fifteen miles away. It's the same difference we saw in New Orleans, the difference between looking at census data about poverty and disability and having people in your social circle carless, poor, and housebound. The difference between headlines about war in Iraq and your own kin sustaining a brain injury from an IED.

The increasing complexity of financial markets and the massive explosion in securitization created a way to link together the fates of an impossibly attenuated chain of players bound to one another inextricably but invisibly. The financial distance between a working-class grandmother in South Carolina with an adjusted rate mortgage and a Norwegian pensioner whose fund had purchased a slice of her loan was radically shrunk, while the immense social distance remained. And since there was no other institution or mechanism for mediating that distance, genuine disaster could bloom in the vast dark spaces in between.

Such is the core lesson of the financial crisis: the increasing inequality, compartmentalization, and stratification of America in the post-meritocratic age served to seduce those at the top into an extremely dangerous, even pathological, kind of complacency. The ship sprung a leak down in the lower decks, flooding the servants' quarters, and no one up top realized that it would bring down the whole thing. The cocktails continued to flow, the band continued to play, and the party rollicked on Wall Street throughout the housing bubble, even as subprime borrowers drowned, as their lives and wealth and homes were destroyed. But the water kept coming in, and it climbed deck by deck until, eventually, the music stopped and the party ended, and it looked like the entire thing might go down.

Given what a close call it was for those on that top deck, for the Jamie Dimons and the bankers and the titans of industry and all the members of the 1 percent, you would think that the single most important lesson they would take away from the near miss would be this: You ignore the fate of those on the bottom deck at your peril. An economy divided into "subprime" and "prime" is dangerously precarious; the predations tolerated in the former will, sooner or later, come to feast on those who make up the latter.

And yet, astonishingly, this lesson has gone almost entirely unheeded. We once again have a bifurcated economy, a prime economy and a subprime economy. Our governing institutions responded with nearly unprecedented swiftness and force to save, and then revive, the prime economy. Yet they are letting the subprime economy fend for itself, to suffer through a period of drought and privation as bad as anything in eighty years. "If your personal wealth is predominantly in capital markets," says Damon Linker, a lawyer at the AFL-CIO, who served on the TARP Congressional

Oversight Panel, "well then you had a hell of a scare, but you're 70 percent of the way back to where you were in 2007. If your personal wealth is predominantly in your home, you're fucked. And approximately 80 percent of people in the U.S., their only asset is in their home."

Despite anemic growth in the post-crisis years, stocks are performing at historically high levels and inflation-adjusted corporate profits are at near record highs; the stock market has regained its losses from the crashes and the Dow is back above 13,000. Unemployment for the 30 percent of the adult population with a four-year college degree is a bit above 4.5 percent, which is back to its pre-crisis levels and constitutes full employment for that portion of the society. Large corporate law firms that dramatically cut their signing bonuses for well-credentialed new associates in the wake of the crisis have reinstituted them at levels even higher than before the crisis. Bonuses on Wall Street are once again breaking records.

Meanwhile the "real economy," or "Main Street" as politicians call it, is mired in its worst extended contraction in eighty years. Middle-class professionals find credit constricted in a way that recalls the experience of marginalized inner-city communities in the days before the Community Reinvestment Act outlawed redlining. Personal bankruptcies have been climbing and are near an all-time high, and forty months after the financial crisis, the unemployment rate remains above 8 percent. Broader measures of unemployment, which include those who've given up looking for work, are above 16 percent. Millions of Americans are mired in a long-term unemployment epidemic unprecedented in American history.

Polls consistently rate the economy and jobs as voters' prime concerns. Yet the political system seems more or less completely deaf to any cries for more stimulus and direct job creation. As soon as stocks had recovered and a modicum of growth was restored, the dominant conversation in Washington among both Republicans and Democrats was about how and how much to cut the deficit. The White House spoke of its "pivot" to deficit concerns, while Wall Street, conservative think tanks, and the Republican Party all devoted themselves to sounding increasingly dire alarms about the size of the U.S. government's debt and advocating a radical deconstruction of the country's basic framework for providing social insurance.

The bet that those who run the prime economy are making is the same bet they made during the years that preceded the crash: that they can continue to profit enormously even as the broader economy fails to deliver real and steady gains for the majority of its participants. The last time around this produced a housing and credit bubble that ended in ruin for most and almost took the financial elite with it. So one might think that rebooting this same program is a wildly irrational if not genuinely psychopathological proposition.

But the real lesson of the financial crisis and the bailouts that followed is that when the subprime economy threatens to bring down the prime economy, the government will step in with overwhelming force to make sure the prime economy is saved. If that's the case, then there's simply no real reason for Wall Street and the chamber of commerce and the rest of the elite superstructures of American capitalism to worry about a repeat of the boom-bust cycle that nearly did them in. Even if the ship sinks, they know they've reserved sufficient life rafts for themselves, so why fret about the icebergs?

Democracies will always struggle to protect the rights and interests of minorities from being swallowed up by majority rule. Along the way, democratic societies will engage in brutal and, in hindsight, indefensible ignorance of the plight of those who are in its darkest corners. So it was with gay men facing the AIDS crisis in the 1980s, the infirm and carless residents of New Orleans, and subprime borrowers.

But what we confront in the post-crisis era is far more grave. No longer is ours a ruling majority that has lost sight of the plight of a hated or invisible minority. The ratio has flipped. The majority of Americans now feel deeply as if they have been relegated to minority status. We are all subprime now.

We now see ourselves ruled by a remote class. They may not wear flowing robes, or carry miters, but they are marked in their own way as separate and distinct. The distance between those who will be bailed out and those who will not is the ultimate social distance, and it has grown so vast it now strains the bonds of representation that hold the republic and its people together.

Chapter 7

REFORMATION

OVER THE COURSE OF THE TWO PLUS YEARS IT'S taken me to write this book, I've had hundreds of conversations with friends and acquaintances about its main theme. Given my own social circles, the majority of my interlocutors were themselves produced by institutions of meritocratic formation, and though mostly liberals, many of them had come to view the basic framework of the meritocracy as so obvious it was almost transparent. "OK," they would often say, "I agree things are pretty messed up. Something about our system and institutions isn't working. But if you are so down on the meritocracy, what's your solution? If not meritocracy, then what?"

At its most basic, the logic of "meritocracy" is ironclad: putting the most qualified, best equipped people into the positions of greatest responsibility and import. It would be foolhardy to toss this principle out in its entirety. You certainly wouldn't want surgeons' licenses to be handed out via lottery, or to have major cabinet members selected through reality TV–style voting. Anyone who's ever worked in an organization of any kind has seen firsthand that there are sometimes vast differences between individuals in ability, work ethic, and efficiency. An institution that pays no heed to these differences will almost certainly fare poorly.

But my central contention is that our near-religious fidelity to the meritocratic model comes with huge costs. We overestimate the advantages of meritocracy and underappreciate its costs, because we don't think hard enough about the consequences of the inequality it produces. As Americans, we take it as a given that unequal levels of achievement are natural, even desirable. Sociologist Jerome Karabel, whose work looks at elite formation, once said he didn't "think any advanced democracy is as obsessed with equality of opportunity or as relatively unconcerned with equality of condition" as the United States. This is our central problem. And my proposed solution for correcting the excesses of our extreme version of meritocracy is quite simple: make America more equal.

TWO ERAS OF EQUALITY

It's important to recognize that the history of America over the last seven decades is a story of remarkable, improbable, even transcendent progress toward equality. Since World War II, we've seen two distinct eras of equality in which a whole host of deeply embedded, overwhelmingly powerful systems of inequality were dramatically weakened, and in some cases all but destroyed.

The first era of equality, from the end of the Second World War to the early 1970s, represented a period of historically unprecedented growth, mass affluence, and middle-class expansion that has not been duplicated since. Income inequality markedly declined, even as the economy posted a nearly unmatched level of annual GDP growth. Union density rose as high as 34 percent (the highest it's ever been), while the ratio between average CEO compensation and average production worker compensation hovered around 25 (by 2009 it was 185), and people up and down the income scale saw remarkable material gains.

Between 1947 and 1979 real family income grew for everyone but it grew the most for the poorest 20 percent of the population. Compare that to the period from 1979 to 2009, when real family income declined for those in the lowest income quintile, while increasing annually by 1.2 percent for those in the top quintile. During the Great Compression income gains were relatively evenly distributed, while in the three decades after 1979, the top 10 percent captured *all* of the income gains, while incomes for the bottom 90 percent declined.

The fact that the first era of equality—with its strong middle class, manufacturing base, union density, but also "traditional families," higher levels of church attendance, and far less tolerance for sexual identities outside rigidly prescribed norms—has something to recommend to both the left and the right means that we are gripped by a tangled kind of nostalgia politics. "Here, in the first decade of the twenty-first century," writer Brink Lindsey observed in a 2006 essay, "the rival ideologies of left and right are both pining for the '50s. The only difference is that liberals want to work there, while conservatives want to go home there."

Lindsey, a libertarian, prefers the values of the second era of equality, the period from the mid to late 1970s until now that follows the contours of our meritocratic model: more equality along lines of race, gender, and sexual orientation, with far greater inequality and segregation in skills, wages, and wealth: More women law students, more black doctors, more openly gay millionaires.

I don't share Lindsey's politics, but I do think there's much to celebrate now. It's senseless to pine for a bygone era of Jim Crow,

Mad Men–style casual sexual harassment and gender apartheid, police raids of underground gay bars and sodomy prosecutions, and laws against interracial marriage.

The second era of equality has dismantled many (though certainly by no means all) of the legal and cultural structures that regulated and enforced these brutal inequalities of race, gender, and sexual orientation. Women entered the workforce in unprecedented numbers, and trends suggest that in the very near future, women will surpass men in all levels of educational attainment. While women still make on average 23 percent less than men, that gap has shrunk markedly since 1980, when women made on average 40 percent less.

As for racial equity, the gains are decidedly more mixed, but one unambiguous achievement of the second era of equality is that the elite has undoubtedly become more diverse. In 1975, only 1.4 percent of black households made more than $100,000. By 2006, it was more than six times that, a considerably faster rate of growth than that of white households. The number of black officeholders doubled between 1975 and 1993. And of course, there is what many view as the crowning achievement of the Civil Rights era: the first black president of the United States.

Equality for LGBT people hardly existed as a political issue during the first era of equality, while during the second the strides have been historic and remarkable: in 2003, the Supreme Court in *Lawrence v. Texas* struck down sodomy laws as unconstitutional. Eight states plus the District of Columbia have legalized gay marriage, while 58 percent of Fortune 500 companies offer benefits to same-sex partnerships. As of 2011, gays and lesbians can serve openly for the first time in the history of the United States military.

So the first era of equality produced an unprecedented reduction in economic inequality, a reduction that did not last, but that was, in some senses, replaced by a dramatic, if patchy and incomplete, reduction in inequality along the lines of gender, race, and sexual orientation.

Given this history, the path forward is clear, if not exactly easy: we need to bring about a social order that combines the best things about each era of equality, one that shrinks the yawning social distance that now makes elite failure inevitable.

The first step is persuading the public—including the elites themselves—that the ideology of meritocractic achievement stands in the way of social progress. The first commandment of the post-1970s meritocracy can be summed up as follows: "Thou shall provide equality of opportunity to all, regardless of race, gender, or sexual orientation, but worry not about equality of outcomes."

But what we've seen time and time again is that the two aren't so neatly separated. If you don't concern yourself at all with equality of outcomes, you will, over time, produce a system with horrendous inequality of opportunity. This is the paradox of meritocracy: It can only truly come to flower in a society that starts out with a relatively high degree of equality. So if you want meritocracy, work for equality. Because it is only in a society which values equality of actual outcomes, one that promotes the commonweal and social solidarity, that equal opportunity and earned mobility can flourish.

Such was the setting of England after World War II, when Michael Young first coined the term "meritocracy." In recalling his education in England during that era, the late historian Tony Judt noted that his cohort got to experience a kind of meritocratic honeymoon period, a time of unrivaled social equality, when old class boundaries were being torn down but the rigor and seriousness of the ancien educational régime remained. "We got both the traditions and the transgressions," he wrote, "the continuities and the change. But what we bequeathed to our successors was something far less substantial than what we ourselves had inherited."

It is the internal contradictions of such a system that accounts for its fragility. The Iron Law of Meritocracy means that over time, the inequality that such a system celebrates and prizes will lead to its dissolution. In England, Judt says educational institutions responded to increasing social inequality outside the university walls by doubling down on equality within it; but in doing so they lost precisely the spirit of rigor that had made them such engines of social mobility and intellectual force during his time: "Equality of opportunity and equality of outcome are not the same thing. A society divided by wealth and inheritance cannot redress this injustice by camouflaging it in educational institutions—by denying distinctions of ability or by restricting selective opportunity— while favoring a steadily widening income gap in the name of the free market. This is mere cant and hypocrisy."

The same pertains in the United States. As inequality has grown, as its negative consequences have become harder and harder to ignore, our response has been to put more and more weight on the educational system, to look to school reform as the means of closing the "achievement gap" and of guaranteeing the increasingly illusory promise of equal opportunity. We ask the education system to expiate the sins of the rest of the society and then condemn it as hopelessly broken when it doesn't prove up to the task. Because education lies on the opportunity side of the opportunity/outcome divide, it is the only place where we see sustained and genuine bipartisan consensus on domestic policy. From Ted Kennedy cosponsoring No Child Left Behind, to Mitt Romney praising President Obama's Race to the Top, there is an elite consensus that education, and specifically a certain vision of education reform, can provide the equality of opportunity that is so scandalously absent at present.

To urge that we consider equality of outcomes, however, is heresy, and for no small reason. There are ample historical examples of societies ideologically committed to equality of outcomes that resulted in a small, corrupt, and morally bankrupt ruling class and widespread penury and immiseration. Taken to its absolute extreme, a commitment to complete equality of outcomes is summed up by the Maoist adage "The tall stalk gets cut down."

Clearly I'm not saying we should do whatever it takes to ensure a perfect equality of outcomes. But as a democratic society we should care much, much more than we currently do about achieving them. We can't continue to tell ourselves that all is well as long as we're working for "equality of opportunity."

The good news is that achieving greater equality is, from a policy perspective, eminently doable. Computer programmers use the term "solved problem" to describe a particular programming challenge that may be difficult to implement but is one that someone, somewhere, has already figured out. When you're working on a solved problem, you know that no matter how difficult the task is, it can be done. In this crucial sense, creating a more equitable nation is a solved problem.

The policies needed to reduce inequality aren't particularly mysterious. In Latin America, neoliberal reforms and financial crises in the 1990s increased inequality on a continent that was already the most unequal in the world. But over the last decade a variety of leaders were elected to power on explicitly egalitarian platforms. They went to work putting their platforms into practice with an emphasis on increasing redistribution via payments to the poor, and the result is that across the continent, inequality fell. This at the same time inequality was increasing almost everywhere else in the world.

The experience of Brazil, in particular, shows that with a political leadership committed to reducing inequality, it is possible to produce high levels of growth while simultaneously shrinking the gap between rich and poor, even as inequality expands across the globe. Former trade unionist and social democrat Ignácio Lula da

Silva inherited one of the most unequal nations in the world when he was elected in 2002; he instituted a variety of programs that succeeded in shrinking that gap considerably. As *Newsweek* noted in 2009, "Between 2003 and 2008, the top 10 percent of Brazilians got 11 percent richer, while the bottom tenth saw their earnings jump 72 percent."

Much of this is due to a straightforward program of downward redistribution called the Bolsa Família. The program uses general government revenue collected through progressive taxation to pay for cash subsidies to the poorest Brazilians, so long as they send their kids to school and go for regular checkups at free federal health clinics. The Lula government also increased pension payouts, as well as the minimum wage, by a whopping 50 percent.

Since Brazil is a developing economy (and a very fast-growing one at that), it may not be the best model for the United States. But with the exception of England, every other industrialized democracy has higher levels of income equality than the United States. Data from the OECD shows one consistent, general principle: The higher the taxes in a given country, the less inequality. This makes obvious and intuitive sense. Taxation is the primary method for redistribution, and as a general rule, the more taxation, the more redistribution; the more redistribution, the more equality. The United States collects a far smaller share of the national income in taxes than nearly every other industrialized democracy, and in recent years that rate has been dropping. Total tax revenue as percentage of GDP in the United States is at 24.8 percent, down from 29.5 percent in 2000. You can compare that to Denmark, which has the highest level of tax revenue as a percentage of GDP (48.2 percent) and the most equality out of any OECD country.

Over the last thirty years or so we've seen rising inequality in pre-tax income, which means that before the government even starts its taxing, spending, and redistribution, there has been a profound and accelerating gap between high income earners and everyone else. The rich are earning more, while the non-rich's earnings stagnate or decline. But these pre-tax earnings are run through the redistributive mechanisms of the state. And during the same time that pre-tax inequality has been growing, our tax system has grown less redistributive, further amplifying inequality rather than mitigating it.

This shouldn't be all too surprising, since we've seen how inequality is autocatalytic. Those at the top can use their relative power to alter and manipulate existing institutions so as to further consolidate their gains and press their advantage. We've seen this in our own society, so much so that even the most "low-hanging fruit" of meritocratic policy has been abandoned.

Take the estate tax. The estate tax is designed to only affect those with vast fortunes, estates of more than $5 million. And its logic is clear: We don't want an aristocracy of birth—that's the very system our founders repudiated when they created a republic. Conservative Winston Churchill argued that an estate tax provided "a certain corrective against the development of a race of idle rich," and it was out of an ideological commitment to a kind of proto-meritocratic vision of equality of opportunity that robber baron Andrew Carnegie, opponent of income and property taxes, argued for a steep and confiscatory tax on inheritance:

> As a rule, a self-made millionaire is not an extravagant man himself. . . . But as far as sons and children, they are not so constituted. They have never known what it was to figure means to the end, to live frugal lives, or to do any useful work. . . . And I say these men, when the time comes that they must die . . . I say the community fails in its duty, and our legislators fail in their duty, if they do not exact a tremendous share.

And yet, over the past decade, this fundamental and basic means of gently enforcing some modicum of a level playing field has been gutted. In 2002, the rate for estates of more than $1 million was 50 percent, but it was diminished each year, until it was entirely phased out in 2009. It has since been restored (extended in December 2010 only for two years, for now), but at the historically rock-bottom rate of 35 percent, with a $10 million exemption for married couples. The *New York Times* said House Democrats opposed the deal brokered by Obama and congressional Republicans in the lame-duck congressional session of 2010 because it "would cost $68 billion, help only the richest of the rich—an estimated 6,600 households—and do nothing to stimulate the economy while adding to the national debt."

Same goes for the top marginal tax rate. If there is one single trend identifiable in the second era of equality it is the sharp decline in the rate that the very rich pay in income taxes. Not only has the top marginal rate fallen from 70 percent during the Carter administration to 35 percent at the end of this last decade, but the tax code has been shot through with a host of deductions and exemptions— from mortgage interest deduction to corporate jet depreciation breaks—which also disproportionally benefit the wealthy. All of this has combined to sharply reduce the system's progressivity. According to analysis produced by Pulitzer Prize–winning tax reporter David Cay Johnston, the four hundred richest filers paid an average effective tax rate of 16.6 percent. A worker making in the middle quintile of income can generally expect to pay an effective tax rate of around 22 percent.

In other words, the tax system, the most straightforward means of restraining inequality, has been subverted, so as to become a tool for maintaining and expanding it.

But of course, even if, in theory, a straightforward program of higher taxes and more redistribution would make America more equal, prescribing it as a solution begs the question, because any vision of egalitarian policies isn't worth much without a vision for how to create the political space for their adoption.

The first set of obstacles has to do with public opinion, or, at least, perceptions of public opinion. It is a widely held view that America's less egalitarian social structure is a manifestation of a certain kind of American exceptionalism, a shared cultural belief that with enough pluck and gumption anyone can end up on the top. Politicians and advocates feel they must frame their egalitarian arguments within the confines of the meritocratic framework— equal opportunity, level playing field, a fair shake for those who work hard and play by the rules—rather than the straightforward language of social solidarity.

Sherron Watkins, the Enron whistle-blower, cites exactly this fundamental aspect of the American character in explaining just why it's so hard to institute reforms of CEO compensation that might curtail the high-level fraud that spelled Enron's doom. When you start to go after excessive compensation, she argues, you run smack-dab into the powerful and ubiquitous ideology of the meritocracy: "The masses," she says, "think the CEO has a moral right to his money when they don't know the game's been rigged."

This conception of the American public is extremely widespread, and yet, while it's true that most Americans don't know in graphic and precise detail the extent to which the game has been rigged, they do, remarkably, want a more equal society. In 2010, economists Michael Norton and Dan Ariely studied Americans' perceptions of wealth distribution, asking survey participants to identify the distribution of wealth that prevailed in the United States (what percentage of wealth the top 20 percent owned, for instance). Norton and Ariely also had their subjects model their own ideal distributions: Just how equal would they like America to be? The results were striking:

First, respondents dramatically underestimated the current level of wealth inequality. Second, respondents constructed ideal wealth distributions that were far more equitable than even their erroneously low estimates of the actual distribution. Most important from a policy perspective, we observed a surprising level of consensus: All demographic groups—even those not usually associated with wealth redistribution such as Republicans and the wealthy—desired a more equal distribution of wealth than the status quo.

Of course, it is the nature of American democracy that we do not distribute wealth and resources via plebiscite. But public opinion also shows that there is a surprising amount of support for exactly the one policy that would most quickly reduce inequality: higher taxes.

In poll after poll, when asked how they want to reduce the deficit, Americans reliably choose cutting military spending and raising taxes on the wealthy as their two most favored approaches. In fact, raising taxes on the wealthy is one of the single most durably popular policy positions in the country. During the health care bill debate in 2009, 57 percent of respondents in an Associated Press poll said they favored a health surtax on the richest among us. More recently, 81 percent of respondents in a February 2011 NBC News/Wall Street Journal poll said "placing a surtax on federal income taxes for people earning over one million dollars a year" is a most acceptable way to reduce the federal budget deficit.

This suggests something remarkable and remarkably overlooked about the nature of American public opinion. We are more egalitarian than we, ourselves, realize.

So the obstacle to more equality isn't the absence of possible models for equality-enhancing policies, and it is not widespread public opposition to a more egalitarian society. The obstacle is simply that people and institutions who benefit most from extreme inequality have outsize power they can use to protect their gains from egalitarian incursions. The most pressing challenge for those who desire a better-functioning, more representative nation is conceiving not of policies that will ultimately enhance equality but of mechanisms by which the power of the current elite might be dramatically reduced.

Because the meritocratic winners are reluctant to part with their power, they must be convinced that the current status quo is unsustainable. Normalcy is what keeps the system moving and its inequities unaddressed—so normalcy must be disrupted. The social distance between the current beneficiaries of our postmeritocratic social order and its victims must be annihilated.

THIS WAS the approach that ACT UP used to great success in the 1980s and 1990s while confronting the devastation of the AIDS crisis. AIDS was a disease that was allowed to flourish in the dark vastness of social distance that separated gay men and drug users from "mainstream culture" and the power elite. And ACT UP's strategy was to shrink that social distance by disrupting the normalcy and comfort of the elite. Through die-ins in intersections and protests on cathedral steps, ACT UP brought the AIDS crisis to the doors of the powerful. They made themselves impossible to ignore.

This was the same tactic that Occupy Wall Street used so successfully in the fall and winter of 2011. By occupying public spaces in cities and towns across the country, the protesters disrupted the basic normalcy of everyday life. Mayors and police and media and fellow citizens had to, if nothing else, pay attention. And while the message may have been polarizing or sometimes lost between the various incidents of police violence and bullying, the basic effort was successful in dramatically expanding public consciousness of the basic problem of inequality and the rigged game it had created. Across America, people tuned in to their local nightly news to see people in the streets, decrying the basic unfairness of the system.

But disruption as disruption isn't enough. In order to actually effect deep and lasting change, those opposed to the current social order must locate another base of power that can credibly challenge the power of incumbent interests. I think the answer lies in a newly radicalized upper middle class.

One of the most interesting features of our current political moment is that a significant gulf has opened up between, roughly, the top 40 percent and the top 1 percent, between the middle class, upper middle class, professionals, and the mass affluent and the genuine plutocrats.

In fact, the two most energetic and important political movements of the aughts draw their popular constituency from the upper middle class: people with graduate school degrees, homes, second homes, kids in good colleges, and six-figure incomes. This frustrated, discontented class has spent a decade with their noses pressed against the glass, watching the winners grab more and more for themselves, seemingly at the upper middle class's expense.

On the left, the most durable new force in the last ten years is the Netroots, which includes a host of new progressive institutions, like MoveOn.org, and the diarists and readers of progressive blogs, like *Daily Kos*. Polling, surveys, and studies all suggest that its base is rooted in the professional upper middle class. A 2005 Pew study of more than eleven thousand Howard Dean volunteers and donors found that 80 percent had four-year college degrees and that 45 percent earned more than $75,000. The audience of *Daily Kos* and the more radical website *Firedoglake* are roughly similar.

More recently there is Occupy Wall Street, whose activists skew much younger, but who, if my experience in speaking with them is representative, are drawn from a similar class profile as MoveOn members and *Daily Kos* diarists. Most are college educated, now saddled with tens of thousands of dollars in college debt and no job prospects. They face a fundamental mismatch between their abilities and their opportunities. These are middle- and upper-middle-class young people with middle- and upper-middle-class expectations that are being dashed, and it is this frustration with a social contract that does not deliver that so often sows the seeds of revolutionary movements. "You have a lot of kids graduating college, can't find jobs," Mayor Bloomberg observed in September 2011 as Occupy Wall Street was first seizing the nation's attention. "That's what happened in Cairo. That's what happened in Madrid. You don't want those kinds of riots here."

On the right, there is the Tea Party movement, whose demographic was summarized in 2010 by the *New York Times* with the headline POLL FINDS TEA PARTY BACKERS WEALTHIER AND MORE EDUCATED.

Both the Netroots and the Tea Party, though obviously different in many ways—geographic distribution, political heritage, ideology, and whom they blame their lot on—share a uniting frustration. It is the anger of an upper middle class that finds itself increasingly dispossessed. A group of people who feel that those with more power and access are getting away with things. Decades of deindustrialization and globalization have already squeezed and battered the poor and working classes. But the professional class that makes up the core of the new insurrectionists had, until recently, been able to escape the vise of wage stagnation and foreshortened horizons. But no longer. They are now the class that feels most keenly the sense of betrayal, injustice, and dissolution that the Crisis of Authority has ushered in.

They share a sense that they are no longer in control, that some small, corrupt core of elites can launch an idiotic war, or bail out the banks, or mandate health insurance, and despite their relative privilege and education and money and social capital, there's not a damn thing they can do about it.

There are few forces more powerful in politics than downward mobility, the dispossession of the formerly privileged. As my father, a community organizer, once told me, the most difficult task an organizer faces when organizing the poor or working class is convincing people that they are entitled to something better, that they can assert their own claims and have them be taken seriously. America's upper middle class needs no such provocation.

The most militant and effective political mobilizations of our last decade were, for the most part, upper-middle-class uprisings (often partially bankrolled, it should be noted, by plutocrats), and while they were occasioned by a litany of specific triggers—the Iraq War, the deception of the Bush administration, the financial crisis, and the gently liberal agenda of the new Democratic president— they gained their momentum from their specific class origins. The resonance of their complaints is echoed by Tea Party activist Terri Hall: that the game is rigged. The Others, whether they be the "losers" that CNBC host Rick Santelli ranted about, who didn't pay their mortgages, or the bank CEOs and Halliburton and Blackwater executives, have unshackled themselves from the rules that bind everyone else. Such epiphanies are often the predicate for radicalization. And radicalization in its peculiar American, postmodern form is what we've seen much of in this past decade.

This is the rage of the insurrectionist class. The people who, to quote a favorite Bill Clinton phrase, have "worked hard and played by the rules" only to find the hard work for naught, the rules of the game rigged against them. And if reform is going to come, of the scope that it must to save our elites from themselves, it will come, I think, from this class.

Overall, however, the radicalization at the margins hasn't been enough to radically alter the status quo. The Tea Party has been quite successful in electing allied representatives and in pushing Congress to pursue a wildly destructive (and plutocratic) austerity agenda, but it has done little to alter the fundamental rules of the game. Special interests retain their control, the lobbying industrial complex remains alive and well. Activists of the left were able to channel anger at America's failed war in Iraq into electing Democrats to Congress and then the White House, but weren't able to actually end the war until December 31, 2011, a date arranged in negotiations by the Bush administration. Anger at growing inequality and concentration of power among the 1 percent has provided a boost to Occupy Wall Street and its sister occupations across the country, but the power of the 1 percent remains firmly intact.

The challenge, and it is not a small one, is directing the frustration, anger, and alienation we all feel into building a trans-ideological coalition that can actually dislodge the power of the post-meritocratic elite. One that marshals insurrectionist sentiment without succumbing to nihilism and manic, paranoid distrust. One that avoids the dark seduction of everything-is-broken-ism. One that leverages the deep skepticism of elites into a proactive, constructive vision of a moral, equitable, and connected social order.

The most obvious obstacle to building a potent coalition of the radicalized upper middle class is the deep partisan and ideological division that runs between conservatives and liberals. They have seemingly incompatible worldviews, with strongly held beliefs about the proper role of government, about who is to blame for the nation's ills, and who can and cannot be trusted. Our fractured media environment means that left and right also receive a constant stream of competing information and interpretation about the effects and causes of the Crisis of Authority.

Doubtless, mobilizing a grassroots egalitarian movement is far easier to do on the left, which has an ideological and historical commitment to equality. MoveOn wants higher taxes, the Tea Party views them as theft. The left wants increased Medicaid and money for health care for the poor, the right sees this as the vanguard of tyranny. And any time the natural class resentment toward the top 1 percent threatens to manifest itself within the ranks of the Tea Party and the right, the most trusted voices quickly rush in to warn them away from the vile spectacle of class warfare. Glenn Beck became righteously indignant over "mob rule" at the congressional hearing over post-bailout bonuses at AIG, and Rush Limbaugh described the outrage over the bonuses as "a lynch mob." When Obama moved to repeal the corporate jet tax breaks, Beck complained of Obama's "sheer unadulterated disgust for the wealthy, the successful, and anyone who's ever tried to do anything with their life," and Limbaugh warned that Obama's "dangerous" idea put "corporate jet owners in the crosshairs again." And on and on.

But major social change throughout the country's history has often emerged from strange and ideologically contorted coalitions. Abolitionists drew from former slaves like Frederick Douglass, women's suffragists, ministers, and intellectuals. Women's suffrage bound together Democrats and rebel factions of the Republican Party. Prohibition involved anti-Catholic moral crusaders and progressive suffragists. Its repeal was brought about by lifelong non-drinkers like John D. Rockefeller Jr. and lifelong alcoholics like Ernest Hemingway.

There have been occasional, fleeting hints of this in our own time. Tea Party–sympathetic libertarians and antiwar progressives have formed coalitions of convenience on opposition to continuing the war in Afghanistan, and the continued forward march of the War on Terror national security state. A strange bedfellows left-right coalition voted down the first TARP and reunited to force the Federal Reserve to submit to an audit and release records about the details of the extraordinary actions it took in the fall of 2008 to keep the global financial system from collapsing.

As activists of these alienated classes deepen their work, the full spectrum of our institutional dysfunction may challenge their assumptions about just who it is that is on their team. Spend time with lefty activists in New Orleans and you hear far more withering and damning indictments of government bureaucracy than you will ever hear from a Cato Institute position paper or a Republican member of Congress. Similarly, some of the Tea Party activists I've spoken with over the past few years show an increasing realization that Big Business is not their ally, and may be as much of a problem as Big Government. "Ultimately I figured out that the real enemy of the people, while government is a tool, it's really about the special interests," Terri Hall told me in March 2010. "The lobby makes sure they grease the wheels on both sides of the aisle. They work with and buy off anybody. It's almost like you can't characterize it as David and Goliath. It's a giant ten times the size of Goliath."

Each side sees itself as David and the other as Goliath. But they are united in a desire to see the giant slain, to see the old order held to account, the incumbents—broadly construed—swept out. "Accountability" is the word the comes up most in conversations with the new insurrectionist activists. We cannot achieve equality without first achieving some measure of accountability for those at the top.

It is easy to list dozens of reasons why such a coalition will not, cannot, work. But in the wake of some exogenous shock to the system that may change. The most recent and most imaginative of the movements borne of the crisis of authority, Occupy Wall Street, seems to understand that if change is to happen, it must come about through a very fundamental reconceptualization of our most basic political divisions. "It's about class," Occupy Wall Street organizer Andrew Smith told me. "People can't unify around party or religion, but we can unify around class."

The history of American politics would suggest otherwise. But as the investment ads all say: Past performance is no guarantee of future returns.

The nature of the post-meritocratic elite is that it can't help but produce failure. It is too socially distant to properly manage the institutions with which it has been entrusted. We are, as I write this, hurtling toward the certain crisis of catastrophic global climate change. Our elites and institutions have proven themselves entirely incapable of addressing and forestalling the immiseration and destruction that now approach like a meteor. Our financial system has grown only more concentrated in the wake of the financial crisis; the biggest banks have gotten bigger, the logic of too big to fail even more deeply embedded. Inequality has gotten worse in the wake of the crisis, and we remain wildly overextended in our military commitments, chained to eighteenth-century technology to power our way of life.

There is, I fear, more crisis to come. The imbalances of our society make it unavoidable.

And when the next crisis does come, there will once again be a brief moment in which, like that strange day on Capitol Hill after Lehman Brothers collapsed, normal politics give way to the idiosyncratic politics of the extraordinary. And in that context, who knows what strange new forces for equity and accountability might emerge?

Crisis is not something to be longed for or embraced: as we've seen, war, financial crisis, natural disaster visit their most punitive blows upon the weakest, the poorest, the least powerful members of society. But political crises, moments when the keystone of authority of some major governing institution is whisked away like a

Jenga block, can produce a tumbling cascade of new forms of politics. We've been looking at the tower for so long we forget it's made of blocks; we forget it can be put back together in a different way.

Previous crises of authority in America produced not just concerted movements to reform the institutions of the time, but organic bouts of institutional innovation that created fundamentally new ways of coordinating work and life. On the plains in the nineteenth century, farmers created co-ops and mutual aid societies that could share risk and smooth the volatilities of agricultural life when the government provided no such aid. Laborers in the bustling industrial cities began to form labor unions, and after the turn of the century, credit unions and local social clubs came across the sea with immigrants from Europe, providing something novel to American life in the crowded urban centers of the Industrial Age.

Often, institutional innovation precedes social reform. In the early years of the New Deal, a doctor named Francis Townsend came up with the idea of ending the Depression by creating a national pension for the elderly. Like a door-to-door Bible salesman, he traveled the country, pushing the idea and creating a legion of pension-fund missionaries who proselytized the gospel of the pensions. He founded a private company called the Old Age Revolving Pensions, Ltd., which boasted a membership at its peak of more than 2 million Americans. This was in a country with a total population of senior citizens of just over 10 million. The movement was so strong and the political pressure so acute, there's evidence that Roosevelt introduced the Social Security Act when he did as a means of sapping the Townsend Plan's momentum.

The good news is that in our own time, we have seen an explosion of institutional innovations. The common thread that runs through the most promising institutional innovations of this decade is, of course, the Internet. Nearly every single one of the most transformational new approaches to coordinating human interaction over the last ten years could not have happened without the Internet: the political organizing and fund-raising of MoveOn, blogs, and Obama for America, just to name a few.

Wikipedia provides a genuinely new form of authority during a time when traditional sources of authority have suffered a historic decline in trust. This is no small accomplishment. In his eccentricity and slightly quixotic zeal, Wikipedia's founder Jimmy Wales is something of a Francis Townsend for this age. The crucial difference being that while Townsend hoped to have the government implement his vision, Ayn Rand devotee Wales was able to implement his "plan" without having to convince a single legislator of its efficacy. We can imagine and hope that organic, Internet-facilitated cooperation can create new institutions that disrupt and break the monopolies of the old ones. A world of Craigslist and peer-to-peer micro-finance lenders, of distance learning via YouTube.

The Internet plays a huge role in allowing people to self-organize in non-hierarchical ways, but it's not a necessary precondition. Even without the Internet, people can find new ways to come together. It is striking that both the Tea Party and Occupy Wall Street describe themselves, insistently, as leaderless. In fact the Tea Party has taken as its organizational manifesto a book called *The Starfish and the Spider: The Unstoppable Power of Leaderless Organizations*. The idea behind the book is that if you have a leader, then the organization is only as good as that leader's decision-making, whereas if you decentralize power, you are no longer pegged to the flaws of a small elite. It's a way to rewrite Michels's Iron Law. "In American politics, radical decentralization has never been tried on so large a scale," wrote *National Journal*'s Jonathan Rauch. "Tea Party activists believe that their hive-like, 'organized but not organized' (as one calls it) structure is their signal innovation and secret weapon, the key to outlasting and outmaneuvering traditional political organizations and interest groups. . . . No foolish or self-serving boss can wreck it, because it has no boss. Fragmentation, the bane of traditional organizations, actually makes the network stronger. It is like a starfish: Cut off an arm, and it grows (in some species) into a new starfish. Result: two starfish, where before there was just one."

On the other side, Occupy Wall Street's official manifesto proclaimed it is a "leaderless resistance movement." Its commitment to equality and antipathy to hierarchy was so intense that participants created a laborious process of collective consensus decision-making called the General Assembly. Every evening, across the country, different local Occupy outposts got together for the nightly GA meeting, which served as the self-governing body for the occupation. All decisions were made collectively. Anyone at the GA had the ability to block a decision, and anyone had as much of a right to speak as anyone else. There were no representatives, no officials, and few of the mechanisms of "organization" that Robert Michels identified as sliding naturally toward the empowerment of the few over the many. The commitment to this process was so total it was done even at the cost of efficiency. Meetings took a very long time; decisions could not be made quickly and efficiently. But that's the whole idea. "You're creating a vision of the sort of society you want to have in miniature," David Graeber, a radical anthropologist who's been active in planning Occupy Wall Street since its inception, told the *Washington Post*'s Ezra Klein. The occupiers, Graeber said, wanted to "create a body that could act as a model of genuine, direct democracy to contrapose to the corrupt charade presented to us as 'democracy' by the U.S. government."

If we are going to find our way out of the present crisis, we will need more of this kind of political imagination. We will need to imagine a different social order, to conceive of what more egalitarian institutions would look like. We will need to construct coalitions, institutions, and constituencies that militate not only against the status quo but for equality. Our post-meritocratic inequality is the defining feature of the social contract to which we are all a party. And the terms of that contract must be renegotiated on a society-wide level. There is no withdrawing from this reality, no sidestepping it. The most fundamental institutions—our educational system, the federal government, the national security state, and Wall Street—must be confronted and reformed directly. Power must be distributed against the tooth, nail, and knife opposition of those who wield it most closely and those who benefit from it most exorbitantly. Organic grassroots coordination between citizens is a necessary means to achieve this end, but it cannot be the end itself.

Should America undergo the necessary upheaval and social transformation to bring about the third Era of Equality, we will not have arrived at some permanent state of bliss or end of history. The implacable hydraulic forces that draw power to collect and pool will continue to do their work. New tendencies for corruption will manifest themselves, and eventually, decades hence, people will find themselves pining for the good old days or decrying their broken institutions once again. This is the cycle of a dynamic society. Equality is never a final state, democracy never a stable equilibrium: they are processes, they are struggles.

Our task now is to recognize that that struggle is ours.

Acknowledgments

One of the more insidious aspects of meritocratic indoctrination is that it teaches you to believe that you wholly own your accomplishments. As I've tried to make clear in the book, it's a tempting notion but a dangerous one. As is the case with any project of this size, this book is the product of the labor of far, far more people than the one person whose name appears on the cover. A Nate Silver post at his old site FiveThirtyEight, that showed General Social Survey data about America's declining trust in their institutions over time, first crystallized the idea for the book. And it was during a long, loquacious walk I took with Dan Benaim through Washington, DC, in 2009 that I was first able to articulate just what it was I wanted to write a book about.

Throughout the development of the book, I've had hundreds of conversations with friends and colleagues about its main themes, and those conversations inform every page of the work. Our crew in DC comprised an intellectually vibrant and loving community during our time there: the aforementioned Dan Benaim, Meg Rooney, Dan Lurie, Elizabeth Drew, Kareem Saleh, Emily Parker, Elana Berkowitz, Ed Al-Husseiny, and Phoebe Connelly. Ezra Klein provided indispensable feedback and encouragement, particularly during the grueling proposal process, and Ryan Grim gave me wonderful advice about navigating the process. Josh Segall is the single best person in the world to sit on a long drive with and talk ideas for three hours. Dave Moore and Brian Cook read more of the Internet than I do, and it's my full-time job. Each offered constant intellectual support. Dan Berwick gave me a place to crash and an endless supply of sharp insights during my trips to Cambridge. Issa Kohler-Hausmann, Cassie Fennell, Eric Klinenberg, Jeff Lane, and Tom Schaller generously allowed me to borrow their vast academic knowledge. Other friends have also kindly engaged my years-long monomaniacal obsession with institutional distrust and elite failure: the Hunter crew, who I've known since adolescence and look forward to growing old with, Andrei Scheinkman, Elise Zelechowski, Paul Smith, and Michelle Mills, and our many beloved Chicago friends.

A number of people read early portions of the manuscript. Henry Farrell slogged his way through the entirety of an early version and gave characteristically astute (but gentle!) criticism. Steve Teles, Father Bill Dailey, Heather Parton (better known as Digby), Paul Smith, Rick Perlstein, and Nick Reville all read chapters in various stages and offered criticisms, observations, and feedback that made the book immeasurably better. The indefatigable and omnivorous Jonathan Lewinsohn devoured as many chapters as I could send him and was a constant source of encouragement throughout. My old history teacher Irving Kagan not only set me on my current path when he introduced me to political philosophy at the age of fourteen, he graciously helped me think through the chapter on Hunter.

Steve Coll and Andres Martinez gave me an institutional home and access to a host of fascinating thinkers at New America Foundation. Despite my lack of academic pedigree, Lawrence Lessig was gracious enough to invite me into the fold of the Edmund J. Safra Foundation Center for Ethics at Harvard, where I spent a year as a nonresident fellow in the lab on institutional corruption. The imaginative and generous scholars to whom I was exposed during my time there had a huge influence on the direction the book took.

Over the two years it's taken me to write the book, I've been blessed with talented and industrious research assistants. Ryan Rafaty, Laura Stampler, Laura Dean, Lauren North, Casey Scharf, Eric Naing, and Emma Dumain helped me find sources, facts, publications, and ideas.

The kind and fastidious Chuck Wilson did a comprehensive fact check on the book and handled the notes and citations. His attention to detail was remarkable and he saved me from more than a few embarrassments. Whatever errors managed to make it through are, of course, my doing and mine alone.

Katrina vanden Heuvel nurtured me as a writer and continues to be a stalwart mentor, advocate, and friend. Betsy Reed, Richard Kim, Roane Carey, and the rest of the *Nation* posse are the best coworkers and friends a writer could have.

At MSNBC, Phil Griffin had enough faith in me to entrust me with four hours a week on his network, and it's the best job I've ever had. Rachel Maddow has been a comrade and a role model: her generosity and integrity are an inspiration. The entire amazing staff of *Up* has tolerated my stressed-out, distracted multitasking while trying to bring this book to fruition.

Will Lippincott is fiercely loyal, savvy, and perhaps the most charming man I know. In other words, he is the perfect agent. His wisdom, judgment, humor, and support have made all of this possible.

Perhaps Will's greatest stroke of genius was steering me toward Vanessa Mobley, who has been more than an editor, she has been an intellectual copilot for the entirety of the journey. From our very first conversation, when she invoked Rorty in the first two minutes, we've shared the same vision. When I signed my contract, many of her current and former authors e-mailed me to tell me I'd ended up with the best editor in New York. They were right. Molly Stern, Julie Cepler, Penny Simon, and the entire team at

Crown have been remarkably supportive and proactive in getting this book into the hands of as many readers as possible.

My family—my parents, Aunts Linda, Alex, Diana, and Sheila, Uncles Don, Billi, and Ronnie—have all been the primary focus group for the book's main themes and arguments. I talked to them about it, I tested ideas and arguments and stories with them, and I shaped the text based on what they responded to. I wrote it, in large part, for them. My in-laws, Mary, Andy, Emily, and EB Shaw and Jim Furman, have been endlessly supportive, providing everything from child care to wise career advice. Even though he's younger than me, I look up to my brother, Luke, who every day does the grueling, indispensable work of citizenship with grace, humor, cheer, and passion.

At the age of eighteen, I met a girl who I thought was the most beautiful, fascinating, electrifying, and brilliant person I'd ever met. For the past fourteen years I've been lucky enough to spend my life with her, and each day reveals just how much I underestimated her. I think the way I do, write the way I do, and am the person I am because of my wife, Kate. Her depthless compassion, kindness, strength, and openness have taught me how to be a better, fuller person. There is not a sentence in this book in which she is not present.

When this book was conceived, our remarkable daughter, Ryan, hadn't yet been, but the human gestation period is shorter than the literary one, so our daughter made it into the world before the text. Ryan, you are everything to your mother and me. I'm sorry I'm going to raise you a Cubs fan.

Notes

CHAPTER 1. THE NAKED EMPERORS

1 *median household income*: See "Income and Poverty Rate at 1990s Levels," *New York Times*, September 23, 2011.

1 *optimism that today's young people*: See Elizabeth Mendes, "In U.S., Optimism About Future for Youth Reaches All-Time Low," Gallup .com, May 2, 2011.

3 *4,500 Americans and 100,000-plus Iraqis, and $800 billion*: The figure on American deaths was obtained through the Department of Defense, http://www.defense.gov/news/casualty.pdf, accessed December 27, 2011; for Iraqi deaths, see "AP Exclusive: Secret Tally Has 87,215 Iraqis Dead," Associated Press, April 23, 2009. The article explains that "figures show that more than 110,000 Iraqis have died in violence since the 2003 U.S.-led invasion." For cost of the war, see Amy Belasco, "The Cost of Iraq, Afghanistan, and Other Global War on Terror Operations Since 9/11," Congressional Research Service, March 29, 2011.

3 *"a really big number"*: Cited on p. 13 of *Meeting on Priorities for the Next Administration: Use of TARP Funds under EESA*, Committee on Financial Services, U.S. House of Representatives, 11th Congress, (Washington, D.C.,: U.S. Government Printing Office, January 13, 2009).

4 *worst unemployment rate in nearly thirty years*: See "Annual Average Unemployment Rate, Civilian Labor Force 16 Years and Over (percent)," Bureau of Labor Statistics, http://www.bls.gov/cps/prev_yrs .htm, accessed January 17, 2012.

4 *"Almost nothing is going the way that most people have been told that it will"*: Cited in David Carr, "Olbermann, Impartiality and MSNBC," *New York Times*, November 8, 2010.

4 *"hard to have faith in that right now"*: Press conference by the President, East Room, November 3, 2010, http://www.whitehouse.gov/the -press-office/2010/11/03/press-conference-president, accessed December 28, 2011.

5 *"We've created this situation where we've created so much mistrust in government"*: Author interview.

5 *"I've always defended corporations"*: Author interview.

6 *"I'm 31, an Iraq war veteran"*: Thomas L. Day, "Penn State, My Final Loss of Faith," *Washington Post Guest Voices* blog, http://www.washington post.com/blogs/guest-voices/post/penn-state-my-final-loss-of -faith/2011/11/11/gIQAwmiIDN_blog.html, accessed January 17, 2012.

7 *"We saw how quickly the whole things can fall apart"*: Author interview.

7 *"offered to come and help us"*: Author interview.

7 *"It's just block after block after block of abandoned homes"*: Author interview.

7 *the real figure was closer to 50 percent*: For corroboration of Azikiwe's figures, see Mike Wilkinson, "Nearly Half of Detroit's Workers Are Unemployed," *Detroit News,* December 16, 2009.

8 *"I can't remember when I last heard someone genuinely optimistic about the future"*: Charles Simic, "The New American Pessimism," *New York Review of Books,* March 10, 2011, http://www.nybooks.com/blogs /nyrblog/2011/mar/10/new-american-pessimism/, accessed January 18, 2012.

8 *"an agent for angst"*: Author interview.

8 *"a permanent D.C. ruling class"*: "Le Hameau de la Potomac," http:// digbysblog.blogspot.com/2009/10/le-hameau-de-la-potomac-by -digby-i-have.html, accessed January 18, 2012.

9 *"For years, the right has worshipped markets"*: Author interview.

9 *"Go all the way back to Sumerian civilization"*: Author notes.

10 *"In retrospect we were all illiterate!"*: Author interview.

10 *"Behind all the questions of politics"*: James Reston, "The Hypocrisy of Power," *New York Times,* April 8, 1970.

10 *By 2007—even before the financial crash—both Gallup and the General Social Survey showed public trust in nearly every single major institution at or near an all-time low*: See "Americans' Confidence in Congress at All-Time Low," Gallup.com, June 21, 2007, and "Confidence in Congress: Lowest Ever for Any U.S. Institution," Gallup.com, June 20, 2008.

11 *the British Crown was almost certainly more widely trusted in the colonies at the time of the revolution*: See Lawrence Lessig, *Republic, Lost: How Money Corrupts Congress—and a Plan to Stop It* (New York: Hachette Book Group, 2011), p. 247.

11 *anti-government sentiment has its own ideological and partisan basis*": See "Distrust, Discontent, Anger, and Partisan Rancor: The People and Their Government," Pew Research Center for the People & the Press, April 18, 2010, http://www.people-press.org/2010/04/18/distrust-discontent-anger-and-partisan-rancor/, accessed April 5, 2012.

11 *A 2010 study conducted by the Harvard Institute of Politics*": See "Survey of Young Americans' Attitudes Toward Politics and Public Service: 17th Edition," Institute of Politics, Harvard University, Key Findings & Highlights presented at The Brookings Institution, March 9, 2010, http://www.iop.harvard.edu/var/ezp_site/storage/fckeditor /file/010308_IOP%20Spring%202010_powerpoint.pdf, accessed January 19, 2012.

11 *"The moral for that story is*": Author interview.

12 *In 1979, newspapers were one of the most trusted institutions in America, with ratings over 50 percent: today they're one of the least*: See "Confidence in Institutions," Gallup, http://www.gallup.com/poll/1597/confidence -institutions.aspx, accessed January 19, 2012.

14 *"end the mind-set that got us into war in the first place*": Obama's comments were made in the January 31, 2008, CNN Democratic Debate.

15 *"sapping of confidence across our land*": See Transcript: Barack Obama's Inaugural Address, *New York Times*, January 20, 2009, www.nytimes .com/2009/01/20/us/politics/20text-obama.html, accessed February 22, 2012.

16 *"We are in a time when the American public is highly suspect of any institution*": Peter Baker, "Education of a President," *New York Times Magazine*, October 12, 2010.

17 *"Left or right, but up or down*": Author interview.

17 *"it seemed that the United States was blessed with mature, skillful economic leaders*": Paul Krugman, *The Great Unraveling* (New York: W. W. Norton Company, 2004), p. xxxii.

18 *"pulled down to the ground their monarchy*": Edmund Burke, *The Works of the Right Honorable Edmund Burke,* vol. 5 (London: F. and C. Rivington, 1801), pp. 57 and 59.

18 *"the institutionalist has a deep reverence"*: See David Brooks, "What Life Asks of Us," *New York Times,* January 26, 2009.

19 *"Americans' distrust of politicians"*: See "Farewell Address by Senator Christopher Dodd, The Senate Chamber," Federal News Service, December 29, 2010.

19 *"'bankers, bankers, bankers'"*: See Matthew Dalton, "A Banker's Plaintive Wail," Davos Live, *Wall Street Journal Blogs,* January 27, 2011, http://blogs.wsj.com/davos/2011/01/27/a-bankers-plaintive -wail/, accessed January 19, 2012.

19 *"My own trust in our political leaders is at a personal low"*: David Brooks and Dick Cavett, "In Whom Can We Trust?" *Opinionator: Exclusive Online Commentary from The Times,* http://opinionator.blogs.nytimes .com/2010/03/05/in-whom-can-we-trust/, accessed January 19, 2012.

21 *"Obama's faith lay in cream rising to the top"*: Jonathan Alter, *The Promise: President Obama, Year One* (New York: Simon & Schuster, 2010), p. 64.

22 *"Meritocracy is a parody of democracy"*: Christopher Lasch, *The Revolt of the Elites and the Betrayal of Democracy* (New York: W. W. Norton, 1996), p. 41.

23 *"Who's going to feel confident about the government"*: Author interview.

24 *"We and our children walking around in ankle-deep water"*: Author interview.

26 *the number of kindergartners whose parents requested vaccination exemptions*: Cited in See Rong-Gong Lin II and Sandra Poindexter, "Drop in Vaccinations Raises Risk at Some California Schools," *Los Angeles Times,* March 29, 2009.

26 *2010 outbreak of the illness killed ten infants in California*: See "Pertussis (Whooping Cough)," Centers for Disease Control and Prevention, http://www.cdc.gov/pertussis/outbreaks.html, accessed January 19, 2012.

26 *A comprehensive Pew poll*: See "Fewer Americans See Solid Evidence of Global Warming," Pew Research Center for the People & the Press, October 22, 2009, http://pewresearch.org/pubs/1386/cap -and-trade-global-warming-opinion, accessed January 19, 2012.

27 *"Those institutions are now corrupt"*: Cited in "Science Scorned," *Nature,* September 9, 2010.

28 *Bonuses and profits are near record levels*: Shira Ovide, "More Evidence Wall Street Pay at Near or Record Levels," *Deal Journal,* February 23, 2011, http://blogs.wsj.com/deals/2011/02/23/more-evidence-wall -street-pay-at-near-record-levels/, accessed January 18, 2012.

28 *"they frankly own the place"*: Cited in Joe Weisenthal, "Senator Admits That Bankers Own Capitol Hill," *The Business Insider,* May 1, 2009.

CHAPTER 2. MERITOCRACY AND ITS DISCONTENTS

31 *"Goldman Sachs is a meritocracy"*: See "Why Goldman Sachs?" http://www2.goldmansachs.com/careers/why-goldman-sachs/our-culture/index.html, accessed January 5, 2012.

32 *only 185 are offered admission*: Figures provided by Hunter College High School director of admissions Kyla Kupferstein Torres.

33 *"I feel guilty"*: The entire speech is accessible through the *New York Times* website, at www.nytimes.com/packages/pdf/speech.pdf.

34 *Jennifer J. Raab . . . stayed seated*: In an interview with the author Raab confirmed that she stayed seated.

34 *"The Joyful Elite"*: Katharine Davis Fishman, "The Joyful Elite," *New York*, January 18, 1982.

34 *"I came from a family where"*: Author interview.

36 *just 3 percent black and 1 percent Hispanic by 2009*: Cited in Sharon Otterman, "Diversity Debate Convulses Elite High School," *New York Times,* August 4, 2010.

36 *"The teachers are disconcerted"*: Author interview.

36 *"When you look at what happens in classrooms"*: Author interview.

37 *"Honestly, [admissions] is based"*: Cynthia Bau quoted in Belinda Zhou, "Graduation Speech Ignites Heated Debate," *What's What,* October 26, 2010.

38 *"The rhetoric that accompanied the birth of the ETS"*: Nicholas Lemann, *The Big Test: The Secret History of the American Meritocracy,* rev. pbk. ed., New York: Farrar, Straus & Giroux, 2000), p. 344.

38 *"We're still using this method of identifying children"*: Author interview.

38 *"one of the best ways to predict a student's SAT score is to look at his parents income"* ETS data as analyzed by Daniel Pink, http://www.danpink

.com/archives/2012/02/how-to-predict-a-students-sat-score-look-at-the-parents-tax-return.

39 *"imported the year-round enrichment programs of the Far East"*: See Javier C. Hernandez, "The Big Cram for Hunter High School," *New York Times,* January 3, 2009.

39 *In 1965, the school's administrators at the City University of New York*: Elizabeth Stone, *The Hunter College Campus Schools for the Gifted: The Challenge of Equity and Excellence* (New York: Teachers College Press, 1992), p. 3

40 *The result is that just 10 percent of Hunter High School's students are poor enough to qualify for free or reduced-price lunch*: Hunter College Campus Schools 2009 Basic Educational Data Systems Report http://hces.hunter.cuny.edu/BasicEdDataSysReport_2009.pdf.

41 *"we frankly recognize that democracy can be no more than aspiration"*: Michael Young, *The Rise of the Meritocracy* (1958 repr, New Brunswick, N.J.: Transaction Publishers, 1994), p. 11.

42 *"The book was a satire meant to be a warning"*: Michael Young, "Down with Meritocracy," *Guardian,* June 28, 2001.

42 *"The Americans never use the word peasant"*: See Alexis de Tocqueville, *Democracy in America,* vol. 1 (London: Longmans, Green, and Co., 1875), p. 321.

43 *"I agree with you that there is a natural aristocracy among men"*: *The Essential Jefferson,* ed. Jean M. Yarbough (Indianapolis: Hackett Publishing, 2006), p. 215.

43 *"The gradual development of the principle of equality"*: See *The Tocqueville Reader: A Life in Letters and Politics* (Malden, Mass.: Blackwell Publishers, 2002), p. 67.

44 *"As the circle of those who decide is narrowed"*: C. Wright Mills, *The Power Elite* (New York: Oxford University Press, 1956), p. 21.

45 *"History is the graveyard of aristocracies"*: Cited in Joseph V. Femia, *Pareto and Political Theory* (New York: Routledge, 2006), p. 71.

46 *"A bedrock American principle"*: See Ben Bernanke, "The Level and Distribution of Economic Well-Being," speech before the Greater Omaha Chamber of Commerce, Omaha, Nebraska, February 6, 2007, http://www.federalreserve.gov/newsevents/speech/bernanke 20070206a.htm, accessed January 5, 2012.

46 *"unpleasant term, like that of 'equality of opportunity'"*: Young, *Rise of the Meritocracy,* p. 11.

47 *"the levelers . . . only change and pervert the natural order of things"*: Edmund
    Burke, *Reflections on the Revolution in France, and on the Proceedings in Cer-*
    tain Societies in London Relative to That Event (London: J. Dodsley, 1790),
    p. 72.

48 *"Think about every problem, every challenge, we face"*: Cited in Lori Cox
    Han, *A Presidency Upstaged: The Public Leadership of George H. W. Bush*
    (College Station, Tex.: Texas A&M University Press, 2011), p. 181.

48 *"We are living in a world where what we earn is a function of what we learn"*: Bill
    Clinton, "Remarks at the Opportunity Skyway School-to-Work
    Program in Georgetown, Delaware," September 3, 1993, in *Public*
    Papers of the Presidents of the United States, William J. Clinton, 1993, Bk. 2,
    August 1 to December 31, 1993 (Washington, D.C.: United States Gov-
    ernment Printing Office, 1994), p. 1434.

48 *"a good education is no longer just a pathway to opportunity"*: Barack Obama,
    Address to Joint Session of Congress, February 24, 2009, http://
    www.whitehouse.gov/the press_office/Fact-Sheet-Expanding
    -the-Promise-of-Education-in-America, accessed January 6, 2012.

49 *"There's no greater challenge than to make sure that every child"*: George W.
    Bush, "Remarks on Signing the No Child Left Behind Act of 2001
    in Hamilton, Ohio," January 8, 2002, in *Public Papers of the Presidents*
    of the United States, George W. Bush, 2002, January 1 to June 30, 2002 (Wash-
    ington, D.C.: U.S. Government Printing Office, 2005), p. 23.

50 *"that salutary branch of business education"*: See Andrew Carnegie, *The Em-*
    pire of Business (New York: Doubleday, 1913), pp. 3–4. The speech
    was initially given to students at Curry Commercial College in
    Pittsburgh in June of 1885.

50 *"I found not only that most bankers came from a few elite institutions"*: Karen
    Zouwen Ho, *Liquidated: An Ethnography of Wall Street* (Durham, N.C.:
    Duke University Press, 2009), pp. 43–44.

50 *Between 2000 and 2005 about 40 percent of Princeton students*: Cited in Ho,
    Liquidated, p. 44. For Harvard numbers, Ho cites a statement from
    the university's Office of Career Services in 2005, indicating that
    close to half of Harvard students go through "the recruiting process
    to vie for investment banking and consulting jobs."

50 *"American CEOs looked very different"*: Benjamin Wallace-Wells, "The
    Romney Economy," *New York*, October 23, 2011.

52 *"It's the easiest way to see who was lucky enough to get a good elementary school*

education": Quoted in Belinda Zhou, "Graduation Speech Ignites Heated Debate," *What's What,* October 26, 2010.

52 *"The idea of meritocracy may have many virtues"*: Amartya Sen, "Merit and Justice," in *Meritocracy and Economic Inequality,* ed. Kenneth Arrow et al. (Princeton, N.J.: Princeton University Press, 2000), p. 5.

52 *"meritocratic feedback loop"*: Ho, *Liquidated,* p. 57.

52 *Grover Norquist likened progressive taxation . . . to Hitler's treatment of the Jews*: The dialogue is quoted in Michael J. Graetz and Ian Shapiro, *Death by a Thousand Cuts: The Fight Over Taxing Inherited Wealth* (Princeton, N.J.: Princeton University Press, 2006), pp. 213–14.

54 *"Our workers' organization has become an end in itself"*: Cited in John Kilcullen, "Robert Michels: Oligarchy," http://www.humanities.mq.edu.au/Ockham/y64l11.html, accessed January 6, 2012.

55 *"The most formidable argument against the sovereignty of the masses"*: Robert Michels, *Political Parties: A Sociological Study of the Oligarchical Tendencies of Modern Democracy,* trans. Eden and Cedar Paul (New York: The Free Press, 1962), p. 65.

55 *"In the great industrial centers"*: Ibid., p. 65.

55 *"gulf which divides the leaders from the masses"*: Ibid., p. 70.

56 *"The Iron Law of Oligarchy"*: Ibid., p. 342.

56 *"It is organization which gives birth"*: Ibid., p. 365.

56 *"The treasure in the fable may well symbolize democracy"*: Ibid., p. 368.

58 *"At least one third of the students at elite universities"*: Daniel Golden, *The Price of Admission: How America's Ruling Class Buys Its Way into Elite Colleges— and Who Gets Left Outside the Gates* (New York: Three Rivers Press, 2007), p. 6.

59 *"affirmative action for rich white people" . . . "elites mastering the art of perpetuating themselves"*: Ibid., pp. 6 and 10.

59 *"The Great Divergence"*: See Paul Krugman, "Introducing This Blog," http://krugman.blogs.nytimes.com/2007/09/18/introducing-this-blog/, accessed January 7, 2012.

59 *In 1928, the top 10 percent of earners captured 46 percent of national income. . . . Between 1979 and 2005, nearly 88 percent of the entire economy's income gains went to the top 1 percent*: Emmanuel Saez, "Striking It Richer: The Evolution of Top Incomes in the United States," March 15, 2008, http://www.econ.berkeley.edu/~saez/saez-UStopincomes-2006prel.pdf,

accessed January 7, 2012, and Arloc Sherman and Chad Stone, "Income Gaps Between Very Rich and Everyone Else More Than Tripled in Last Three Decades, New Data Show," Center on Budget and Policy Priorities, http://www.cbpp.org/cms/?fa=view&id=3220, accessed January 7, 2012.

60 *"while seemingly an exclusive group":* Jacob S. Hacker and Paul Pierson, *Winner-Take-All Politics: How Washington Made the Rich Richer—and Turned Its Back on the Middle Class* (New York: Simon & Schuster, 2010), p. 16.

60 *Adjusted for inflation, the top 0.1 percent:* Cited in Ibid, p. 16, from the research of economists Thomas Piketty and Emmanuel Saez.

61 *"as inequality has increased . . .":* Alan B. Krueger, "The Rise and Consequences of Inequality in the United States," January 12, 2012, http://www.americanprogress.org/issues/2012/01/curbing_inequality.html, accessed April 5, 2012.

61 *"Intergenerational Economic Mobility in the U.S., 1940 to 2000":* Daniel Aaronson and Bhashkar Mazumder, "Intergenerational Economic Mobility in the U.S, 1940 to 2000," Federal Reserve Bank of Chicago, revised February 2007, http://www.chicagofed.org/digital_assets/publications/working_papers/2005/wp2005_12.pdf, accessed January 7, 2012.

61 *Another pair of economists, from the Boston Federal Reserve:* See Katherine Bradbury and Jane Katz, "Trends in U.S. Family Income Mobility, 1967–2004, Boston Federal Reserve, http://www.bostonfed.org/economic/wp/wp2009/wp0907.htm.

61 *A study carried out by economist Tom Hertz of more than six thousand American families over two generations:* See Tom Hertz, "Understanding Mobility in America," Center for American Progress, http://www.americanprogress.org/kf/hertz_mobility_analy-sis.pdf, accessed January 8, 2012.

61 *"The gap between median black family income and median white family income":* Author interview.

62 *A report based on the research of Bruce Western and Becky Pettit:* "Collateral Costs: Incarceration's Effect on Economic Mobility," The Pew Charitable Trusts, http://www.economicmobility.org/assets/pdfs/EMP_Incarceration.pdfaccessed, accessed January 8, 2012.

62 *"Germany is 1.5 times more mobile than the United States":* Isabel Sawhill and

John E. Morton, "Economic Mobility: Is the American Dream Alive and Well?" Economic Mobility Project, http://www .economicmobility.org/assets/pdfs/EMP%20American%20 Dream%20Report.pdf, accessed January 8, 2012.

62 *"In America only 32% take such a fatalistic view"*: "Ever Higher Society, Ever Harder to Ascend: Whatever happened to the belief that any American could get to the top?" *The Economist,* December 29, 2004.

62 *an occasional CBS News/New York Times poll*: See CBS News/New York Times Poll, "The American Dream," Monday, May 4, 2009, 6:30 P.M., and Peter L. Callero, *The Myth of Individualism: How Social Forces Shape Our Lives* (Lanham, Md.: Rowman & Littlefield, 2009), p. 93.

63 *"The socialists might conquer, but not socialism"*: Michels, *Political Parties,* 355. Michels's book was initially published in 1915.

CHAPTER 3. MORAL HAZARDS

65 *"The bargain has been breached"*: Quoted in James Oliphant, "Biden Likens Occupy Wall Street to Tea Party, Blasts BofA," *Los Angeles Times,* October 6, 2011.

65 *Andrew Joseph Stack*: The account of the Andrew Joseph Stack case was drawn from several sources, including "Pilot's Communication with Tower Before Crash into Office Building," *Austin Statesman,* February 20, 2010.

66 *"his alienation is similar to that we're hearing"*: Jonathan Capehart, http://voices.washingtonpost.com/postpartisan/2010/02/_joseph _stack_was_angry.html, accessed January 8, 2012.

66 *"just like any liberal Democrat"*: Premiere Radio Networks' *The Rush Limbaugh Show,* February 19, 2010, http://mediamatters.org/mmtv /201002190029, accessed January 8, 2012.

67 *"made it extremely difficult for information technology professionals to work as self-employed individuals"* and *"This law has ruined many people's lives"*: David Cay Johnston, "Tax Law Cited in Software Engineer's Suicide Note," *New York Times,* February 18, 2010.

68 *"started getting disillusioned and feeling not so good about my government"*: Author interview.

70 *"The social line between the laborer and the capitalist"*: Cited in John Micklethwait and Adrian Wooldridge, *The Company: A Short History of a Revolutionary Idea* (New York: Random House Digital, Inc., 2005), p. 74.

70 *And yet while U.S. employment declined by 8.8 million during this recent recession*: See Christopher J. Goodman and Steven M. Mance, "Employment Loss and the 2007-2009 Recession: An Overview," *Monthly Labor Review*, April 2011,pp. 3-12, http://www.bls.gov/opub/mlr/2011/04 /art1full.pdf, accessed January 9, 2012.

70 *Ken Lewis of Bank of America*: See Colin Barr, "BofA CEO: $53 Million Retirement Score," CNNMoney, October 2, 2009, http://money .cnn.com/2009/10/01/news/newsmakers/lewis.payout.fortune /index.htm, accessed January 9, 2012.

70 *Even Dick Fuld*: See Lucian A. Bebchuk et al., "The Wages of Failure: Executive Compensation at Bear Stearns and Lehman 2000–2008," *Yale Journal on Regulation* 27 (2010): 257–82. This article estimates that Fuld earned $461 million from the sale of more than 12 million shares of Lehman stock.

70 *America incarcerates a larger percentage of its citizens . . . With less than 5 percent of the world's population, we account for nearly 25 percent of the world's prison population*: Cited in Adam Liptak, "Inmate Count in U.S. Dwarfs Other Nations'," *New York Times*, April 23, 2008.

74 *"Skilling thought he was on his way to building a perfect meritocracy"*: Kurt Eichenwald, *Conspiracy of Fools: A True Story* (New York: Broadway Books, 2005), p. 49.

74 *"We hire very smart people and we pay them more than they think they are worth"*: Executive quoted in Richard Foster and Sarah Kaplan, *Creative Destruction: Why Companies That Are Built to Last Underperform the Market— and How to Successfully Transform Them* (New York: Doubleday, 2001), p. 150.

74 *"rank and yank"*: For a defense of the ranking process, see Richard C. Grote, *Forced Ranking: Making Performance Management Work* (Cambridge: Harvard Business Press, 2005), pp. ix–xiii.

74 McKinsey Quarterly *singled out the policy in 1997 for playing a large role in Enron's success*: Timothy Bleakley, David S. Gee, and Ron Hulme, "The Atomization of Big Oil," *McKinsey Quarterly*, May 1997, http://

www.mckinseyquarterly.com/The_atomization_of_big_oil_217, accessed January 9, 2012. The authors praised Enron's "new breed of tightly focused and vertically specialized 'petropreneuers.'"

75 *"I thought Enron was a fabulous experiment"*: Author interview.

75 *"It was an exhilarating atmosphere"*: Author interview.

75 *"I'm incredibly nervous that we will implode"*: Sherron Watkins memo to Ken Lay, August 15, 2001, http://cdm15017.contentdm.oclc.org /cdm4/document.php?CISOROOT=/p15017coll21&CISOPTR= 4319&REC=1, accessed January 19, 2012.

75 *"I knew either this woman was a lunatic or I was sitting on a corporate nuclear bomb that was going to explode"*: Author interview.

78 *"The beginning was absolutely the worst"*: Author interview.

79 *"It poisoned the well of what was already a fairly toxic relationship"*: Author interview.

81 *"little or no federal inspection"*: Quoted in Jim Salisbury, "Phillies Get Warning from Fehr," *Philadelphia Inquirer,* March 1, 2009.

82 *"This guy could Hula Hoop inside a Cheerio"*: David Wells, *Perfect I'm Not: Boomer on Beer, Brawls, Backaches, and Baseball* (New York: William Morrow, 2003), p. 54.

82 *"What the hell was this monster eating?"*: Ibid., p. 54.

83 *"If they wanted to know about steroids, they knew who to ask"*: Ibid., p. 136.

83 *"Learning Unethical Practices from a Co-worker: The Peer Effect of Jose Canseco"*: Eric D. Gould and Todd R. Kaplan, "Learning Unethical Practices from a Co-worker: The Peer Effect of Jose Canseco," Institute for the Study of Labor, Discussion Paper No. 3328, January 2008, http://ftp.iza.org/dp3328.pdf, accessed January 10, 2012.

84 *"I didn't help these players earn millions of dollars"*: Kirk Radomski, *Bases Loaded: The Inside Story of the Steroid Era in Baseball by the Central Figure in the Mitchell Report* (New York: Hudson Street Press, 2009), pp. 3–4. Radomski achieved notoriety when, under investigation by the FBI, he wore a wire and then spoke to baseball's official investigator George Mitchell and named names.

84 *"People who are not using them can't compete against people who do"*: Ibid., chapter 4.

84 *"Where did you get all that muscle?"*: See Jeff Pearlman, *Love Me, Hate Me: Barry Bonds and the Making of an Anti-Hero* (New York: HarperCollins, 2006), p. 213.

85 *"Talking to professional athletes about steroids"*: Radomski, *Bases Loaded,* page 59.

85 *Ken Caminiti, who estimated that at least half the league was using*: Tom Verducci, "Totally Juiced," *Sports Illustrated,* June 3, 2002.

86 *"What about the apartment I've leased?"*: Author interview.

88 *"The owners had been smart enough not to chase steroid use out of the game"*: Canseco, *Juiced,* p. 199.

88 *"they were much more concerned about the serious economic issues facing baseball"*: See George J. Mitchell, "Report to the Commissioner of Baseball of an Independent Investigation into the Illegal Use of Steroids and Other Performance Enhancing Substances By Players in Major League Baseball," December 13, 2007, http://extras.mnginteractive .com/live/media/site36/2007/1213/20071213_120215_mitchrpt .pdf, accessed January 19, 2012.

88 *"Steroids speculated by GM"*: Cited in Dylan Hernandez, "Dodgers Deeply Implicated," *Los Angeles Times,* December 14, 2007.

89 *In 2007, the average team was worth $472 million*: See Michael K. Ozanian and Kurt Badenhausen, "The Business of Baseball," Forbes.com, April 16, 2008, http://www.forbes.com/2008/04/16/baseball-team -values-biz-sports-baseball08-cx_mo_kb_0416baseballintro .html, accessed January 19, 2012.

89 *Levitt used test score fluctuations in Chicago public schools*: See Brian A. Jacob and Steven D. Levitt, "Rotten Apples: An Investigation of the Prevalence and Predictors of Teacher Cheating," *Quarterly Journal of Economics,* August 2003, p. 843.

90 *"High-powered incentive schemes"*: Ibid.

91 *The odds of winning the Powerball grand prize were better*: Jack Gillum and Marisol Bello, "When Standardized Test Scores Soared in D.C., Were the Gains Real?" *USA Today,* March 27, 2011.

92 *"that good and bad coin cannot circulate together"*: Cited in Henry Dunning Macleod, *The Theory and Practice of Banking* (London: Longmans, Green, Reader & Dyer, 1866), p. 219.

94 *"If you wanted a stellar reputation as a baseball player"*: Author interview.

94 *Steve Wilstein . . . wrote an article questioning whether the drug*: See Steve Wilstein, "McGwire Legend Grows in Season-Long Home Run Derby," Associated Press, August 15, 1998, and "'Andro' OK in Baseball, Not Olympics," Associated Press, August 22, 1998.

96 *"Lehman's failure is a story, in large part, of fraud"*: The video of this testimony is available at http://www.c-spanvideo.org/appearance/598024924, accessed January 19, 2012.

96 *"If Countrywide did not offer a product offered by a competitor"*: See Securities and Exchange Commission v. Angelo Mozilo, David Sambol, and Eric Sieracki, United States District Court, Central District of California (filed June 4, 2009), p. 10.

97 *"the most dangerous product in existence and there can be nothing more toxic..."* and *"milk of the business"*: See March 28 and April 13, 2006, e-mails in "Excerpts of E-Mails from Angelo Mozilo," U.S. Securities and Exchange Commission, http://www.sec.gov/news/press/2009/2009-129-email.htm, accessed February 22, 2012.

97 *"Countrywide fashioned itself a meritocracy"*: Adam Michaelson, *The Foreclosure of America: Life Inside Countrywide Home Loans and the Selling of the American Dream* (New York: Penguin, 2010), p. 182.

98 *"He steals money from California to the tune of about a million"*: Cited in Joel Roberts, "Enron Traders Caught on Tape," *CBS Evening News,* December 5, 2007, http://www.cbsnews.com/stories/2004/06/01/eveningnews/main620626.shtml, accessed January 19, 2012.

99 *"jokingly call the steroid injections 'B12 shots'"*: Canseco, *Juiced,* p. 211.

99 *"got the joke"*: See Jack Abramoff, *Capitol Punishment: The Hard Truth About Washington Corruption from America's Most Notorious Lobbyist* (Washington, D.C.: WND Books, 2011), p. 65.

99 *"IBGYBG"*: Cited in Maurice Mullard, *The Politics of Recession* (Northampton, Mass.: Edward Elgar Publishing), p. 119.

100 *"Anyway, not feeling too guilty about this"*: Steve Eder and Kary Wutkowski, "Goldman's 'Fabulous' Fab's conflicted love letters," Reuters, April 26, 2010.

100 *"Manipulate projections so credit ratings are reasonable"*: See Ho, *Liquidated,* p. 106.

101 *"If that case were to present itself, we'd have to deny it, huh?"*: See Mark Zachary v. Countrywide Financial Corporation, Plaintiff's Second Amended Complaint.

101 *"There were more morons than crooks, but the crooks were higher up"*: Michael Lewis, *The Big Short: Inside the Doomsday Machine* (New York: W. W. Norton, 2011), p. 158.

CHAPTER 4. WHO KNOWS?

103 *"There are no more arbiters of truth"*: Cited in Jonathan Martin and John F. Harris, "A New Era of Innuendo," *Politico,* April 28, 2011.

104 *A recent study of Medicare patients*: See Daniel R. Levinson, "Adverse Events in Hospitals: National Incidence Among Medicare Beneficiaries," Department of Health and Human Services, November 2010, http://oig.hhs.gov/oei/reports/oei-06-09-00090.pdf, accessed January 19, 2012.

104 *sixteen times as many as are killed by drunk drivers*: In 2009, 10,839 people were killed in alcohol-impaired driving crashes. See "Impaired Driving: Get the Facts," Centers for Disease Control and Prevention, http://www.cdc.gov/motorvehiclesafety/impaired_driving /impaired-drv_factsheet.html, accessed January 19, 2012.

104 *a Philadelphia pathologist named John Kolmer*: See Paul A. Offit, *The Cutter Incident: How America's First Polio Vaccine Led to the Growing Vaccine Crisis* (New Haven: Yale University Press, 2007), pp. 16–17.

104 *Tenet Healthcare paid $395 million*: Kevin McCoy, "Tenet to Pay $395M to Former Patients," *USA Today,* December 21, 2004.

106 *"The bulk of our knowledge"*: See Russell Hardin, "Democratic Epistemology and Accountability," *Social Philosophy and Policy* 17, no. 1 (2000).

110 *"abject pacifism"*: See The Editors, "Time Out," *New Republic,* January 30, 2003.

111 *"history will not easily excuse us"*: David Remnick, "Making a Case," *New Yorker,* February 3, 2003.

111 *"Bush administration officials were the most frequently quoted sources"*: See Danny Hayes and Matt Guardino, "Whose Views Made the News? Media Coverage and the March to War in Iraq," *Political Communication* 27, no. 1 (Routledge, 2010): 59–87.

112 *"possible for home prices to fall as they did in a couple of quarters in 1990"*: See "Remarks by Chairman Alan Greenspan at the Annual Convention of the Independent Community Bankers of America, Orlando, Florida," March 4, 2003, http://www.federalreserve.gov/boarddocs /speeches/2003/20030304/, accessed January 19, 2012.

112 *"There is No U.S. Housing Bubble"*: See Norman Williams et al., "In Focus This Quarter: Housing Bubble Concerns and the Outlook

for Mortgage Credit Quality," FDIC Outlook, 2004, www.fdic
.gov/bank/analytical/regional/r020041q/na/infocus.html, accessed
February 22, 2012.

112 *"largely reflect strong economic fundamentals."*: Cited in Nell Henderson,
"Bernanke: There's No Housing Bubble to Go Bust," *Washington
Post,* October 27, 2005.

113 *"the impact on the broader economy"*: Testimony of Ben S. Bernanke,
"The Economic Outlook: Before the Joint Economic Committee,
U.S. Congress," March 28, 2007.

113 *"There is no evidence here"*: Cited in "U.S. House Prices Rose 13 Percent
Over Year," Associated Press, September 1, 2005.

113 *"was enough to put even the most ardent believer"*: See "Meeting of the Federal Open Market Committee, December 13, 2005," http://www
.federalreserve.gov/monetarypolicy/files/FOMC20051213meeting
.pdf, accessed January 19, 2012.

113 *"housing prices declined by a third nationwide"*: See S&P/Case-Shiller Home
Price Indices, http://www.standardandpoors.com/indices/sp-case-
shiller-home-price-indices/en/us/?indexId=spusa-cashpidff--p-
us----, accessed January 19, 2012.

113 *"Everybody missed it"*: Cited in Rich Miller and Josh Zumbrun,
"Greenspan Takes Issue with Yellen on Fed's Role in House Bubble," Bloomberg, March 27, 2010.

115 *"has provided most of the front page exclusives"*: Charles Layton, "Miller
Brouhaha," *American Journalism Review,* March/April 2003.

115 *"psychologically stable guy"*: See Bob Drogin and John Goetz, "How U.S.
Fell Under the Spell of 'Curveball,'" *Los Angeles Times,* November 20,
2005.

116 *"Buy Bear!"* and *"Open the darn Fed window"*: The two videos of Jim Cramer
are available at http://bigpicture.typepad.com/comments/2007/08
/cramer-pleads-f.html, accessed January 19, 2012.

117 *"We committed journalistic malpractice on a grand scale"*: See Jon Talton,
"Journalism's Culpability in the Economic Crisis," *Encyclopedia Bri-
tannica Blog,* March 4, 2009, http://www.britannica.com/blogs/2009
/03/journalisms-culpability-in-the-economic-crisis/, accessed February 23, 2012.

117 *"missed the biggest story on the beat"*: Dean Starkman, "How Could 9,000
Business Reporters Blow It?" *Mother Jones,* January/February 2009.

119 *"One of the frightening effects"*: See Letters to the Editor, *New York Times*, October 4, 1973.

120 *"must be meticulously followed"*: See letter of Luciano Storero, January 31, 2007, http://graphics8.nytimes.com/packages/pdf/world/Ireland-Catholic-Abuse.pdf, accessed January 19, 2012.

121 *Jeff Anderson, a Minneapolis lawyer*: Author interview.

121 *"When I first started dealing with my abuse"*: Author interview.

122 *"I was here in Boston in 2002 when the shit hit the fan"*: Author interview.

124 *in 1969, after several young boys alleged they had been sexually abused*: John Stucke and Benjamin Shors, "Cover-Up at Gonzaga: Leary Left after '69 Police Ultimatum," *Spokesman Review*, September 9, 2006.

125 *"The World's Largest Hedge Fund Is a Fraud"*: See Harry Markopolos, "The World's Largest Hedge Fund Is a Fraud: November 7, 2005 Submission to the SEC, Madoff Investment Securities, LLC," November 7, 2005, www.scribd.com/doc/9189340/The-Worlds-Largest-Hedge-Fund-Is-a-Fraud, accessed February 22, 2012.

126 *"A private individual can force a national security agency to disgorge information it does not want to release"*: Author interview.

127 *"The world of secret knowledge is larger than the world of public knowledge"*: Author interview.

127 *Roughly 850,000 people hold top secret security clearances*: See "Top Secret America: A *Washington Post* Investigation," http://projects.washingtonpost.com/top-secret-america/, accessed January 19, 2012.

127 *"Top Secret America"*: Dana Priest and William M. Arkin, "A Hidden World, Growing Beyond Control," *Washington Post*, July 19, 2010.

127 *the market for over-the-counter derivatives grew 74 percent . . . the market for over-the-counter derivatives had grown 122 percent*: See "BIS Releases Latest Statistics on OTC Derivatives," Futuresmag.com, November 15, 2010.

128 *A 2010 report from the Federal Reserve Bank of New York*: See Zoltan Pozsar, et al., "Shadow Banking," *Federal Reserve Bank of New York Staff Reports*, no. 458 (July 2010): p. 65.

129 *"As a student of Kafka, Koestler, and Solzhenitsyn"*: Raffi Khatchadourian, "No Secrets," *New Yorker*, June 7, 2010.

130 *"We deplore WikiLeaks"*: Quoted in Jim Garamone, "Pentagon Prepares for Possible WikiLeaks Publication," *Armed Forces Press Service*, October 22, 2010.

130 *"We're not in the mess we're in, in the world, because of too many leaks"*: Video and transcript available at http://www.ellsberg.net/archive/daniel -ellsberg-on-colbert-report, accessed January 19, 2012.

131 *"What we want people to do is fight with the truth"*: See "WikiLeaks on 'Climategate,'" YouTube, www.youtube.com/watch?v=w17dw_aJEWU, accessed April 5, 2012.

132 *"It doesn't matter what we think"*: Ibid.

132 *"If your gut said"*: Cited in "Beck's 'Brand-New Reality' on Climate Change Relies on Distorting Apparently Stolen E-Mails," *Media Matters for America*, November 23, 2009.

133 *"rigour and honesty"*: Cited in Justin Gillis, "British Panel Clears Scientists," *New York Times*, July 7, 2010.

133 *"long after the damage is done, revealed as utterly bereft of substance"*: See David Roberts, "What We Have and Haven't Learned from 'Climategate,'" *Grist*, March 1, 2011.

133 *In the UK, a quarter of the population is "unconvinced" that the planet's temperatures are warming*: Cited in Steve Doughty, "Global Warming Skepticism Doubles in U.K.," *Daily Mail*, January 29, 2011.

133 *"In the United States, roughly two-thirds of the population are unconvinced that global warming is "a very serious problem."*: See "Energy Update: 30% Say Global Warming a Very Serious Problem," Rasmussen Reports, January 7, 2012, http://www.rasmussenreports.com/public _content/politics/current_events/environment_energy/energy _update, accessed January 20, 2012.

133 *"At no other time in U.S. history were the news media more influential"*: Gene Roberts and Hank Klibanoff, *The Race Beat: The Press, the Civil Rights Struggle, and the Awakening of a Nation* (New York: Random House, 2007), p. 7.

134 *"there is no doubt"*: Ibid., p. 6.

135 *"We're marching over the cliff"*: See interview with Noam Chomsky in "Peak Oil and a Changing Climate," Videonation, www.youtube .com/watch?v=UUmwy0VTnqM&feature=player_embedded, accessed February 22, 2012.

135 *"State and Terrorist Conspiracies"*: Available at http://cryptome.org/0002 /ja-conspiracies.pdf, accessed January 19, 2012.

136 *"Institutions are very important"*: "Frost Over the World: Julian Assange Interview," Aljazeera, http://www.aljazeera.com/programmes/frost

overtheworld/2010/12/201012228384924314.html, accessed January 19, 2012.

CHAPTER 5. WINNERS

137 *"We are the 1%"*: See "Board of Trade Has a Message for Occupy Chicago," *Chicagoist,* http://chicagoist.com/2011/10/05/board_of_trade_has_a_message_for_oc.php, accessed January 22, 2012.

138 *"I should sooner live in a society governed by the first two thousand names in the Boston telephone directory"*: See William F. Buckley, *Rumbles Left and Right* (New York: Putnam, 1963), p. 134.

138 *"pointy-headed intellectuals"*: See Charles Schutz, *Political Humor: From Aristophanes to Sam Ervin* (Madison, N.J.: Farleigh Dickinson University Press, 1977), p. 35.

138 *"effete corps of impudent snobs"*: "The Vice Presidency: Agnew Unleashed," *Time,* October 31, 1969, http://www.time.com/time/magazine/article /0,9171,839090,00.html, accessed January 22, 2012.

138 *references on Fox News to the "media elite" outnumber references to the corporate or business elite by forty to one*: Cited in Geoff Nunberg, "Where the 'Elites' Meet," *Fresh Air,* NPR, April 25, 2008.

138 *"seditious taste in cheese and beverages"*: Ibid.

139 *"some are marked for subjection and some for command"*: Cited in Will Durant, *The Story of Philosophy* (New York: Simon & Schuster, 1961), p. 65.

140 *"As one advances in life"*: José Ortega y Gasset, *The Revolt of the Masses* (1930 repr., New York: W. W. Norton & Company, 1994), p. 65.

140 *"Insofar as national events are decided"*: Mills, *Power Elite,* p. 18.

142 *John Paulson made $2.4 million per hour in the year 2010*: Cited in Zaid Jilani, "Hedge Funder John Paulson Earns More Hourly Than Most Americans Do in a Lifetime and Pays a Lower Tax Rate," *ThinkProgress,* May 13, 2011, http://thinkprogress.org/politics/2011 /05/13/166068/hedge-funder-john-paulson/, accessed January 22, 2012.

142 *"there is concentration of output among a few individuals"*: Sherwin Rosen, "The Economics of Superstars," *American Economic Review* 78, no. 1: 845.

143 *In 2003, that top 1 percent . . . took 56 percent of the concert pie*: Cited in Vic-

tor Ginsburgh, ed., *Handbook of the Economics of Art and Culture,* vol. 1 (Amsterdam: Elsevier, 2006), p. 684.

143 *"earn $10 million or more a year"*: Nathan Koppel and Vanessa O'Connell, "Pay Gap Widens at Big Firms as Partners Chase Star Attorneys," *Wall Street Journal,* February 8, 2011.

143 *Between the 1970s and early 2000, the ratio of the pay of the top 10 percent of CEOs*: See Table 3 of Carola Frydman and Raven E. Saks, "Executive Compensation: A New View from a Long-Term Perspective," http://web.mt.edu/frydman/www/trends_frydmansaks_rfs.pdf, accessed April 5, 2012.

143 *A 2006 study found that the ratio*: Ibid.

144 *"Freedom of the press belongs to those who own one"*: Cited in C. Edwin Baker, *Media Concentration and Democracy: Why Ownership Matters* (New York: Cambridge University Press, 2007), p. 199.

145 *"lawyers, accountants, lobbyists, wealth management agencies"*: Jeffrey A. Winters, *Oligarchy,* (New York: Cambridge University Press, 2011), p. 213.

145 *"senators appear to be considerably more responsive to the opinions of affluent constituents"*: Larry M. Bartels, "Economic Inequality and Political Representation," http://www.princeton.edu/~bartels/economic.pdf, accessed January 22, 2012.

146 *"are fairly strongly related to the preferences of the well-to-do"*: Martin Gilens, "Inequality and Democratic Responsiveness," *Public Opinion Quarterly* 69, no. 5 (2005): 788, http://poq.oxfordjournals.org/content/69/5/778.full.pdf, accessed January 22, 2012.

147 *With nearly 15 million weekly listeners, Rush Limbaugh*: See estimate of Michael Harrison, and its rationale, in Paul Farhi, "Limbaugh's Audience Size? It's Largely Up in the Air," *Washington Post,* March 7, 2009.

147 *800 million Facebook users*: See http://www.facebook.com/press/info.php?statistics, accessed January 22, 2012.

148 *"The American government is not"*: C. Wright Mills, *The Power Elite* (New York: Oxford University Press, 2000), p. 170.

149 *"Grover is at the switchboard"*: John Pitney quoted in Jill Zuckman, "Conservative Operative Is in the Right Place at the Right Time," *Orlando Sentinel,* June 15, 2003.

149 *Economist Jamie Galbraith found*: See James K. Galbraith, "Inequality, Unemployment, and Growth: New Measures for Old Controver-

sies," UTIP Working Paper no. 48, p. 39, http://utip.gov.utexas .edu/papers/utip_48.pdf, accessed February 23, 2012.

150 *"They'll say to you"*: Author interview.

150 *nearly half of all members of Congress have a net worth north of a million dollars*: See Eric Lichtblau, "Economic Downturn Took a Detour on Capitol Hill," *New York Times,* December 26, 2011, and Peter Whoriskey, "Growing Wealth Widens Distance between Lawmakers and Constituents," *Washington Post,* December 26, 2011.

151 *According to an August 2010 study*: See pp. 5–6 of Jordi Blanes i Vidal, Mirko Draca, and Christian Fons-Rosen, "Revolving Door Lobbyists," Centre for Economic Performance: London School of Economics, http://cep.lse.ac.uk/pubs/download/dp0993.pdf, accessed April 5, 2012.

151 *"A telegenic young lawmaker with a wide network of relationships"*: Michael Barbaro and Louise Story, "Merrill Lynch Guaranteed Ford Annual Pay of at Least $2 Million," *New York Times,* February 25, 2010.

152 *Sarah Palin ... made a reported $12 million*: See Matthew Mosk, "Sarah Palin Has Earned an Estimated $12 Million Since July," ABC News, April 23, 2010.

152 *Rahm Emanuel ... amassed a fortune of more than $18 million*: See Michael Luo, "In Banking, Emanuel Made Money and Connections," *New York Times,* December 3, 2008.

153 *Jack Lew, who spent four years at Citigroup and received a bonus of $950,000 in 2009*: Cited in Daniel Halper, "New Chief of Staff: Former Hedge Fund Exec. at Citigroup, Made Money Off Mortgage Defaults," *Weekly Standard,* January 9, 2012.

153 *that gig paid him $5.2 million a year, or more than $100,000 per week, for one day of work a week*: Cited in Louise Story, "U.S. Economy Chief Had Inside View of Wall Street," *International Herald-Tribune,* April 7, 2009.

154 *Axelrod reported income of $1.5 million*: Cited in "All the President's Millionaires: Disclosure Reports Show That Many in Barack Obama's Inner Circle Have More Than Just a City in Common," *Chicago Tribune,* April 9, 2009.

154 *Valerie Jarrett ... reported a money market fund that held between $1 million and $5 million*: See "White House Wealth: President Barack Obama's Team Virtually All Chicago Millionaires," *Chicago Tribune,* April 9, 2009.

155 *"Even the supporters of apartheid were the victims of the vicious system"*: Desmond Tutu, *No Future Without Forgiveness* (New York: Doubleday, 1999), p. 103.

157 *"The point about Davos is that it makes everyone feel wildly insecure"*: Anya Schiffrin, "Jealous Davos Mistresses," Reuters, January 25, 2011.

158 *"You have met the phenomenon of an Inner Ring"*: See C. S. Lewis, *Weight of Glory* (New York: HarperCollins, 2001), pp. 145–46.

159 *A 2011 poll of millionaires commissioned by Fidelity*: See "Fidelity Survey Finds Millionaires' Outlook for Economy at Highest Level Since 2006," Fidelity.com, March 14, 2011, http://www.fidelity.com /inside-fidelity/individual-investing/millionaire-outlook-2011, accessed January 23, 2012.

160 *"compare themselves to their peer group"*: See Helen Kearney, "Oddly Enough: U.S. Millionaires Say $7 Million Not Enough to Be Rich," Reuters, March 14, 2012.

161 *"He really believes that he is looked down upon by those who admire and fear him"*: Tom Junod, "Why Does Roger Ailes Hate America?" *Esquire,* January 18, 2011.

161 *"And I—I mean—you know, my dad"*: See "Republican Presidential Candidates Participate in a CNN-Sponsored Debate," *Political Transcript Wire,* January 20, 2012.

162 *"It was always a business where you had to have an edge"*: Steve Fishman, "The Madoff Tapes," *New York,* February 27, 2011.

162 *"I am an important person"*: Jean M. Twenge et al., "Egos Inflating Over Time: A Cross-Temporal Meta-Analysis of the Narcissistic Personality Disorder," *Journal of Personality* 76, no. 4 (2008): 878.

162 *"People with insecure high self-esteem"*: Kate Pickett and Richard Wilkinson, *The Spirit Level: Why Greater Equality Makes Societies Stronger* (New York: Bloomsbury), p. 37.

164 *"not that smart and kind of a bully"*: See Jeffrey Rosen, "The Case Against Sotomayor," *New Republic,* May 4, 2009.

166 *"meritocratic feedback loop"*: Ho, *Liquidated,* p. 57.

166 *"There's 100 percent no question"*: Author interview.

168 *"the outstretched arms of J.P. Morgan's H.R. department"*: Matthew L. Siegel, "Dress for Success: The I-Banker Has No Clothes," *Harvard Crimson,* October 30, 2003.

168 *"the most powerful man you've never heard of"*: Chitra Ragavan, "Cheney's Guy," *U.S. News and World Report,* May 21, 2006.

168 *"The boy seemed terribly, terribly bright"*: See Jane Mayer, *The Dark Side: The Inside Story of How the War on Terror Turned into a War on American Ideals* (New York: Random House, 2009), p. 57.

169 *"He was always right"*: Ibid., p. 64.

170 *"Pollack manages to eschew the cant, stupidity, and obfuscation"*: Joshua Micah Marshall, "The Reluctant Hawk: The Skeptical Case for Regime Change in Iraq," *Washington Monthly,* November 2002.

170 *"argument for invading Iraq is surely the most influential book of this season"*: Bill Keller, "The I-Can't-Believe-I'm-a-Hawk Club," *New York Times,* February 8, 2003.

170 *"I was 21 years old and kind of a jerk"*: Matthew Yglesias, "Four Reasons for a Mistake," *ThinkProgress,* August 19, 2010.

171 *"If you [the average investor or the average corporation] don't know anything"*: Ho, *Liquidated,* p. 40.

171 *"improper dependency"*: Lessig, *Republic, Lost,* p. 245.

173 *what Jane Jacobs described as the Guardian Syndrome*: See Jane Jacobs, *Systems of Survival: A Dialogue on the Moral Foundations of Commerce and Politics,* (New York: Vintage, 1992).

174 *"At some point after incomes in the financial sector took off"*: Thomas Ferguson and Robert Johnson, "When Wolves Cry 'Wolf': Systemic Financial Crises and the Myth of the Danaid Jar," http://andrewgelman .com/movabletype/mlm/Ferg-John%20INET%20Conf%20 Cambridge%20UK%20April%202010%20final%20%20pdf-1.pdf, accessed January 23, 2012.

175 *"Mishkin even took $124,000 from the Iceland Chamber of Commerce"*: See Annie Lowrey, "The Economics of Economists' Ethics," *Slate,* January 5, 2011, http://www.slate.com/articles/business/moneybox/2011 /01/the_economics_of_economists_ethics.html, accessed January 23, 2012.

175 *"adapted to the new environment with the most agility and creativity"*: Janine R. Wedel, *Shadow Elite: How the World's New Power Brokers Undermine Democracy, Government, and the Free Market* (New York: Basic Books, 2009), p. 14.

CHAPTER 6. OUT OF TOUCH

177 *"He grabbed a quart of milk, a light bulb and a bag of candy"*: Andrew Rosenthal, "Bush Encounters the Supermarket, Amazed," *New York Times,* February 5, 1992.

178 *"Bush had no idea how 'Joe Six-Pack' lived"*: William F. Levantrosser and Rosanna Perotti, eds., *A Noble Calling: Character and the George H. W. Bush Presidency* (Westport, Conn.: Greenwood Publishing Group Inc., 2004), p. 122.

178 *only 18 percent of respondents in a CBS News/New York Times poll*: See Robin Toner, "Poll Shows Price Bush Pays for Tough Economic Times," *New York Times,* January 10, 1992.

179 *"I think—I'll have my staff get to you"*: Jonathan Martin and Mike Allen, "McCain Unsure How Many Houses He Owns," *Politico,* August 21, 2008.

179 *"The fact that John McCain"*: Spokesman Hari Sevugan, cited in "Dems Pounce on McCain Admission He Doesn't Know How Many Houses He Owns," washingtonpost.com, August 21, 2008.

179 *Among those who ranked "cares about people like me"... Obama beat McCain 73–19*: See "FOX News Poll: Obama's Edge Over McCain Narrows," October 30, 2008.

180 *"He has forbidden his Governors to pass Laws of immediate and pressing importance"*: See http://www.archives.gov/exhibits/charters/declaration _transcript.html, accessed January 23, 2012.

182 *"A small representation can never be well informed as to the circumstances of the people"*: See http://www.constitution.org/afp/fedfar07.htm, accessed January 23, 2012.

186 *Chicago has the fourth highest level of black-white segregation in the entire nation*: See Matthew Hall et al., "Racial and Ethnic Residential Segregation in the Chicago Metropolitan Area, 1980–2009," in Institute of Government & Public Affairs, University of Illinois, *Changing American Neighborhoods and Communities Report,* Series 2, p. 2.

186 *26 percent of Americans lived in what Bishop calls "landslide counties"*: Bill Bishop, *The Big Sort: Why the Cluster of Like-Minded America Is Tearing Us Apart* (Boston: Houghton Mifflin Harcourt, 2009), p. 9.

187 *Dick Fuld... had a separate elevator that was commandeered*: See "A Look Back at the Collapse of Lehman Brothers," PBS *NewsHour,*

http://www.pbs.org/newshour/bb/business/july-dec09/solman
lehman_09-14.html, accessed January 23, 2012.

188 *"They help him focus on the real problems people are facing"*: See Stephen
Splane, " 'Dear President Obama': The President Reads 10 Letters a
Day from the Public, with Policy Ramifications," ABC News, Feb-
ruary 23, 2009.

190 *The high-power group were far more likely to draw an "E" as if they were reading it*
themselves: Adam Galinsky et al., "Power and Perspectives Not Taken,"
Psychological Science 17, no. 12 (2006): 1069, http://www.kellogg
.northwestern.edu/faculty/galinsky/power%252520and%252520
perspective-taking%252520psych%252520science%2525202006
.pdf, accessed January 23, 2012.

190 *"made more accurate inferences about emotion"*: Michael W. Kraus et al.,
"Social Class, Contextualism, and Empathic Accuracy," *Psycho-*
logical Science 20, no. 10 (2010): 2, http://www.rotman.utoronto.ca
/facbios/file/Kraus%20C%C3%B4t%C3%A9%20Keltner%20PS%20
in%20press.pdf, accessed January 13, 2012.

191 *3.5 percent of priests accused of sexual abuse had allegedly molested more than ten*
victims: See "The Nature and Scope of the Problem of Sexual Abuse
of Minors by Catholic Priests and Deacons in the United States:
A Research Study Conducted by the John Jay College of Criminal
Justice," http://www.jjay.cuny.edu/churchstudy/main.asp, accessed
January 23, 2012.

192 *"Yours has been an effective life of ministry"*: See Jason Berry and Gerald
Renner, *Vows of Silence: The Abuse of Power in the Papacy of John Paul II*
(New York: Free Press, 2004), p. 51.

193 *"The matter of your concern is being investigated"*: Cited in Walter V. Rob-
inson and Michael Rezendes, "Crisis in the Church: Law Recalls
Little on Abuse Case, Says Under Oath He Delegated Geoghan
Matter to Other Bishops," *Boston Globe,* May 9, 2002.

193 *"The bishop will resign next year"*: See Steven Erlanger, "Belgian Church
Leader Urged Victim to Be Silent," *New York Times,* August 29, 2010.

194 *" facing a storm that most of us have feared"*: See transcript, "New Orleans
Mayor, Louisiana Governor Hold Press Conference," CNN Break-
ing News, August 28, 2005.

195 *"the failure of citizenship in the Ninth Ward"*: See *Countdown,* MSNBC,
March 5, 2007.

195 *"Where can you go if you don't have a car?"*: See Frank Bass, "Katrina's Worst-Hit Victims Much Poorer Than Rest of America, Census Analysis Shows," Associated Press, September 4, 2005.

196 *"I've only got like $80 to my name"*: *Morning Edition*, National Public Radio, September 2, 2005.

196 *Among the poor nationwide, 20 percent live in households that don't have access to a car, and among the poor in the city of New Orleans that number was 47 percent*: See Alan Berube et al., "Economic Difference in Household Automobile Ownership Rates: Implications for Evacuation Policy," pp. 7–8, http://socrates.berkeley.edu/~raphael/BerubeDeakenRaphael .pdf, accessed January 23, 2012.

197 *"a lot of people live on fixed income, be it a Social Security check or a retirement check"* . . . *"It is not the role of the federal government to supply five gallons of gas"*: See U.S. House of Representatives, *A Failure of Initiative: Final Report of the Select Bipartisan Committee to Investigate the Preparation for and Response to Hurricane Katrina* (Washington, D.C.: U.S. Government Printing Office, 2006), p. 106. http://www.gpoaccess.gov/serialset/creports /pdf/hr109-377/evac.pdf, accessed February 23, 2012.

197 *"direct and compel, by any necessary and reasonable force"*: This excerpt from the New Orleans Plan is quoted in *A Failure of Initiative*, p. 109, http://www.gpoaccess.gov/serialset/creports/pdf/hr109-377/evac .pdf, accessed February 23, 2012.

198 *In his landmark study of the disaster*: Eric Klinenberg, *Heat Wave: A Social Autopsy of Disaster in Chicago* (Chicago: University of Chicago Press, 2002).

199 *"It's hot, but let's not blow it out of proportion"*: See Sharon Cohen, "Chicago's Heat Tragedy: 'I've Never Seen So Many Dead People,'" Associated Press, July 22, 1995.

199 *"the longest sustained combat in American history"*: See Elisabeth Bumiller, "Gates Fears Wider Gap Between Country and Military," *New York Times*, September 29, 2010.

199 *enough money to pay the inflation-adjusted cost of Roosevelt's New Deal twice over*: The inflation-adjusted cost of the New Deal was about $500 billion. See Katrina vanden Heuvel and Eric Schlosser, "America Needs a New New Deal," *Nation*, September 27, 2008. The inflation-adjusted cost of the Marshall Plan was $115.3 bil-

lion. See "Big Budget Events," CNBC.com, http://www.cnbc.com
/id/27717424/Big_Budget_Events, accessed January 24, 2012.

199 *more than 6,000 Americans have been killed in action . . . 47,000 troops have been*
wounded, and 1,400 have had a limb amputated: See http://www.defense.gov
/news/casualty.pdf, and Hannah Fischer, "U.S. Military Casualty
Statistics: Operation New Dawn, Operation Iraqi Freedom, and
Operation Enduring Freedom," September 28, 2010, http://www
.fas.org/sgp/crs/natsec/RS22452.pdf, accessed January 23, 2012.

200 *During the Gulf War, service members were also typically deployed only*
once, for an average of 153 days: For Gulf War deployment statistics, see Richard Thomas et al., "Particulate Exposure During
the Persian Gulf War," May 2000, http://www.dtic.mil/cgi-bin
/GetTRDoc?AD=ADA382643, accessed January 23, 2012. For
current deployment statistics, see Samuel G. Freedman, "Minister-
ing to Soldiers, and Facing Their Struggles," *New York Times,* July 1,
2011.

200 *A 2007 study by the Brookings Institution found that 27 percent of soldiers:* Cited
in Michael O'Hanlon, "U.S. Military Check-Up Time," *Washington*
Times, May 4, 2008.

200 *"stretched the U.S. military dangerously thin":* See "U.S. Military Stretched
Dangerously Thin by War: Poll," Reuters, February 19, 2008.

200 *"by supporting and signing expensive spending and tax legislation, President George*
W. Bush": Robert D. Hormats, *The Price of Liberty: Paying for America's*
Wars (New York: Times Books), p. xix.

201 *1.4 million active duty soldiers:* See "Armed Forces Strength Figures
for November 30, 2011," http://siadapp.dmdc.osd.mil/personnel
/MILITARY/ms0.pdf, accessed January 24, 2012.

201 *"as family income increases, the likelihood of having ever served in the military de-*
creases": Amy Lutz, "Who Joins the Military?: A Look at Race, Class,
and Immigration Status," *Journal of Political and Military Sociology* 36,
no. 2 (2008): 167–88.

202 *"Whatever their fond sentiments for men and women in uniform":* Cited in
Charley Keyes, "Joint Chiefs Chair Warns of Disconnect Between
Military and Civilians," CNN, January 20, 2011.

202 *"alienation that impoverishes citizenship on both sides":* Author interview.

203 *Writing in the* Chronicle of Higher Education, *political scientist Michael*

Nelson argues: Michael Nelson, "Warrior Nation," *Chronicle of Higher Education,* October 24, 2010.

203 *"The college campuses in 1969 were hotbeds of activism":* Author interview.

204 *"There's no question in my mind that this president and this administration would ever have invaded Iraq":* "Rangel Will Push to Bring Back the Draft," Associated Press, February 11, 2009.

204 *"There's a long-standing debate in American foreign policy circles":* Author interview.

205 *"What's the point of you saving this superb military you're always talking about if we can't use it?":* Colin Powell with Joseph E. Persico, *My American Journey* (New York: Ballantine Books, 1995), p. 561.

206 *An immigrant from the Caribbean, she mentioned to him that she and a sister owned six townhomes in Queens:* Lewis, *Big Short,* pp. 98–102.

208 *"He went to talk to Martin about it":* Author interview.

208 *"We published a paper in 2006":* See Ellen Schloemer et al., "Losing Ground: Foreclosures in the Subprime Market and Their Cost to Homeowners," Center for Responsible Lending, December 2006, http://www.responsiblelending.org/mortgage-lending/research-analysis/foreclosure-paper-report-2-17.pdf, accessed January 24, 2012.

208 *"At that time":* Author interview.

208 *Between 2006 and 2010:* See Debbie Gruenstein Bocian et al., "Lost Ground, 2011: Disparities in Mortgage Lending and Foreclosures: Executive Summary," Center for Responsible Lending, p. 2, http://www.responsiblelending.org/mortgage-lending/research-analysis/Lost-Ground-exec-summary.pdf, accessed January 25, 2012.

209 *In July 2005, he said that the "fundamentals" . . . "We expect the housing market to cool, but not to change very sharply":* Cited in David Leonhardt, "Greenspan and Bernanke: Evolving Views," *New York Times,* August 22, 2007.

209 *"I don't think people realize how much information the regulators had":* Author interview.

209 *"It wasn't until it started happening on blocks":* Author interview.

213 *Personal bankruptcies have been climbing:* See "Influence of Total Consumer Debt on Bankruptcy Filings, Trends by Year 1980–2010," http://www.abiworld.org/statcharts/Consumer%20Debt-Bankruptcy 2011FINAL.pdf, accessed January 25, 2012.

CHAPTER 7. REFORMATION

218 *"think any advanced democracy is as obsessed with equality of opportunity or as relatively unconcerned with equality of condition"*: See Alexander Stille, "The Paradox of the New Elite," *New York Times,* October 22, 2011.

218 *Union density rose as as high as 34 percent*: Cited in Michael Wachter, "The Rise and Decline of Unions," *Regulation,* Summer 2007, p. 27.

219 *the ratio between average CEO compensation and average production worker compensation hovered around 25 (by 2009 it was 185)*: See "Ratio of Average CEO Total Direct Compensation to Average Production Worker Compensation, 1965–2009," Economic Policy Institute, May 16, 2011, http://www.stateofworkingamerica.org/charts/view/17, accessed January 25, 2012.

219 *Between 1947 and 1979 real family income grew for everyone but it grew the most for the poorest 20 percent of the population*: See "Family Income Growth in Two Eras," Economic Policy Institute, http://stateofworkingamerica.org/charts/real-annual-family-income-growth-by-quintile-1947-79-and-1979-2010/, accessed January 25, 2012.

219 *from 1979 to 2009, when real family income declined for those in the lowest income quintile, while increasing annually by 1.2 percent for those in the top quintile"*: Ibid.

219 *The top 10 percent captured all of the income gains*: See "When Income Grows, Who Gains?" Economic Policy Institute, http://stateofworkingamerica.org/who-gains/#/?start=1979&end=2008,accessed January 25, 2012.

219 *"the rival ideologies of left and right are both pining for the '50s"*: Brink Lindsey, "Liberaltarians," *New Republic* online, December 4, 2006.

220 *women still make on average 23 percent less than men, that gap has shrunk markedly since 1980, when women made on average 40 percent less*: See "The Gender Wage Gap: 2010," Institute for Women's Policy Research, http://www.iwpr.org/publications/pubs/the-gender-wage-gap-2010-updated-march-2011, accessed January 25, 2012.

220 *In 1975, only 1.4 percent of black households made more than $100,000. By 2006, it was more than six times that, a considerably faster rate of growth than that of white households*: See "Distribution of Household Income by Race," *U.S. Census Bureau: Income, Poverty and Health Insurance Coverage in the*

United States: 2006, http://www.infoplease.com/ipa/A0104552.html, accessed January 25, 2012. The $100,000 figure represents 2006 inflation-adjusted dollars.

220 *The number of black officeholders has doubled between 1975 and 1993:* See Steven F. Lawson, *One America in the Twenty-first Century* (New Haven: Yale University Press, 2009), p. xxiii.

220 *58 percent of Fortune 500 companies offer benefits to same-sex partnerships:* Cited in Tara Siegel Bernard, "For Gay Employees, an Equalizer," *New York Times,* May 20, 2011.

221 *"We got both the traditions and the transgressions":* Tony Judt, "Meritocrats," *New York Review of Books,* August 19, 2010.

224 *"Between 2003 and 2008, the top 10 percent of Brazilians got 11 percent richer, while the bottom tenth saw their earnings jump 72 percent":* "The Land of Less Contrast: How Brazil Reined in Inequality," *Newsweek,* November 27, 2009.

224 *The Lula government also increased pension payouts, as well as the minimum wage, by a whopping 50 percent:* See Perry Anderson, "Lula's Brazil," *London Review of Books* 33 (March 31, 2011).

224 *Total tax revenue as percentage of GDP in the United States is at 24.8 percent, down from 29.5 percent in 2000. You can compare that to Denmark, which has the highest level of tax revenue as a percentage of GDP (48.2 percent):* See Revenue Statistics—Comparative Tables, "Tax Revenue as Percentage of GDP," Organization for Economic Cooperation and Development, http://stats.oecd.org/Index.aspx?DataSetCode=REV, accessed January 26, 2012.

225 *"a certain corrective against the development of a race of idle rich":* Cited in Martin J. Daunton, *Just Taxes: The Politics of Taxation in Britain* (Cambridge: Cambridge University Press, 2002), p. 124.

225 *"As a rule, a self-made millionaire is not an extravagant man himself":* See the full text of Carnegie's speech in "Wealth Tax Views in Notable Talks," *New York Times,* December 14, 1906.

226 *"would cost $68 billion, help only the richest of the rich":* See "Inheritance and Estate Taxes," http://topics.nytimes.com/top/reference/timestopics/subjects/i/inheritance_and_estate_taxes/index.html, accessed January 25, 2012.

226 *an average effective tax rate of 16.6 percent:* See David Cay Johnston, "9 Things the Rich Don't Want You to Know About Taxes," Asso-

ciation of Alternative News Media, April 14, 2011, http://www
.altweeklies.com/aan/9-things-the-rich-dont-want-you-to-know
-about-taxes/Story?oid=3971382, accessed January 25, 2012.

227 *"The masses,"* she says: Author interview.

228 *"First, respondents dramatically underestimated the current level of wealth inequality"*: Michael I. Norton and Dan Ariely, "Building a Better
America—One Wealth Quintile at a Time," *Perspectives on Political Science* 6, no. 1 (2011): 9, http://www.people.hbs.edu/mnorton
/norton%20ariely.pdf, accessed January 26, 2012.

228 *"placing a surtax on federal income taxes for people earning over one million dollars a year"*: NBC News/Wall Street Journal Survey, February 2011,
p. 16, http://issuu.com/wsj.com/docs/wsj-nbcpoll03022011.pdf, accessed January 26, 2012.

230 *A 2005 Pew study of more than eleven thousand Howard Dean volunteers and
donors found that 80 percent had four-year college degrees*: See "The Dean
Activists: Their Profile and Prospects," Pew Research Center
for People & The Press, April 6, 2005, http://www.people-press
.org/2005/04/06/the-dean-activists-their-profile-and-prospects/,
accessed January 26, 2012.

230 *The audience of Daily Kos and the more radical website Firedoglake are
roughly similar*: See demographic statistics at http://www.quantcast
.com/firedoglake.com, and http://www.quantcast.com/dailykos.com,
accessed February 22, 2012.

231 *"You have a lot of kids graduating college, can't find jobs"*: See Kate Taylor,
"Bloomberg, on Radio, Raises Specter of Riots by Jobless," *New York
Times,* September 16, 2011.

231 *"POLL FINDS TEA PARTY BACKERS WEALTHIER AND MORE EDUCATED"*:
Kate Zernike and Megan Thee-Brenan, "Poll Finds Tea Party Backers Wealthier and More Educated," *New York Times,* April 14, 2010.

234 *"sheer unadulterated disgust for the wealthy"*: The clip is available at http://
mediamatters.org/mmtv/201106300012, accessed January 26,
2012.

235 *"Ultimately I figured out that the real enemy of the people"*: Author interview.

237 *boasted a membership at its peak of more than 2 million*: See Edwin Amenta,
When Movements Matter: The Townsend Plan and the Rise of Social Security
(Princeton, N.J.: Princeton University Press, 2006), p. 1.

238 *"In American politics, radical decentralization has never been tried on so large a*

scale": Jonathan Rauch, "Group Think: Inside the Tea Party's Collective Brain," *National Journal,* September 11, 2010.

239 *"You're creating a vision of the sort of society you want to have in miniature"*: See "You're Creating the Sort of Society You Want to Have in Miniature," Ezra Klein's *Wonkblog, Washington Post,* October 3, 2011.

Selected Bibliography

Akerlof, George A., et al. "Looting: The Economic Underworld of Bankruptcy for Profit." *Brookings Papers on Economic Activity 1993,* no. 2: 1–73.

American Society of Civil Engineers Hurricane Karina External Review Panel. *The New Orleans Hurricane Protection System: What Went Wrong and Why.* Reston, Va.: American Society of Civil Engineers, 2007.

Arrow, Kenneth, Samuel Bowls, and Steven Durlauf, eds. *Meritocracy and Economic Inequality.* Princeton, N.J.: Princeton University Press, 2000.

Baker, Dean. *False Profits: Recovering from the Bubble Economy.* Sausalito, Calif·: PoliPointPress, 2010.

Baltzell, E. Digby. *The Protestant Establishment: Aristocracy & Caste in America.* 1964. Reprint, New Haven, Conn.: Yale University Press, 1987.

Bottomore, Tom. *Elites and Society.* 2nd ed. London and New York: Routledge, 1993.

Brooks, David. *Bobos in Paradise: The New Upper Class and How They Got There.* New York: Simon & Schuster, 2000.

Canseco, José. *Juiced: Wild Times, Rampant 'Roids, Smash Hits, and How Baseball Got Big.* New York: HarperCollins, 2005.

Doyle, Thomas P. *Sex, Priests, and Secret Codes: The Catholic Church's 2000-Year Paper Trail of Sexual Abuse.* Los Angeles: Volt Press, 2006.

Eichenwald, Kurt. *Conspiracy of Fools: A True Story.* New York: Broadway Books, 2005.

Fainaru-Wada, Mark, and Lance Williams. *Game of Shadows: Barry Bonds, BALCO, and the Steroids Scandal That Rocked Professional Sports.* New York: Gotham, 2006.

Feaver, Peter D., and Christopher Gelpi. *Choosing Your Battles: American Civil-Military Relations and the Use of Force.* Princeton, N.J.: Princeton University Press, 2004.

Frank, Robert H., and Philip J. Cook. *The Winner-Take-All Society: Why the Few at the Top Get So Much More Than the Rest of Us.* New York: Penguin, 1995.

Golden, Daniel. *The Price of Admission: How America's Ruling Class Buys Its Way into Elite Colleges—and Who Gets Left Outside the Gates.* New York: Three Rivers Press, 2007.

Heclo, Hugh. *On Thinking Institutionally.* Boulder, Colo.: Paradigm Publishers, 2008.

Heerden, Ivor Van. *The Storm: What Went Wrong and Why During Hurricane Katrina—the Inside Story from One Louisiana Scientist.* New York: Viking, 2006.

Ho, Karen Zouwen. *Liquidated: An Ethnography of Wall Street.* Durham, N.C.: Duke University Press, 2009.

Investigative Staff of the *Boston Globe. Betrayal: The Crisis in the Catholic Church.* New York: Little, Brown and Company, 2002.

Jacobs, Jane. *Systems of Survival: A Dialogue on the Moral Foundations of Commerce and Politics.* New York: Vintage, 1992.

Jones, Thomas M. "Ethical Decision Making by Individuals in Organizations: An Issue-Contingent Model." *Academy of Management Review* 16, no. 2 (April 1991): 366–95.

Judis, John B. *The Paradox of American Democracy: Elites, Special Interests, and the Betrayal of Public Trust.* New York: Routledge, 2001.

Lasch, Christopher. *The Revolt of the Elites and the Betrayal of Democracy.* New York: W. W. Norton, 1996.

Lemann, Nicholas. *The Big Test: The Secret History of the American Meritocracy.* New York: Farrar, Straus & Giroux, 1999.

McNamee, Stephen J., and Robert K. Miller Jr. *The Meritocracy Myth.* Lanham, Md.: Rowman & Littlefield Publishers, Inc., 2004.

Michaelson, Adam. *The Foreclosure of America: Life Inside Countrywide Home Loans and the Selling of the American Dream.* New York: Penguin, 2010.

Michels, Robert. *Political Parties: A Sociological Study of the Oligarchical Tendencies of Modern Democracy.* Translated by Eden and Cedar Paul. New York: The Free Press, 1962.

Mills, C. Wright. *The Power Elite.* New York: Oxford University Press, 1956.

Moynihan, Daniel Patrick. *Secrecy: The American Experience.* New Haven, Conn.: Yale University Press, 1998.

Pareto, Vilfredo. *The Rise and Fall of Elites: An Application of Theoretical Sociology.* 1968. Reprint, New Brunswick, N.J.: Transaction Publishers, 1991.

Putnam, Robert D. *The Comparative Study of Political Elites.* Englewood Cliffs, N.J.: Prentice Hall, Inc., 1976.

Schleef, Debra J. *Managing Elites: Professional Socialization in Law and Business Schools.* Lanham, Md.: Rowman & Littlefield Publishers, Inc., 2006.

Specter, Michael. *Denialism: How Irrational Thinking Hinders Scientific Progress, Harms the Planet, and Threatens Our Lives.* New York: The Penguin Press, 2009.

Trevino, Linda Klebe. "Ethical Decision Making in Organizations: A Person-Situation Interactionist Model." *Academy of Management Review* 11, no. 3 (July 1986): 601–17.

Victor, Bart, and John B. Cullen. "The Organizational Bases of Ethical Work Climates." *Administrative Science Quarterly* 33, no. 1 (March 1988): 101–25.

Weber, Max. *From Max Weber: Essays in Sociology.* 1946. Translated, edited, and with an introduction by H. H. Gerth and C. Wright Mills. Reprint, New York: Oxford University Press, 1972.

Wedel, Janine R. *Shadow Elite: How the World's New Power Brokers Undermine Democracy, Government, and the Free Market.* New York: Basic Books, 2009.

Wilson, James Q. *Bureaucracy: What Government Agencies Do and Why They Do It.* New York: Basic Books, 1989.

Young, Michael. *The Rise of the Meritocracy.* 1958. Reprint, New Brunswick, N.J.: Transaction Publishers, 1994.

Index

About the Author

CHRISTOPHER HAYES is editor at large of *The Nation* and host of *All In with Chris Hayes* on MSNBC. From 2010 to 2011, he was a fellow at Harvard University's Edmond J. Safra Foundation Center for Ethics. His essays, articles, and reviews have appeared in the *New York Times Magazine, Time, The American Prospect, The New Republic*, the *Washington Monthly,* and the *Guardian.* He lives in Brooklyn with his wife, Kate, and daughter, Ryan.